EXURBIA
NOW

Also by David Masciotra

I Am Somebody:
Why Jesse Jackson Matters

Barack Obama: Invisible Man

Mellencamp:
American Troubadour

Metallica

Working On a Dream:
The Progressive Political Vision
of Bruce Springsteen

EXURBIA NOW

THE **BATTLEGROUND** OF AMERICAN DEMOCRACY

DAVID MASCIOTRA

MELVILLE HOUSE
BROOKLYN • LONDON

EXURBIA NOW: THE BATTLEGROUND
OF AMERICAN DEMOCRACY

First published in 2024 by Melville House
Copyright © 2023 by David Masciotra
All rights reserved
First Melville House Printing: January 2024

Melville House Publishing
46 John Street
Brooklyn, NY 11201

and

Melville House UK
Suite 2000
16/18 Woodford Road
London E7 0HA

mhpbooks.com
@melvillehouse

ISBN: 978-1-68589-089-6
ISBN: 978-1-68589-090-2 (eBook)

Library of Congress Control Number: 2023949505

Designed by Beste M. Doğan

Printed in the United States of America
10 9 8 7 6 5 4 3 2 1

A catalog record for this book is available from the Library of Congress

For Edward R. Ward
A Great Teacher and Friend

"[We are] half-tamed creatures, whose great
moral task it is to hold in balance the angel and
the monster within—for we are both,
and to ignore this duality is to invite disaster."
—GORE VIDAL, 1959

TABLE OF CONTENTS

BORN IN A SMALL TOWN:
AN INTRODUCTION

"The most important battles are fought in places no one cares about," James Lee Burke often writes. Dave Robicheaux is the recurring hero of Burke's crime novels. A former New Orleans cop and Vietnam vet, he is a detective working for the New Iberia sheriff's department who fights to protect the natural environment against avaricious polluters and preserve the dignity of children against sexual predators, and help move America in the direction of democratic idealism and virtue. Transforming his relatively small role into a crusade for justice, he becomes a veritable foot soldier in the war on behalf of a multicultural, multiracial, and ecumenical democracy against bigots and bullies who bedevil New Iberia, Louisiana—a town few care about.

Burke's fictional universe bears a strong resemblance to our own fragile world. New Iberia is a political and cultural cousin of towns across America, particularly those that surround me in the Midwest—those with stories that feature throughout this book: towns that, indeed, few people care about but where our democracy's most important battles are taking place. There are battles for racial justice, as white flight has moved from suburbia to exurbia—a densely populated precinct, not quite rural but far from urban.

Exurbia, as its name would suggest, is excised from the urban center—further from the suburbs than metropolitan culture and commerce, with fewer people. Although it is not monolithic, it has developed as the later stage of suburbia, blending the politics of escape, primarily in the form of white flight, with the economics of corporate homogeneity. Once the land of trailer parks, it is now full of planned communities—new single-family homes in close proximity to wide roads, big box retailers, chain restaurants, and megachurches. Most exurbs lack a downtown, walkable commercial district, and many even have a noticeable absence of sidewalks. It is where Americans go to "bowl alone," as Robert Putnam would have it, or to paraphrase the late Warren Zevon, enjoy their "splendid isolation."

Where civic association and communal culture die, right-wing movements metastasize. It should not register as surprise, then, that exurbia is now the staging and breeding ground for the radical right extremist insurgency troubling the United States by threatening its citizenry and endangering its democracy. A simple reading of an electoral map makes as clear as red and blue crayons that Donald Trump's popularity scales off the charts in exurbia, and that the most malevolent and fascistic members of Congress, from Georgia's Marjorie Taylor Greene to Ohio's Jim Jordan, represent districts that are heavily exurban. Their voters do not want disturbances to their isolation in the form of racial diversity, LGBTQ acceptance, and decisions rendered according to the Constitutional mechanisms of secular democratic governance. They seek an America like the communities that they create and dominate—hostile to outsiders and the public good, ruled by white, Christian authority, and operative in conjunction with the romanticized mores of the pre-Civil Rights, pre-feminist, pre-gay rights 1950s. It is because of anxiety, hatred, and hostility toward democracy, that the rank and file in the January 6 insurrectionist mob was populated heavily with residents of exurban towns.

The right-wing voters placing the Uniited States on the edge of violent tyranny are not the only players in the story. They are reactionary, but also reactive. Exurbia grew as a means to escape not only the big city, but the increasingly liberal suburbs surrounding the cities. As suburbia becomes more diverse, progressive, and cosmopolitan, exurbanites' knuckles grow ever whiter, clutching onto their power and paranoia.

"Something's happenin' in the backwoods / It's spreading out like water / Stone cold rage in the hinterland," Gov't Mule declares in their protest song following the political ascension of Donald Trump. It was not the metropolitan areas, but the exurbs and rural villages that acted as a collective valet of Trump into the White House. The states of the industrial Midwest—for decades reliable territory for the Democratic Party—shifted to the right because of a tilt in suburbs and exurbs where beleaguered residents sought a strongman to assuage their fears, and, tapping into a multi-century tradition of xenophobia and racism, their perception of a threat emanating out of the rapidly diversifying demography of America.

Political forecasters and prognosticators appear in agreement that the genuinely "swing" territory of states like Georgia, Pennsylvania, and Arizona is not the solidly Democratic city centers, or the bloodred rural ground, but the suburbs—some poor, some rich; some a stone's throw from the city, and some only marginally attached to urban energy and commercial activity. The shift of merely a few points toward Democrats in the suburbs was crucial to Joe Biden's 2020 victory. In a violent attempt to nullify the votes of the eighty-one million Americans responsible for the Biden presidency, an insurrectionist insurgency, comprising largely enraged white men from small metro suburbs and exurbs, stormed the Capitol, where they defecated on the floor, attacked police officers, and threatened to lynch public officials, hoping to stop the certification of the election.

Similar to when two armies converged at Gettysburg or a young minister named Martin Luther King organized a boycott of public transit in Montgomery, Alabama, suddenly many people are deeply worried, anxious, and excited about what transpires in places no one used to care about.

THE RIGHT-WING STATES OF MOST EXURBAN AND some suburban counties makes them convenient debate fodder whenever the national discussion turns to "red" and "blue" states, but the consequences are much greater than election results, which typically receive the breathless, and often superficial, coverage of competition in professional sports. Exurbia is no longer the setting of an intriguing subplot in American history. Because it is the recruiting and staging area for the extreme right, it is the battleground of American democracy.

Exurbia Now: The Battleground of American Democracy will give an impressionistic sense of what it is like to live in one part of the Midwest where suburbia and exurbia meet, intermingle, and often collide. It provides a sense of the fight for democracy, on the ground, in the heartland, and how suburbia is changing and exurbia is becoming radically right wing in response. In the shadow of Chicago and stretching into the pastoral villages of Indiana, the geography of Exurbia Now illustrates the erosion, shifting terrain, and fertility of an American democracy that is both beleaguered and yet still full of promise. The stories, arguments, and observations that fill Exurbia Now derive from a writer in a unique position to offer a powerful chronicle. I combine over ten years of journalism and familiarity with academic research into American voting patterns and political alignments with the education of my own life. I came of age in the Chicago suburbs, live in northwest Indiana, and have come to possess a degree of intimacy with the people and places I describe.

A drive through my part of the vast American landscape corrects many of the misperceptions that inhibit political comprehension and conversation. The average Trump supporter, for example, is not a hobo of globalization, merely angry at trade deals and political correctness. The reality is much more insidious. The average small town is not a backwater full of only prejudice and parochial judgment. The reality is much more inspiring.

There are many Americans who do not neatly fall into the increasingly narrow and stereotypical classifications of politics and identity. I am one. My home is in a small town in Indiana, and yet my politics are firmly on the left. My ideology finds traffic with most metropolitan progressives to the extent that one of my most reliable sources of amusement is the hate mail I receive from angry readers who accuse me of membership in the dubious category "coastal elite." Most of the political allies that I find live in Chicago, or another large, urban area, but I prefer to reside in a small town. Once when interviewing Bill Ayers— the antiwar activist, educator, and once leading member of the Weather Underground who briefly became famous in 2008 when Sarah Palin called him a "terrorist"—he asked where I live. When I answered, he looked at me incredulously, and asked, "Why?" The brilliance and eloquence I managed to muster amounted to the simple declaration, "I like it." Ayers took a sip of his coffee.

It is not as if I live in a town not yet discovered by anthropologists. It takes a mere forty minutes by car or train to get to Chicago from my home. My wife, Sarah, and I often visit Art Institute, shop at bookstores, dine out, and attend concerts in jazz clubs and the beautiful Chicago

Theatre. We are also supporters and volunteers with the Rainbow/ PUSH Coalition—the international civil rights and humanitarian organization founded by Jesse Jackson with its headquarters on the southside of Chicago. I am an overjoyed visitor of Chicago, but I do not want to live in Chicago.

My friend, the novelist Tim Hall, once said that every person has an ecosystem in which they thrive. Born and raised in New York City, when he and his wife moved to a tiny town in Illinois, he felt like he was quarantined in a padded cell. He needs the lights, energy, activity, large crowds, and fast pace of the city. When Sarah and I file out of the Riviera Theatre, exit the Art Institute, or pay the tab at Harry Caray's restaurant, I am ready to retreat back to the empty side streets, two-block downtown, and slow movement of our little village where I can see dogs in big yards and children playing in the middle of the road, and when I'm in a solitary mood, can walk outside on a route that enables me to avoid human interaction.

It is something of a ritual in our home for Sarah to ask, "Why do we live here?" Her voice bending on notes of bafflement and distress— "What is wrong with people around here?" She sees the pickup trucks with NRA bumper stickers, "Blue Lives Matter" decals, and large flags flying from the back of the bed. If that sounds too clichéd to be true, come over for dinner some night. I once saw a truck with two stickers, side by side, apparently without a hint of cognitive dissonance—"God Bless Our Troops . . . Especially Our Snipers" and "Jesus Protects Me."

At the height of hostility in the 2016 presidential race, a neighboring town made local news when a bar owner advertised on her business sign—yes, the owner was a woman—"Grab 'Em by the Pussy. Buckets of Beer on Special." The chamber of commerce, along with a petition of nearby residents, pressured her to censor the sign, which she did, but only after protesting that "free speech was under assault" by the "politically correct."

It is often irritating to observe the pride in right-wing ignorance that is visible in provincial America, but that is not the entire story—and it is not the totality of my experience. It is a delight to take a leisurely walk into town, stop for a cup of vanilla custard at the family run dairy stand, or an espresso at the coffeehouse always playing the Grateful Dead while students from the local high school buzz around taking customers' orders, and then buy locally sourced honey from the eccentric chain smoker in high heels who owns a hodge-podge shop next door. I check a book out of the library, while the elderly clerk stocks the shelves, and children in costume run into the back room for a theme party. The waitress at the bar and grill down the road knows my wife's and my drink order before we even lower ourselves into a booth. The restaurant borders a bakery where its Buddhist owner has created an outdoor home for a few stray cats who sleep under its heated roof, and eat out of the bowls of dry food. Throughout the "Main Street" there are hand-painted murals decorating the buildings—the artwork of local painters and high school art students. We can also see advertisements for spaghetti dinners and pancake breakfasts benefitting low-income families, and cancer patients unable to keep up with their medical expenses—a reminder of both the ghastly injustices of American society, and the generosity of the human spirit.

Small towns have the reputation of translucent whiteness—a population so pale that an onlooker might require shades to walk down the street—but our neighbors include a couple who moved from Nigeria, an Illinois implant who married a Japanese immigrant, and a Colombian-born American. In our small neighborhood, there are young couples, elderly widows, and residents of various sexual orientations, political loyalties, and religious beliefs. There are bodybuilders, BMX riders, musicians, and drunkards.

Just as the right wing lies that the "Real America" exists only in towns like the one where I live (it exists everywhere and anywhere that is America—from Big Sky to the "big city"), liberals too often erroneously assert that the country's great diversity is only accessible in large cities, or that small towns are not part of progressive America.

The reality is that small towns have become ground zero for many of the nation's most urgent crises and severe troubles. The Brookings Institute has reported on the "changing geography of poverty," indicating that, in the words of a *Slate* headline, "The suburbs are now where poverty lives." Suburban and exurban sprawl has long initiated and illustrated that environmental devastation of US policy—creating neighborhoods that are unwalkable, prioritizing automobiles over people, increasing pollution, and contributing to the existential threat of climate change. The fight for healthy and locally sourced food—products of sustainable agricultural practices—often begins in small towns where farmers live and work the land. As progressives celebrate the multiculturalism and cosmopolitanism of major metropolitan areas, they should consider that the fight for racial equality, and the acceptance of LGBTQ Americans, is at its most impactful in small towns, where racial minorities often have a tougher time receiving hospitality from their neighbors, and a young gay boy or trans girl is more likely to have come out to a conservative family.

Following the election of Donald Trump, the major newspapers and cable news networks were breathless in their coverage of the "Trump voter," creating profiles that were so repetitive that one can almost write them according to memory, recycling clichéd phrases and common images of white working class privation: The unemployed factory worker stares pensively out the living room window of a dilapidated rental home, taking slow drags off his cigarette before explaining how the town slid into economic decline when the textile mill boarded its doors.

His story is important, but where was the segment on the young Hillary Clinton voter in Youngstown, Ohio—barely able to make student debt payments, and concerned about her uninsured mother ailing from a stroke? Where was the story of the Indiana for Biden volunteer in 2020 who called my home to confirm that my wife and I were going to make it to the polls? Where was the coverage of the activists who have toiled for decades—without profit or fame—to prevent their towns from falling under the manipulative spell of right-wing propaganda and scapegoating by working to engineer class solidarity that transcends racial difference and religious divide?

The story that is lost in the transformation of suburbia, and the traumas and triumphs of the small town, is the power, persistence, and often mere presence, of the small town liberal—the inhabitant of provincial America who believes in equality, celebrates diversity, and enrolls in movements for justice.

By creating a false dichotomy of urban versus rural and suburban, the mainline media amplified the divisive stereotypes of the effete elite in a high rise of Chicago chortling at the troubles of the hick downstate, who keeps his assault rifle safely underneath a Confederate flag in the garage. While these unfortunate characters do populate American cities and villages, they are not wholly representative. There are right-wing racists and homophobic theocrats in Manhattan, and there are acolytes of Jesse Jackson, Harvey Milk, and Dolores Huerta in suburban courthouses and agrarian classrooms. They have stories that are essential to the navigation of America's political and spiritual geography.

The war for the American future, as James Lee Burke would appreciate, is happening in places few people care about. One side is gathering forces and arms in the exurbs, and another is organizing in the cities and moving to the suburbs. Causalities—an ultimate tragedy of warfare - are inevitable. The battlefields are the towns and counties like mine, but the fallout zone stretches all the way around the world.

✳

"I WAS BORN IN A SMALL TOWN..." JOHN MELLENCAMP sings in the opening line of his famous song about his hometown of Seymour, Indiana. Growing up in a region with the nickname "Kentuckiana," Mellencamp become one of rock and roll's greatest songwriters, and a cofounder of Farm Aid, a yearly benefit concert for American farmers. Mellencamp's songs, often dealing with the blight of racism, war, and abuse of the poor on America's political ecology, provide not only entertainment, but also illustrate the inspiring fusion that is possible between art and activism.

"I'm a blue guy in a red state," the music legend told me when I met him in his recording studio in Nashville, Indiana—a town with a "barn dance" as one of its entertainment venues. One of the neighbors of Mellencamp's artistic headquarters was an old man in bib overalls reading the Bible on the front porch. "I like having the opportunity," the songwriter and painter continued, "to communicate with people who don't hold my political beliefs." When he was on VH1 *Storytellers*, a program that encouraged songwriters to give lengthy spoken word introductions to their most popular songs, he argued that what resonated with his audience with "Small Town" was the "truth" of the song. "All I did was look out my window, and sing what I saw," he said before belting out, in his signature rasp, lines like, "I cannot forget from where it is that I come from / I cannot forget the people who really love me..."

Mellencamp believes that, in this instance, the truth made people "feel good about themselves." "Other times," he explained, "I've written songs that told the truth, and people have said, 'Man, why are you being so negative?' No, that's not negative, that's just the truth that you don't want to hear."

I first heard the truth of Mellencamp's music as a thirteen-year-old boy while I was playing basketball in the driveway at a friend's house. We pretended we were in the starting lineup of the Chicago Bulls, alongside Michael Jordan and Scottie Pippen, when my friend's older brother walked into the garage, began working under the hood of his car, and inserted a cassette into a boombox. When the power chords registered in my adrenaline glands, I rushed over to ask what he was playing. Looking irritated at my existence, he handed me the cassette case: John Cougar, *American Fool.*

That was my entrance into the wonderful emporium of rock and roll. It was my introduction to art. It was an early glimpse into a universe of liberal politics with its topography of justice and its cartography of hope. It was all the unpredictable result of one small town rebel—one pastoral progressive—looking out his window, and summoning all his creativity, compassion, and eloquence—to describe what he saw.

And so begins this book.

EXURBIA NOW

WELCOME TO THE EXIT:
A SUBURBAN-EXURBAN TOUR

The United States of America promised an escape from reality. Throughout the second half of the twentieth century, the protection of two oceans, the bounty of natural resources, the exploitation of cheap labor, and a mythmaking machine that would flush the cheeks of Lewis Carroll, allowed Americans to live in the perpetual fantasy of eternal youth and endless wealth. "American exceptionalism," the fraught and destructive update of "manifest destiny," which postulates the United States as an "indispensable nation," different and superior to the dispensable, emanates out of the delusional essence of the American experience. Like two of America's most fantastical creations—Hollywood and Disney—so too does the "American dream" spring out of the "amber waves of grain." Like a drunk stumbling into an insight, the phrase "American dream" includes a certain admirable honesty. Dreams are unreal. They can possess great beauty, as much of the American dream does, especially for the countless immigrants from countless nations who risked life and limb for freedom and opportunity awaiting them on American shores. They can also turn to nightmares. In the American dream, suburbia is the deep REM sleep stage of the dream. If the United

States offers an escape from reality, suburbia, up until recently, always offered an escape from the escape. It is the fantasy of endless growth taken
to its most vivid and pornographic. Suburbia, like any fantasy featuring
the Freudian synthesis of fears and wishes, occupies a bipolar identity
in American culture. Politicians and parents romanticize it, promising
that in the suburbs the family is free to thrive and children are free from
crime, drugs, and danger. Filmmakers, songwriters, novelists, and painters have explored its dark side, transforming the substance of dreams
into the material of night terrors. From Sinclair Lewis's *Main Street* to
David Lynch's *Blue Velvet*, the suburbs threaten to stupefy and horrify.
The irony is that for millions of Americans across generations, including
me, suburbia was the home of, to paraphrase the title of the most famous
movie set in a small town, "a wonderful life."

In the United States, whether it was true or not, mediocre political
leaders convinced the middle class in the second half of the twentieth
century that famine, war, genocide, oppression, and extreme poverty
were the plot twists of melodramatic tales that took place in history
books or countries far away without any connection to life in the land of
the free. The suburbs offered a localized, domestic version of the escapist
dream. Crime, gun violence, deprivation, drug addiction, environmental
degradation, infrastructural decay, and racial discord were problems for
big-city mayors and police departments to handle. They could not—and
would not—invade the suburban fortress. When Donald Trump lit rabid crowds on fire with his nativist, hateful, and imbecilic chant, "Build
the wall!" his suburban and exurban base of voters reacted with excitement. He was speaking their language. For decades they had resided in
American territory they believed would forever enjoy the protection of
walls institutional, ideological, and imaginary.

*

WHEN DEFINING AND DESCRIBING SUBURBIA AND exurbia, and making a distinction between the two related but not identical terms and places, it is necessary to distinguish what suburbia was from what it has become. There are suburbs everywhere in the developed world, but in the United States they took on a unique character in congruence with the unique dynamics of American culture and economics, namely racial segregation and the prioritization of the automobile as the organizing principle of city planning and familial life. Following the Second World War, it became not only possible but popular to construct communities dozens of miles away from men's jobsites and the elements that surrounded those jobsites—traffic, pollution, nightlife decadence, and racial minorities.

When my grandfather returned home from World War II, he used a GI loan to purchase a home in the town where he grew up—Thornton, Illinois. Thornton, about twenty miles outside of Chicago, became a working- and middle-class suburb. Its bankability rested on its proximity to the freeway and also its even closer proximity to the Material Service Quarry—a profitable limestone extraction operation that provided stable, high-wage union employment to thousands of workers, including my grandfather. He and my grandmother would have one child, my mother, Pearl. Like many residents of Thornton, my grandparents were first-generation Americans—the children of Serbian immigrants. Their beige-colored skin was passed down to my mother. Even though her racial category was "white," her appearance as a young girl was brown. There were no Black or Latino families in Thornton. So, in the absence of the real targets of their hatred, the neighborhood bigots began throwing rocks and hurling anti-Black racial epithets at my mother during her morning walks to school. The harassment persisted for years, and the implications of my mother's childhood resound in the study of recent American history. Her experience is emblematic of the dominant trends of the late twentieth century.

One of the great ironies of American politics is that suburban voters are typically more "conservative" than their urban compatriots, and yet the suburbs exist only because of big government spending. My grandfather nearly died in an effort to save civilization from fascism. It isn't as if he did not earn his compensation. The fact remains, however, that he, like millions of other American veterans, helped to build and populate the suburban middle class with the indispensable aid of government subsidy. The staggering amount of young men who entered the real estate market following the Second World War, armed with GI loans, led to a massive boom in property development and housing. From the famous Levittown development of Long Island to the "bedroom communities" surrounding Detroit, real estate magnates took advantage of escalating demand for family homes, and public funding, by creating the suburbs. Whether they were applying at the Material Service Quarry in Thornton, the steel mills of nearby Gary, Indiana, or the automobile plants in Detroit, young men found almost boundless opportunity for backbreaking but secure work with handsome benefits. The victories of organized labor coalesced with additional government subsidy to make suburban living and family rearing ideal. In 1956, President Dwight Eisenhower, himself a World War II veteran, signed the Federal-Aid Highway Act, fully funding the establishment and maintenance of interstate expressways. The expansion of freeways functioned as a jackpot for automobile companies and construction firms. It also enhanced an already prosperous real estate market. Better and bigger highways translate into safer and easier commutes. The suburban middle class was the largest and most successful big government program in the history of the United States.[1]

Economists have an anemic term, "negative externalities," which in direct English means, "consequences." The consequences of the creation of the suburban middle class were smog, the explosion of fossil fuels, the trigger of white fear and resentment as a national political force, and the degradation of communal and civic life through the encouragement of neighborhood isolation and individualistic car culture. Another consequence involves government and taxpayer largesse. When someone receives, someone else does not. Sheryll Cashin, Georgetown law professor, refers to the mechanisms of the multidecade exclusion of Blacks, Latinos, and Native Americans from "white spaces" as "opportunity hoarding," "boundary maintenance," and "stereotype-driven surveillance."[2]

As cruel as it might seem for children to make a young girl like my mother feel hated for the color of her skin, her playground bullies were acting in concert with governors, mayors, bank CEOs, loan officers, and an entire nexus of public policy and economic development. The white neighborhoods and suburbs of Chicago practiced redlining to such a severe extent that the region remains one of the most segregated in modern America. Banks refused to give loans to Black applicants, landlords would not rent to Black tenants, and commercial districts largely remained "white only," even if the signs of Jim Crow never actually hung in the windows. The muscles of economic apartheid flexed throughout the United States, often squeezing the life out of Black mobility and crushing the promise of multiracial democracy.[3] If redlining failed, other cities and suburbs would resort to "blockbusting."[4] One of the most infamous offenses took place near Baltimore, where city officials, police, and neighborhood associations would employ intimidating young men, straight out of hoodlum central casting, to patrol the streets, make noise, and shout threats "coincidentally" when Black families would tour houses on the market. When all else failed and Blacks had the temerity to purchase homes they could afford in towns they desired to live, whites would simply leave like herds of sheep stampeding to the direction of a racist shepherd. The term "white flight" describes what transpired in cities, and then suburbs, across the country. As whites took flight, the property values of the community plummeted due to an oversaturation of the market in real estate supply. Business owners would also move, seeking to retain a white customer base, and thereby deprive the local government of desperately needed tax revenue. When the town would begin to show signs of decline, whites would ignorantly but conveniently blame the situation on the presence of Blacks, e.g., "There goes the neighborhood."

According to numerous studies, the white flight that took place in the south suburbs of Chicago was one of the fastest on national record.[5] And the runways are still ready for lift off. A recent report on the upperclass, professional Chicago suburb of Flossmoor found that in recent years, as more middle-class and wealthy Black families have begun to purchase houses and condominiums, white families have left in droves.[6]

During a conversation with Jesse Jackson, the civil rights leader told me that there is a sequence of institutional and social transformation that many progressives invert. For widespread progress to occur, it is first necessary to change the law; the law then creates a system of rewards and punishments for behavior. Only when behavior changes in reaction to the stimuli of the law do attitudes begin to change. The children who harassed my mother were not only exercising popular prejudices but also reflecting the laws and policies of their community and country. Similarly, the poet Martín Espada describes suffering beatings and endless verbal assault when his family moved from Brooklyn to Long Island and he became the only Puerto Rican student at his otherwise all-white high school. Housing laws, bank practices, and institutional investment told Espada's tormenters, like my mother's harassers, that they were right to practice interpersonal, vigilante "boundary maintenance." They felt that Espada did not belong on Long Island and that my mother did not belong in Thornton. Who would tell them otherwise?

In fact, exclusion and boundary maintenance are also visible and palpable in what town managers and private developers choose *not* to build. Even where sprawl exists, the available housing demonstrates that it is a particular type of sprawl intended for a particular type of resident.

Historian and urban theorist Mike Davis wrote about how neighborhood associations exert legally dubious power over the suburbs of Los Angeles by forbidding homeowners within their association borders to convert houses into rental units.[7] These same associations also convince city councils to strictly prohibit, through zoning laws, the development of apartment complexes, affordable housing, or units that qualify for rent assistance. The construction of single-family homes, especially eyesore McMansions, welcomes a certain demographic to the suburb or exurb—middle- and upper-class families—while pricing out other demographics—low-income families, single parents, and childless adults.

Perhaps nowhere in the United States is exclusionary housing worse than Long Island. In the town of Huntington, single-family homes account for 81 percent of housing stock. A plan to develop an affordable housing complex on Long Island was met with such extreme hostility that Huntington leaders fought it all the way to the Supreme Court.[8] The court ruled in favor of the development plan, but the larger injustice of inadequate housing options in suburbia and exurbia continues to paralyze the poor. Given that for most of American history Blacks and Latinos have experienced disproportionate poverty rates in comparison with whites, the public-private partnership of suburban exclusivity has inflicted greater damage on racial minorities while preserving moderate and reactionary voting patterns where it takes place.

The laws helped to shape the suburban attitude that poet, Michael Blumenthal, described in verse: "Conformity caught here, nobody catches it / Lawns groomed in prose, with hardly a stutter."

It is tempting to use Blumenthal's verse as a functional definition of "suburbia," but the historical pattern calls for more precision. The conventional definition of a suburb is a residential district outlying a large city. As is evident from even a cursory history of suburbia, a suburb is not only a residential community loosely connected to a city but municipally independent of the city; it is a town resulting from deliberate investment in residential growth, planning for middle-to-upper-class populations, commercial development, and exclusion of "undesirable" elements of urban life. This definition, despite its ideological appearance, applies to suburban towns throughout the United States, and it also emphasizes suburbia as refuge—the means of escape for Americans who can afford to invest in an exodus project. Seeking to escape racial diversity, the interference of civic policy in their "personal freedom," pollution, crime, and the dicey issues of managing schools, hospitals, parks, and other public institutions with a multiracial and multireligious polity, Americans could flock to the suburbs.

Developers were more than happy to accommodate the dream of retreat. It is often far more cost effective to build a new subdivision, or stretch the suburb into undeveloped territory, than to provide housing options in already existent residential and commercial districts. Everything from unworn pipes in the ground to freshly paved roads creates an incentive for sprawl. Why spend money on repair when one can maximize profits by starting over? As the authors of *Suburban Nation: The Rise of Sprawl and the Decline of the American Dream* write, "In the case of the city, whiz kids took a complex human tradition of settlement, said 'out with the old,' and replaced it with a rational model that could be easily understood through systems analysis and flow charts. Town planning, until 1930 considered a humanistic discipline based upon history, aesthetics, and culture, became a technical profession based upon numbers."[9]

New communities come with the bonus of lower property taxes. Fewer children in school, low numbers of police officers and firefighters, little to no public transportation, and fully operational infrastructure guarantees low tax rates. The tradition of big-government suburbia continues, especially in exurbia, given that studies and budget analyses routinely show that local, state, and often even federal taxes finance suburban and exurban growth. Within the same suburb, as sprawl begins, tax increases on residents in the old part of town typically subsidize developments in the new part of town. Middle-to-upper-class residents of exurban sprawl are, consequentially, liberated to entertain the delusion that higher tax rates in cities like Chicago or Indianapolis, or even old suburbs, are solely the result of "big government" grifters plotting to dine out on the public dime.

The same antisocial citizens who view taxation as theft will, with all the eloquence of Mel Gibson screaming in *Braveheart*, adopt the word "freedom" as a comprehensive political philosophy. The funny thing about freedom is that other people have it too, and they can use it in ways you might not like. Decades of racist housing policies, even with the enforcement of police patrol, blockbusting tactics, and gentlemen's agreements among landlords, could not prevent Blacks, Latinos, and Asians from acquiring the capability to travel and purchase homes in middle-class suburbs. As the story of Flossmoor indicates, along with towns like Elkhart, Indiana, where an influx of Latinos has shifted the demography, people who are not white also desire to live in suburbia. My own experience illustrates what transpired in counties across the country. When I enrolled at Thornton Fractional South High School in Lansing, Illinois, in 1999, my freshmen class was over 80 percent white. The freshmen class when I graduated was only half white. Meanwhile, suburbs were beginning to capsize in the wake of deindustrialization. The small towns throughout the Rust Belt surrounding cities like Pittsburgh, Youngstown, and Milwaukee that once relied on nearby manufacturing hubs for their own economic security found themselves without a raft as multinational corporations automated production and outsourced the jobs that remained.

Public subsidy and big government investment created the suburbs. Privatization, austerity, and the retraction of public funds are killing them. From 2000 to 2018, the poverty rate in suburbia increased by 55 percent.[10] Likewise, rising crime rates and the opioid crisis demonstrate that social ills associated with poverty do not respect the suburban boundary. Without a robust social welfare state to provide health care, high-quality education, and other social services, young suburban residents have little hope for stability, much less prosperity. Those with the opportunity to leave attend university and seek employment in an urban center with a thriving economy. Sociologists call the lasting effect "brain drain" because it deprives struggling towns of the youthful energy, creativity, and ingenuity that might help them recover.

Meanwhile, older generations are opting for a different kind of escape. Given that they can no longer rely upon the exclusion and isolation of suburbia, they have taken flight—yet again—and landed in exurbia. One can gather from the "sub" in "suburbia" that a suburb is a town falling into a subcategory of its nearby city. The "ex" in exurbia offers similar truth in advertising. It is excised from the city. While the exurbs are not quite rural, because they maintain loose geographic proximity to cities and they are even closer to bustling suburbs, they are desolate. Their planners, typically, embrace sprawl, promising social isolation to residents, with the buffer of suburbs further separating them from Chicago or Detroit or Denver. As the American populace grows more diverse, with many major cities, such as New York, Las Vegas, and Los Angeles, already reaching "majority-minority" status, and as the converging crises of extreme income inequality and global warming threaten not only the United States but the entire world, the exurbs offer an alternative America to its middle- and upper-class, predominantly white and Republican inhabitants. Forever on the run, the world follows the herd wherever it goes. When they turn on the television, they see the apocalypse that their megachurch ministers and favorite right-wing radio hosts have predicted for years—Black and Latino people in power, immigrants crossing the border, gay couples saying their wedding vows, pretty blonde cheerleaders applauding for 6'8" Black men with tattoos, falling rates of religious devotion, NFL players refusing to stand for the national anthem, and transgender people entering the public restrooms of their choice. In the Christian theology popular throughout exurban churches, "the rapture" promises an inevitable, glorious day when God will elevate all of the good, Christian souls off the Earth. While the chosen few enjoy the pleasures of paradise, Jesus Christ, "the Prince of Peace," will command the slaughter of the heretics who remain. Until that beautiful moment arrives, what are the faithful, "real Americans" to do?

"THE FIGHT OR FLIGHT RESPONSE IS TRIGGERED BY A release of hormones either prompting us to stay and fight or run away and flee," Carolyn Fisher, a psychologist with the Cleveland Clinic explains. "During the response, all bodily systems are working to keep us alive in what we've perceived as a dangerous situation."[11]

Sarah Palin, version 1.0 of Donald Trump, anointed white, Christian Americans who live in small towns "real Americans." The "real Americans" have fled from what they perceive as dangerous—and artificially American—for decades. They've ventured far out into the exburbs: towns with only marginal attachment to cities, full of middle- and upper-class housing and commercial chain stores and restaurants, that seek to recreate the suburban fortress at a distance from the now contaminated suburbs. While they enjoy a certain geographic liberation, the political and cultural walls are closing in. Flight is no longer an option in a country with a Black woman as vice president, a married gay man as secretary of transportation, and teachers in schools beginning to tell their children about Black, Indigenous, and LGBTQ history. No longer able to escape, they are now going to fight. They can no longer run from the danger. They must confront it and, ultimately, destroy it. The danger is democracy.

Robert Pape, a political scientist at the University of Chicago and one of the world's leading researchers of terrorism, conducted an exhaustive and microscopic study of the domestic terrorists who broke into the Capitol Building, threatened to murder elected officials, assaulted police officers, and attempted to subvert electoral politics on January 6, 2021. He found that only roughly 10 percent belonged to extremist political organizations, such as white supremacist groups or armed militias. The profile of the average seditionist, almost always white and right-wing, cut across classification in other ways. It was a multigenerational mob of various income classes. Pape found that some of the terrorists were living in borderline poverty with multiple liens against them, while others were relatively wealthy. The most common class of insurrectionist was the petty bourgeois—small business owners, average professionals, and tradesmen who earn over $50,000 per year. Many of them travelled to DC from counties that lean Republican, while others live in "blue" counties. The single most significant commonality among the assembly of would-be fascists was residence in a county where the non-white population is growing. Pape and his colleagues have identified a racially diversifying community as the most active and consistent trigger for right-wing radicalism in the United States.[12]

The Pape study might lead an otherwise uninformed observer to conclude that Trump supporters, QAnon adherents, and "alt-right" sympathizers live in major metropolitan areas. Nowhere in the United States is diversifying faster than cities like Chicago, Los Angeles, and Atlanta. Research has shown that the counties Pape identifies are not urban but suburban and exurban. The far-right voters and activists occupy exurbia, and their counties are becoming more racially and culturally diverse, because of an influx of Blacks, Latinos, and Asians into the suburbs. Jacob Whiton, a political geographer with Georgetown University, scrutinized "where Trumpism lives" for the *Boston Review*, studying the congressional districts that have elected the most fascistic representatives in Congress—those who voted to reject the 2020 election results, sponsor voter-suppression legislation, and are especially hostile to even moderate measures aimed at gun control, LGBTQ rights, or more hospitable immigration procedures. The rogues' gallery of congressmen and -women who appear to despise the institution for which they work, and most of the people it purports to serve, are familiar to anyone who monitors the escalating insanity of American politics: Marjorie Taylor Greene of Georgia, Matt Gaetz of Florida, Lauren Boebert of Colorado, Jim Jordan of Ohio, and similar officials. About these menaces to the Republic, and the voters who installed them in government, Whiton writes:

> The evidence cuts strongly against the common view of the movement as driven by "lumpen" Rust Belt rage and economic despair in the country's shrinking rural hinterland. Rather, the picture that emerges is one of greenfield suburbs that are both fast growing and rapidly diversifying, where inequalities between relatively well-off white households and their non-white neighbors have been shrinking the most . . . In addition to being considerably more suburban than Democratic districts, as all Republican districts are, residents of [2020 election certification] objectors' districts are nearly twice as likely as residents of other Republican districts to live in exurban "sparse suburban areas."[13]

Even if the exurbs are "sparse," they are growing at faster rates than the rest of the country. They include large districts in essential swing states, like the western suburbs, now sprawling into exurbs, of Milwaukee—the largest city in Wisconsin, a state where Trump won in 2016 by about twenty-three thousand votes, and where he lost to Joe Biden by only approximately twenty thousand votes.

With votes, donations, political association, and, as the insurrection of January 6 demonstrated, even violence, the exurban extremists have declared war on democracy, its system of multiracial representation, free and fair elections, and the hope for equality and peaceful coexistence among people of different races and religions. They are responsible for the election of the most destructive members of Congress, and because they often live in swing states, like Wisconsin and North Carolina, they will exert an outsized influence on upcoming presidential races. Whiton finds that it is not only the presence of Blacks, Latinos, Native Americans, and Asians who arouse anger in exurbia, but that right-wing extremism grew the most in "districts where the average Black-white poverty gap shrank." He also concludes that "white homeowners' perception of a loss of status relative to upwardly mobile Hispanic and Asian American households is the social context out of which emerged the nativist politics at the center of Trumpism."

In a sad attempt to obfuscate the centrality of nativism to the modern Republican Party, many mainstream journalists and pundits have created the folklore that Latinos are "drifting right." While it is true that Trump, astonishingly, earned more Latino votes than Mitt Romney, the election data from 2020 and 2022 proves beyond any doubt that two-thirds of Latinos consistently vote for Democrats, and that strong Latino turnout in swing states, such as Pennsylvania, Nevada, and Arizona, was essential to Biden's victory and to the Democratic Party retaining control of the Senate in the 2022 midterms. The insidious nature of the right-wing Latino myth is that it leads uninformed observers to believe that Latinos are the perpetrators of racism. In reality, they are its victims. The Republican Party has become an insurgency of white nationalism, unsurprisingly, due to white voters.

Historian Carol Anderson has written that "Black advancement is the trigger for white rage."[14] Donald Trump exemplifies Anderson's thesis. The exurban-suburban dynamic is crucial to the trigger, because exurbia tends to house wealthier county residents than suburbia. The mainstream media often ran with depictions of the Trump base as the sociopolitical reincarnation of the Joad family, zeroing in on blue-collar individuals while ignoring the larger trend of middle-class and upper-class exurban whites moving to the far-right fringe. On the far-right fringe of the county map, and the political spectrum, exurban whites are now enlisting in a reactionary counterrevolution, fighting for the diminution of the Bill of Rights and the erasure of decades of progress.

I GENUINELY ENJOY LIVING IN A SMALL SUBURB IN Northwest Indiana. Even if the institutional and political origins of a place are not entirely admirable, it can still evolve and progress into something much more communal, charming, and nuanced. If one were to condemn a town or institution because it has a history of racism, exploitation of labor, or homophobia, the entire United States would instantly become irredeemable and unlivable. Even major metropolitan areas with progressive reputations, from New York to San Francisco, could hardly claim innocence. It is not those cities, however, that will determine the survival of democracy within the United States. As the data on voting trends, and volumes of recent journalism, can attest, it is also not rural America that will measure the life span of the American experiment in self-governance. At least in the immediate future, the urban and pastoral have pledged their respective political fealties. In an increasingly polarized America, it is the suburban counties stretching into exurbs that will decide if the country will enlarge its pattern of regularly expanding rights for the previously excluded and abused or allow white rage, paranoia, and autocracy to eliminate all hope for an equal and just society. Many journalists depict the manifestation of the "culture wars" and their political implications happening in suburbia and exurbia as a

subplot in the larger story of American history—trotting out diner cor-
respondences and small-town reportage every four years in the months
leading up to a presidential election. The "swing" status of suburban-
exurban counties makes them convenient for debate fodder whenever
the national discussion turns to "red states" and "blue states," but the
consequences are much greater. Exurbia is no longer the setting of an
intriguing subplot. It is the breeding and staging ground for the far-right
insurgency and, therefore, the battleground of American democracy.

*

IN THE 2016 PRESIDENTIAL RACE, HILLARY CLINTON
carried Lake County, Indiana, where I live, with 57.7 percent of the vote.
Only 37.3 percent of Lake County residents voted for the Trump/Pence
ticket. Four years later, Biden and Harris won 56.7 percent of the vote,
but Trump increased his share to 41.7 percent. During the interim period, the exurbs of the county attracted more residents, and now the
electoral map of Lake County resembles an illustration of blood leak-
ing out of a black eye. The north side of the county, on the edge of the
Illinois border and close to Chicago, is deep blue. Relatively large towns
like Hammond and Gary, which have predominantly Black and Latino
inhabitants and once prospered in the industrial economy, strongly favor the Democratic Party. Their predominantly white and middle-class
neighbors, small towns like Munster and Highland, are also reliably
Democratic, even if the results are more mixed. The blood leaks down in
narrow lines until it reaches the southern portion of the county, where
the exurbs become pools of dark red.[15] In 2021, the Associated Press
reported that the Republican National Committee added the congressional district representing Lake County, Indiana, to its list of seats they
hoped to turn from Democratic to Republican (they failed in the 2022
midterms but will try again).[16]

Exurban resentment gave Republicans a victory in the Virginia race of 2021, where a more palatable version of Trump, Glenn Youngkin, galvanized support with appeals to the fight-or-flight instinct of his voters—simultaneously telling constituents that they could take flight from the brutal realities of American history by eliminating topics of systemic racism from classroom curricula and also that they could fight the artificial Americans—teachers, historians, journalists—with legislative limits on academic freedom. All of these political discussions, even those that involve the preemptive muzzling of teachers, might seem like standard fare, given that debates involving educational policies, banned books, and their electoral effects date back to the Scopes Monkey Trial. When one political party has brazenly adopted authoritarianism as an ideology, hate crimes increase on an annual basis, and the membership roles of militias are swelling; it is as clear as a tornado siren blaring overhead that the stakes are far higher than the average political argument, and that the outcome is potentially catastrophic.

CROWN POINT, INDIANA, ACTS AS THE BORDER BE-tween suburbia and exurbia in Lake County, situated at the center separating the dense suburbs of the north from the sparse exurbs of the south. Crown Point, often called the "hub" of the county because of its charming square surrounding the old country courthouse, is most famous for one of its former visitors. John Dillinger, while on his ruthless armed robbery spree, spent a night on the town's dime in county lockup. The next morning he broke free of law enforcement shackles and hit the road for more theft and mayhem. Johnny Depp attracted screaming fans to Crown Point during the filming of the Michael Mann movie *Public Enemies*, in which he starred as the legendary outlaw. Because Crown

Point has preserved the jail cell where Dillinger resided for twelve hours, Mann and his crew were able to film the scenes in Crown Point with historical accuracy.

Crown Point is also the location of some of my fondest memories. The Lake County Fair at the Crown Point fairgrounds was a can't-miss event every summer during my childhood. My mother and I would go on the carnival rides, walk through the barns to look at the chickens and cows, watch the horse show, and then close the day by dining on the artery-jamming but irresistible feast of large pepperoni pizza slices and elephant ears, which, for the uninitiated, are gigantic, cinnamon-covered pieces of fried dough. When I was in my mid-twenties, one of my closest friends decided to move to New York. We spent one of his final nights in the Chicagoland area, which encompasses Chicago and its surrounding suburbs, stretching from southern Wisconsin to Northern Indiana, drinking shots and beers at Silver Bullet, a Bob Seger–themed bar in the courthouse square, appropriately enough, on Main Street. Live entertainment for the night was the rollicking blues band Dave Weld and the Imperial Flames. So impressed with their performance were my wife and I that we booked them to play our wedding reception a few years later.

Whether it is eating fried food at a picnic table underneath a Ferris wheel or toasting friendship and Bob Seger in a neighborhood bar, Crown Point resonates in my heart as a generous cut of Americana. In 2020, Crown Point briefly became the focal point for millions of Americans, unfortunately for reasons that had nothing to do with carnival games or "Night Moves."

During the political rebellion following the police murder of George Floyd, protest rallies filled the streets of cities large and small. Crown Point was no exception. Amaya Butler, an activist and student at Jackson State University, was on break from school, back in her lifelong hometown of Crown Point, when she watched Floyd's homicide on television. She and other local activists organized a march and demonstration to protest systemic racism and police brutality. "I stand here as a Black woman who is fed up with the tragedies that keep occurring throughout our country," she said. "I am tired of turning on the news only to see another beautiful soul unfairly taken from this earth." Seven million Americans watched video from the Crown Point event but, unfortunately, not to hear Butler and others condemn injustice. It was to react in horror to how some Lake County residents treated Butler and her one hundred fellow marchers.

Twenty-one white men, many of them with camouflage clothing and Osama bin Laden–style beards, lined the protest route holding assault rifles. As the one hundred marchers did nothing more than exercise their First Amendment rights, the gun-toting racists hurled slurs and threats. Several of the protesters said that they felt intimidated, understandably so, and that they suspected that the armed opponents of the march were attempting to escalate the event into a violent confrontation. One of the Black Lives Matter marchers, Bella Gomez, said that the militia-style brigade calmed down only when Crown Point police intervened. She added that "if the cops were not there, I don't know what would have happened." The events in Charlottesville, Virginia, in 2017 and in Washington, DC, on January 6, 2021, might offer a clue as to what *could* have happened. Since the laws of Indiana allow for open carry of shotguns and rifles, the Crown Point chief of police had no choice but to partially surrender to the dangerous insanity of the scene. When asked about the intimidating and threatening display of hatred, he said, "They have a right to do it."[17]

The war for the American future, with one side gathering forces and arms in the exurbs, will create causalities. The battlefields are the towns and counties like mine, but the fallout zone stretches all the way around the world.

THE CONFEDERACY
STRONGHOLD OF
NORTHERN ILLINOIS

Lansing, Illinois, was a picture card. In the 1990s, if one opened the card the message would read like patriotic verse, offering the infectious hospitality of hot dogs on the grill, fireworks on the Fourth of July, and a rambunctious young boy sliding into home. I was fortunate to have my formative experiences in Lansing—a Midwest slice of suburbia twenty-five miles south of Chicago. My parents, our beloved dogs, and I lived in a split-level home within walking distance of several parks, basketball hoops, and ice-cream parlors. When the merciless winter retreated, the spring and summer would invite endless nights of pickup baseball, basketball, or football and afternoons spent on bicycle exploring tiny creeks and short hills as if my friends and I were auditioning for roles as modern incarnations of Lewis and Clark. Using plywood, tree branches, and whatever material, tools, and supplies we could find or commandeer from our parents, we once constructed a humble fort alongside a creek flowing into a muddy bank behind the quiet, residential subdivision where I grew up. The creek ended a few yards from a railroad track, and on the other side was a battered and torn couch. A few teenagers would lounge on the furniture and the surrounding ground smoking cigarettes that emitted a strange, sweet odor. Not keen on having children several years younger within close distance, the oddly hostile potheads would throw rocks at us. If the fort was under heavy fire, we would have no choice but to surrender. One day my friends and I enacted our revenge by taking a bow saw to the sofa and staining what remained with an ample volume of Coca-Cola. A few days later we found our fort in ruins. Turf wars of both the amusing and catastrophic variety stretch back into antiquity. One need only to read the headlines of gang shootings in Chicago, or corporate battles for market share, to learn that among the most permanent of human instincts is the territorial.

Lansing shared one public high school with the nearby town of Lynwood. In an inversion of Chicago's demographic geography, the south side of Lansing was mostly middle class, professional—tree-lined streets and handsome houses with big backyards—while the north side had more apartment buildings, including the universally despised and feared "Section 8" complex. Lynwood recreated the stratification of class dynamic but with a more blue-collar characteristic. Some families sent their children to private academies within close proximity. Those with the motivation of elitism preferred Marian Catholic—a high-tuition, highly exclusive secondary school. Luther East and Illiana Christian attracted pious families who perished the thought of secularism poisoning the minds of their children. Most Lansing households—whether relatively rich or poor—sent their kids to the public high school without much consideration. Thornton Fractional South (TFS), a large and modest building right in the heart of town, gave a good education in the economic diversity of the United States. While it lacked anyone from the extremes, like multimillionaires or the homeless, it schooled children whose parents owned businesses, had medical licenses, and took annual vacations. Sitting alongside those children were the sons and daughters of single moms, blue-collar tradesmen, and hourly wage earners.

When I was a TFS student, from 1999 to 2003, the football team had a running back that no one could catch or bring to the ground—Pierre Thomas. Exercising the brilliant strategy of handing Pierre the ball and letting him run, the football squad made it to the Illinois state championship game for two consecutive years, losing both. Friday nights brought together nearly everyone in Lansing and Lynwood—filling the bleacher seats of the TFS stadium. Teenagers milled around the grounds, halfway paying attention to the gridiron and halfway investing in the triumphs and follies of young lust. Thomas would graduate to play for the University of Illinois and then the Super Bowl–winning New Orleans Saints. Before his athletic glory extended into professional stardom, Lansing sent buses full of children, parents, neighbors, and teachers to the state championship games, hoping for victory. On weeknights, passersby could see Thomas in the parking lot of TFS pulling his mother's used car. With her sitting at the steering wheel and Thomas battling the resistance of the rope tied around his waist, the automobile moved in slow and small circles. Adjacent to the parking lot was a massive stone near the flagpole at the school's front entrance. The "spirit rock," as everyone in town would come to call it, advertised spray-painted messages of school support or communal solidarity—congratulations to a graduating class, well wishes for a sports team, or even words of mourning for a recently deceased teacher or town mainstay.

During my high school years, I never pulled a car around the parking lot but, like Pierre Thomas, I walked into the building, bright and early in the morning, looking at the spirit rock and the flagpole with Old Glory overhead. The Stars and Stripes means many things to many people, but in the early 2000s in Lansing, it too was a symbol and source of unity, especially after the September 11 attacks. Even to present day, the courtyard where the spirit rock sits and the American flag flies is the gathering place for TFS students and staff, whether they are holding a ceremony to memorialize the death of a beloved drama teacher or staging a walkout to protest America's dangerously lax gun laws. For most of the school's history, the courtyard was not harmless and would have made for quite a strange, even disturbing, picture card. The message inside might reference slavery, lynching, and the Civil War. Waving high above TFS, and casting a political and cultural shadow over a small town in Illinois—a state with the slogan "Land of Lincoln"—was the Confederate flag.

TFS's rival, located in the town immediately north of Lansing, was Thornton Fractional North High School (TFN). Even though TFN had the benign nickname of "Meteors," the movers and shakers of the school district thought it clever to give TFS a rebel army moniker and motif. The TFS Rebels studied and played under the Stars and Bars, and throughout the hallways there were murals of Confederate armies, often with the commanding officer "Richie Rebel," a cartoon Confederate general who resembled Yosemite Sam. Needless to say, when TFS opened its doors, almost the entire town of Lansing, along with student body, was white. An obtuse provincialism prevented the school board, town council, school administration, and most residents from realizing how descendants of slaves might feel about sending their children to a school full of tributes to the secessionist military of the South. Lansing never hosted cross burnings in the town square or suffered racial strife that exploded into violence, but the few Blacks and Latinos living within its boundaries in the 1970s and '80s recall an atmosphere of tension, alienation, and subtle but consequential hostility.

Gregory Tejeda, a veteran journalist who covered so-called "Hispanic issues" for United Press International, graduated from TF South in 1980. He writes that he still experiences tremors of embarrassment when he reminisces on his high school days. Then principal Robert Maxeiner would often appear at pep rallies and football games in Confederate clothing, sporting a Stars and Bars vest or dress shirt as if he was first in line for a 1970s Lynyrd Skynyrd concert in Birmingham, Alabama. Tejeda was one of the few Latinos at TFS in the late 1970s, and there were only six Blacks in attendance during his graduating year. In a stroke of luck, none of the Blacks were selected to participate in "Slave Day"—an annual event Tejeda describes as certain students performing favors for other students who had won a contest, such as carrying books or fetching lunch. The TFS alumnus and accomplished journalist doesn't believe that his classmates or teachers were "segregationist wannabes," but that they were profoundly ignorant about the Civil War, Jim Crow, and the historical meaning and political application of the Confederate flag.[1] The ignorance morphed into self-generated stupidity, because no one made any effort to learn. Most astounding, Lansing townspeople fully committed to their ignorance and exercised it as a bludgeon against hospitality and equality.

When the town began to diversify in the 1990s, many Black parents, staff, and students—understandably baffled and outraged—began to demand the removal of all Confederate banners and imagery from school grounds. More than mere protest, Black families, along with a minority of white supporters, petitioned the school board and city halls of Lansing and Lynwood to make the elimination of Confederate iconography official. Recalling historian Carol Anderson's observation that Black progress provokes "white rage" and that Black demands, no matter how reasonable or pedestrian, are typically the impetus for racial collision, the Lansing fiasco seems less absurd.

White families grew outwardly bellicose toward Blacks, even staging a deranged and, given its Union location, rather bizarre march around the high school, brandishing Confederate flags and signage. Many marchers, like the former principal, wore Dixie-themed clothing. Chicago media covered the story, and *American Renaissance*, a flagship publication of the neofascist, white-supremacist right, even wrote a report, citing the "heritage not hate" clichés still popular among politicians in South Carolina, Georgia, and Mississippi. It appeared that a contemporary, suburban Battle of Shiloh was about to break loose, given the obstinance and escalating anger of whites. Like the Confederates at Gettysburg, they soon found themselves outmatched. The pro-Union side enlisted the help of Jesse Jackson, who promised to make a visit to Lansing and also convinced a few members of the Illinois state legislature to reevaluate any state funding for TFS in its budget. To protect state subsidy, and ward off a trip from the intensely feared Jackson, Lansing and Lynwood commissioned a panel of TFS administrators, faculty, and students to debate and vote on the Confederate flag. The nearly unanimous decision was in favor of removal. Had Jackson visited Lansing, he might have provided his audience with the same analysis he gave me in an interview after the South Carolina state government decided to, finally, remove the Confederate flag from government buildings in 2015. "It is good that the flag has come down," Jackson said, "but now the flag agenda must come down with it."

The flag agenda seeks to enforce a racial hierarchy in the distribution of power, prominence, and resources. Given that throughout American history, race is typically only one right turn away from class, and vice versa, the neo-Confederate program also maintains a political culture of aristocratic stratification for workers, voters, and consumers. Historian Heather Cox Richardson, taking into account the oligarchic swing of the early twenty-first century, writes in one of her books, "They [Confederates]were defeated on the battlefields, but their vision of America moved west after the Civil War, where it gathered the strength to regain power." The title of her book: *How the South Won the Civil War.*

The flag agenda also moved north, becoming visible and palpable in a dynamic not too dissimilar from my childhood turf war. The claim of conquest over a town and institution inspires a set of instinctual politics where policymakers pull levers in the background. Democracy insists upon the constant questioning and threatening of ownership claims, creating the mechanisms for collaborative control. The suburbs, especially those in the shadow of large, diverse, and comparably liberal cities, are often an unstudied staging ground for the crash between democratic aims and self-serving authority. Lansing was no exception, and the stakes proved higher than a damaged sofa and destroyed fort.

A SPECIAL COMMISSION COULD VOTE ON THE ELIMI-nation of Confederate iconography from the school, but it could not implement any regulations on townspeople's loyalty or ideology. Simultaneous with the loud fight over symbolism, a quiet exodus took place from Lansing. Whites began leaving town in reaction to the appearance of Black people. As a child, I can recall overhearing many conversations among personal relatives and families of friends that functioned as a racial "Where's Waldo" game, only substituting the word "Blacks" for the name of the striped-sweater-wearing character hiding in plain sight. "I saw Blacks there" and "There were a few Blacks around" became common in everyday vernacular. Talking about human beings with dark skin like UFO believers discussing sightings at a convention in Roswell was more than a perverse hobby for working- and middle-class whites in Lansing. It was announcement of a getaway plan. My family lived in the Monaldi Manor subdivision alongside dentists, small business owners, and school superintendents. The first Black people to purchase a home in Monaldi Manor were a childless couple who kept to themselves. One could ascertain from the man's work truck and clothing that he was a painter, and the sign in his yard indicating support for unions offered a critical detail about his level of income and security. Adjacent to their home, a Black family moved in only a few months later. Their two sons played basketball in the driveway, where I would often join them. The boys' father was a pastor of a midsize church a few towns over, and their mother was a nurse at a Chicago hospital. One wouldn't expect sane adults to find softspoken ministers and maternal health care practitioners menacing, but not long after their arrival, "for sale" signs started decorating Monaldi lawns. Few whites were so brazen to openly declare enmity toward Blacks. Instead, justification turned on a few coded concerns.

First, the entire town began making predictions of "declining property values." Real estate trends and home sales provided no verification of doom-and-gloom forecasting, but the pervasive association of Black people with poverty—even union painters, pastors, and nurses—deceived residents into believing that their town was on the cusp of an instant transformation into Dickensian hell. The second prediction also developed under the influence of the narcotic of stereotyping: a jump in crime. Crime statistics from 1996 to 2021 demonstrate only negligible changes, while the Black population continued to rise in that period.[2]

With perfect timing during the Confederate flag kerfuffle, and the moment the wheels were up for white flight, a Black man in his sixties, after moving into Monaldi Manor, was shot multiple times in his front yard. By some miracle of Herculean strength, he managed to get behind the wheel of his car and drive himself to the nearest emergency room. The attempted murder enhanced the general sense of panic to the extent that the chief of police held an open meeting in which he explained that the shooting was an act of revenge stemming from a personal grievance decades prior. Investigators were unanimous in their conclusion that it was an unfortunate aberration.

The local newspapers—the *SouthtownStar* and the *Northwest Indiana Times*, which despite its name covers Lansing because of its location hugging the Indiana/Illinois state line—ran reportage confirming the veracity of the official discovery. Police detection and journalistic inquiry did little to temper the hysterical mood of Lansing paranoiacs. In what could function as a study of abnormal psychology, information that should have provided comfort actually had the opposite effect.

Throughout town, many otherwise rational people developed the belief that the police and the local press were coconspirators in a massive propaganda campaign. The conspiracy theory went as follows: The Lansing Police Department was keeping major crimes out of public view and denying that they ever took place. The editors and writers for the *SouthtownStar* and the *Northwest Indiana Times* cooperated with law enforcement and mayoral deception by refusing to report on criminality of any significance, instead electing to fill the police blotter page with pedestrian summaries of DUI arrests, shoplifting, and fisticuffs outside the local bars. Given that Lansing was, and remains, a town of roughly thirty thousand people, successfully pulling off a program of secrecy in which acts that, presumably, take place in public, such as drive-by shootings, burglaries, and carjackings, remain unknown to the population would require trickery so sophisticated that Lenin and Houdini would stand in awe. The illogic of the premise driving the exodus out of Lansing was that the mere presence of Blacks would cause property rates to plummet and crime to skyrocket. Rather than observing reality, townspeople were actually defining irony.

The *Park Place Economist*, an economic journal from Illinois Wesleyan University, in 2010 published a study titled "The Effects of White Flight and Urban Decay in Suburban Cook County." Nearly all inspections of white flight in the Chicagoland area examine the city itself. Lindsay Haines, then a graduate student, completed one of the few studies of white flight in the south suburbs. Her research confirmed what mainstream publications in the news media, including *The New York Times*, *Chicago Tribune*, and *The Chicago Reporter*, had found decades earlier—that the flight of whites from the Chicago suburbs was one of the largest and fastest on record. More fascinating, Haines reviewed the relevant literature, in addition to compiling her own numbers, to find that white flight actually creates the conditions that white fliers incoherently claim they are attempting to escape.

To wit, the oversaturation of housing inventory when dozens of families list their homes within the same short time span immediately weighs down what the market will bear, causing a reduction in property values. When homes sell at artificially lowered rates, the buyers are often in lower income strata than the previous demographic of the neighborhood. If the houses are old, new buyers will then have less ability to make improvements and updates, causing another drop in prices. Seeing decay on and of the walls, business owners will then leave for what they perceive to be more ideal customer bases. Desperate storefront owners, looking to replace their leases, will lower their rates, and shops and restaurants will acquire a more blue-collar facade and character—the bookstore becomes a bodega, the bistro becomes a burger joint.[3]

In the case of Lansing, and other south suburbs that went through similar white-flight patterns, nearby Northwest Indiana was happy to play hospitable host. Republicans have controlled state government in Indiana for decades and ensure that property taxes remain at a minimum by enforcing strict limits on how much a county can increase taxation, regardless of need. Low property taxes certainly have a benefit. Young couples, single adults, and retirees on a fixed income can afford a newer and larger home, as compared to what the market offers in Illinois, because they anticipate an annual savings of thousands of dollars.

The advantages of low property taxes are real, but they often mask an uglier side to the suburban face. One of the best-kept secrets of American life is that the taxes and fees on residents of large cities, and more storied suburbs, often subsidize the residential and commercial development of suburban sprawl and exurban birth. In the "Illiana," area, where Northern Illinois meets Northern Indiana, an economic policy that might glaze over the eyes of most voters actually acted as an injection of toxins into the sociopolitical bloodstream. First, it provided cover for the prejudices of many Chicagoland residents hoping to flee the "threat" of diversity, and it then enhanced the magnetic effect, attracting whites and others with a genuine desire for lower taxes and newer houses. Because infrastructure, including everything from water pipes to roads, is cheaper to maintain in a new development, taxes remain low for the foreseeable future. Meanwhile, the tax base shrinks in the suburbs suffering from the exodus, provoking yet another spike in property tax rates, which then makes the town a tougher sell for new home buyers and entrepreneurs.

Public policy has created a series of incentives for middle- and upper-class earners that function as a communal suicide note. Low taxes and new housing developments, offering understandable and undeniable appeal, encourage suburban sprawl and pollution even as the planet heats, enhance personal and familial isolation even as social scientists warn of the increasingly severe symptoms of communal breakdown, and exacerbate class stratification, further separating the working and middle classes from each other. They also create exurbia. Population statistics in Indiana show that the population numbers for Lake County, positioned closest to the Illinois border and city of Chicago, stayed relatively even from the 1980s to the 2010s. The county gained residents from Illinois while losing beleaguered buyers and renters in Gary, Hammond, and East Chicago—three formerly prosperous manufacturing towns now rife with poverty, crime, and smog. The population of Porter County tells a different story. The formerly rural region to the east of Lake County exploded from around 120,000 inhabitants in the 1980s to about 164,000 in 2010.[4]

Valparaiso, Indiana, rests at the center of Porter County. The charming and pastoral town would make an ideal location for a heartwarming television series about the town-and-gown dynamic of a quiet village. The arteries of life in Valparaiso are the square, where farm-to-fork restaurants, boutique shops, an ice-skating park, an outdoor concert space, and a community theater surround the courthouse, and Valparaiso University—one of the country's largest Lutheran institutions of higher education (where I earned my master's degree). "Valpo," as Hoosiers often call it, is a real-life incarnation of Garrison Keillor's Lake Wobegon, minus the body of water. By sheer coincidence of the name, it inspired a different literary creation—the Don DeLillo play *Valparaiso*, which tells the story of a businessman intending to travel to Indiana but instead winding up in Valparaíso, Chile. The traveler would have missed the Valparaiso Popcorn Festival in Indiana, an annual event since 1979 paying tribute to the town's most beloved native, Orville Redenbacher, the deceased agricultural scientist whose methods of popping corn helped make possible the addictively salty and buttery snack famous in movie palaces all over the world. The popcorn festival, drawing families and teenage couples from across the region, boasts of live entertainment, endless food vendors, a gigantic beer garden, and one of the country's two "popcorn parades." Local businesses and organizations compete for a prize with the best popcorn-themed float.

In addition to creating new popcorn flavors and educating Lutherans, Porter County became a Tea Party stronghold in the Midwest during the Obama presidency. I attended several Tea Party rallies in Valparaiso, and reported on one of the more bizarre gatherings for a website devoted to small-town journalism. The keynote speaker claimed he was a "bestselling author." My research found that he had written one self-published book of little regard. Even worse than his own résumé padding was his recitation of the racist conspiracy theory that then-president Obama was born in Kenya and, from his illegally held position in the White House, was plotting US destruction on behalf of "radical Muslims." Demented and paranoid claims of Obama as a Manchurian candidate provoked wild applause.

The ostensible purpose of the Tea Party was advocacy of low tax rates and pro-business policies to assist modest entrepreneurs. There was almost no discussion of economic issues from any of the speakers or attendees, but there was a constant refrain of Obama's Luciferian war against freedom, "American values," and "our rights." When I would request specific examples, presenting questions with the neutral delivery of a curious reporter while concealing my fretful astonishment, the Tea Party supporters would react with incredulous laughter, as if I was denying the existence of gravity. Without citing any examples or evidence, they would admonish me to "pay attention to what is going on."

Lawrence Rosenthal, the chairperson and lead researcher for the Center for Right-Wing Studies at the University of California, Berkeley, writes that the Tea Party was not a movement for the enlargement of capitalistic opportunity or prosperity but an outburst of fear, particularly fear of non-white, non-Christian usurpation of its members' power and infringement on their territory.[5] As the first Black president with a name bearing phonic resemblance to Arabic, Barack Obama, despite his relatively moderate, center-left policy agenda, became the ideal symbol and foil in a fight against multicultural America and its seemingly multiracial and secular democracy. One of the Tea Party foot soldiers who graced me with a conversation uttered the words, "Government ruins everything it touches." He was wearing a T-shirt advertising Yellowstone National Park.

It is easy to ridicule the transparent ignorance and hypocrisy of the right wing but wiser to measure and mitigate the escalation of the threat that it presents to any hope for racial harmony, economic progress, and social democracy. Rosenthal concludes that the Tea Party died on May 26, 2016—the day that Trump sealed his victory as Republican nominee to the presidency. Despite his clownish appearance and incoherence, and the mockery it encouraged, Trump managed to consolidate the most important and voluminous constituencies of the Republican electorate into one campaign, demonstrating a Svengali power to create a personality cult without precedent in American politics. Because of a fascination with "hillbillies" who possessed exotic qualities to the antiseptic reporters in the mainstream media, there is a widespread tendency to equate Trump cultists with rural voters and impoverished, down-home

Americana. The increasingly fascistic coalition of the Republican Party organization certainly includes angry voters in desolate outposts of the Deep South and Heartland, but the story that I observed and intuited as a child, adolescent, and young adult provides a clear but often uninspected background to the American right's brazen turn toward white rage and nationalism. It is a twisted turn that Alexander Laban Hinton, one of the world's leading experts on genocide, describes as portending mass violence in the United States.[6] Consistently rising levels of hate crimes, including targeted massacres of Latinos in El Paso, Jews in Pittsburgh, and Blacks in Buffalo, right-wing plots to execute public officials, and the insurrection of January 6 should disabuse any naïfs of the notion that scholars like Hinton are falling prey to alarmism.

Minimally lucid spectators of the right wing might have also noticed, despite the mainstream media's addiction to the economic motivation theory, that almost all discussion of class issues vanished from far-right circles during the Trump presidency. A stylish and long-legged blonde business owner sitting outside her women's clothing shop, sipping on a Budweiser in a miniskirt and high heels and watching, with incredulity, the Tea Party rally that I covered , saw through the lie pretty easily, telling me, "These people claim they are all about small business. I've never seen them around here before in my life." She waved her arms toward all the independent shops that surrounded hers as she offered her assessment, and then added a final note while I jotted down her remarks with delight: "They're taking up too many parking spaces."

A WIDE RANGE OF DEMOGRAPHIC STUDIES, ACADEMIC analyses, and journalistic reports coalesce to confirm that the most rabid and radical members of the right-wing insurgency are small metro suburban and exurban in their geographic and income profile. Suburbia always had a dominant streak of social conservatism, but it manifested itself in an overwhelming, and often unreflective, docility. Conservatism, in the classic Edmund Burke sense and contemporary George Will iteration, placed a premium on the maintenance of order in the name of social stability. To conserve the institutions and hierarchies of society was the most important function of civil life, even if those institutions and hierarchies were patently unfair and unjust. The repression of suburbia became fodder for endless satire.

In 1922, Sinclair Lewis presented the first satirical exploration of suburban foibles with the novel *Babbitt*. Zenith, a fictional Midwest city that serves as *Babbitt*'s setting, has so many shades pulled down, and so many collars buttoned up, it is almost difficult to read the story without feeling claustrophobic. The main characters, including the eponymous protagonist, lead lives in self-generated prisons of quiet misery and desperation or thoughtless and reckless rebellion that manifest in violence and other forms of cruelty. Only Babbitt's son, Ted, demonstrates the independence necessary to genuinely exercise the American opportunity for freedom. His father transitions from despising him to begrudgingly respecting him for having the strength he has always lacked. *American Beauty*, a 1999 film set in the Chicago suburbs, acts as a cultural reincarnation of *Babbitt*. Lester and Carolyn are two middle-class professionals, barely able to conceal their mutual contempt even as they have dinner with their sullen teenage daughter. Their surroundings abound with characters masking their homosexuality with outward expressions of hatred for gay neighbors, hollow careerism, and communication under the guise of a meaningless sociological script.

One of the most unpredictable changes of American life in the twenty-first century is that the suburbs and exurbs transformed from "Pleasantville," as yet another cinematic satire of suburban, middle-class morality calls it, into the staging ground for insurrection, running on fumes of vulgarity, hatred, and weird bellicosity. School board meetings where parents insult and threaten elected officials over pandemic safety protocols and classroom curricula, armed marauders patrolling Black Lives Matter protests, and brazenly misogynistic and nativist chants at Trump rallies indicate a shocking irony. It is now ideological liberals and progressives who behave more like classic conservatives—demonstrating trust in institutions and exercising restraint while moving through conventional channels for political reform—than the newly radical right, which according to several polls now operates according to the belief that the use of force is justifiable in the service of political ambition.

My next-door neighbor, a Japanese immigrant, told me that she took her son to a nearby park. Two mothers, while watching their children jump and climb on the same playground, were smoking cigarettes. My neighbor, with characteristic politeness, asked if they could take a few steps back from the children after watching her son run through a cloud of secondhand smoke. The mothers not only refused her request but also mocked her Asian accent. When they pulled out of the parking lot a few minutes later, my neighbor noticed a bumper sticker that declared in red, white, and blue lettering, MURICA! There is a cultural collision between those who prefer to live in America versus inhabitants of Murica. The former celebrates the enforcement and spirit of the Bill of Rights and strives toward greater freedom and justice for all, while the latter believe that kindness, reciprocity, and communal interaction with a foundation of respect are antiquated notions, no longer even worthy of aspiration. Stories of parents chanting, "Build the Wall!" at a high school in Elkhart, Indiana, while their children played basketball against a neighboring school with a mostly Latino student population provide additional insight into the procedural routine of Murica—a routine that went national on January 6, 2021.

It would appear that all of the repression, strained civility, and passive acceptance of life's inconvenient rules and regulations that, for so long, defined suburbia and inspired its artistic chroniclers was merely a bargain for power. Sigmund Freud submits in *Civilization and Its Discontents* that repression and sublimation are the price human beings pay for life in civilized society. Many on the American right, even those who appear to have undergone middle-class socialization in suburbia, no longer care for their civilization if they have to share it with a set of "undesirables"—Blacks, gays, immigrants from the Global South. They've cut loose of their constraints. In 2004, the brilliant and late writer David Foster Wallace articulated concern that America had lost its "shame hobble." He posited with consternation that "only time will tell how far we'll go."[7]

Time has telegraphed moral freefall and social arson. The story forms a clear picture, but much of mainline journalism and political commentary refuses to interlock the jagged pieces of the jigsaw puzzle. Reportage announces explanation with the subtlety and insight of a cyborg. Continuing to act against evidence, many on the left and right attribute the insurgent characteristic of the contemporary Republican Party to financial aggrievement. While economics is never irrelevant, and troubled times always exert influence and pressure on the system and its subjects, the truth is easier to ascertain in my hometown battleground of the Confederacy. Like a clichéd "dark and stormy night" at the beginning of a bad cable movie, Lansing residents marching around their alma mater while waving the banner of slavery and secession, foreshadowed an apocalyptic evening on the American calendar.

The hallmarks of the fascist right were all evident in the Rebel banner brouhaha and its accompanying suspicions toward diversification: 1) deliberate insensitivity to American history of oppression, and to the oppressed people themselves, that morphs into racist hostility; 2) refusal to consider redress through the democratic system, instead opting for menacing displays of exclusion; 3) the easy acceptance and proliferation of wild conspiracy theories—"City hall, law enforcement, and local media refuse to acknowledge crime"; 4) with minimal provocation, the willingness to adopt hate speech and symbols as everyday political expression; 5) white fear of minority replacement, and the transformation of political debate into a volatile struggle over ownership of turf.

Given the tension in Lansing over the use of the Confederate flag, occurring simultaneously with an influx of Blacks and Latinos, it is lucky that no confrontation turned violent. One of the most frightening and sickening episodes of recent American history is the 2017 Unite the Right rally in Charlottesville, Virginia. The families of Lansing were and are not the equivalent of Klansmen, skinheads, and armed anti-government militia members, but they shared certain reasoning and beliefs. Even though the Charlottesville white supremacists and neo-Confederates were brazen enough to chant "Jews will not replace us!" while surrounding a Black church and beating a transgender student at the University of Virginia, they claimed that they were merely acting to preserve their "heritage." They only wanted to "protect" the statue of a Confederate leader. Then-president Donald Trump, in his infamous and insidious remarks following the Charlottesville Unite the Right rally, claimed that there were "very fine people" on both sides of the march the day that a neo-Nazi murdered Heather Heyer, an anti-racist activist, by plowing his automobile into a crowd of demonstrators. He then articulated the same historically illiterate justification, saying, "People went because they felt very strongly about the monument to Robert E. Lee, a great general."

The Lansing Confederates offered two defenses of TFS continuing to fly the banner. First, they claimed that it had nothing to do with the South. It was merely a mascot and theme for the school. While there was some nominal truth to that defense, they would contradict themselves by also arguing that even if it did have connection to hate iconography, the flag represents Southern ancestry more than slavery, secession, or Jim Crow. The argument resurfaced when I was a student at TFS, because a small Confederate flag remained on a mural in the cafeteria, and a group of students and parents demanded its erasure. Many white students not only defended the placement of the flag but also claimed that the Civil War was not about slavery. It was about "states' rights." That the only right in contention was the ability to purchase and keep slaves was an inconvenient nuance, but even the states' rights assertion—still popular in classrooms throughout the South and Midwest—is merely a rephrase of turf war. Southern slaveholders believed that they had full ownership of not only their land but their states and communities. The federal government, no matter if it was democratically elected and acting in accordance with the Constitution, had no right to invade and occupy their territory with new laws and prohibitions. Similarly, the extremity of white flight, and the paranoia that precedes and propels it, submits that Blacks have no right to invade and occupy suburban territory with their mere presence, and especially not new desires and concerns.

Many commentators, left and right, have bristled at comparisons between Republican officials and voters with self-identified white supremacists. From the "Southern strategy" and anti-Semitism of Richard Nixon to Ronald Reagan's theatrical warnings about "welfare queens," the Republican Party has long lived in the same neighborhood as hate movements and, depending on the political demands of the season, a handful of blocks or maybe a couple of miles away. Donald Trump, and his acolytes in Congress and the media, merely packed the party's bags and moved it into the house next door. Few Americans can better testify to the proximity between mainstream right-wing behavior and violent extremism than Christian Picciolini.

Picciolini, the son of Italian immigrants, grew up in Blue Island, Illinois, during the 1970s and '80s. Blue Island is a working-class suburb that sits right on the border of the far South Side of Chicago. Blue Island, rich in history, features a picturesque main street in the middle of charming residential surroundings. The classic Americana qualities of its city center have enticed a few of Hollywood's greatest directors, including Paul Schrader and Clint Eastwood, to use the town for provincial settings. Although Blue Island has suffered an economic decline by losing a significant portion of its manufacturing base, Picciolini did not experience abuse or privation as a teenager. His parents were, generally, supportive and cultivated a stable lifestyle for their household, but because they worked seven days a week as small business owners, they devoted little time or attention to their sons. As a consequence, Picciolini had a close and tender bond with his baby brother but he also felt neglected, alienated, and lonely. Serving as a target for playground bullying during his formative years certainly did not help him generate an edifying identity.

One night in a literal dark alley, while taking a drag off a joint at the age of fourteen, a charismatic and intimidating man in his twenties approached Picciolini, imploring him to snuff out the marijuana. The imposing but charming stranger explained that Picciolini was full of potential, and that wasting it on drugs and delinquency would only serve the interests of the villainous forces destroying his community and country. Those forces were the Jews, and the man was a skinhead leader and recruiter. Offering Picciolini the seduction of a sense of belonging, purpose, and power, he pulled him into Chicago Area Skinheads (CASH), the first skinhead gang in the United States. Picciolini would eventually rise to the top, helping CASH to become one of the country's largest neo-Nazi organizations by facilitating its merger with the notoriously violent Hammerskins. He would also write songs and sing lead vocals for the "hate rock" band the Final Solution. With its horrific name, the band would eventually headline a white power festival in Germany not far from where Hitler ordered a genocide that resulted in the butchery of nine million people, six million of whom were Jews. Through a long hero's journey full of danger, fatherhood, fear, grief, love, and remorse, Picciolini left the hate movement at the age of twenty-two. For over twenty years, he has worked as a committed anti-racist leader and one of America's leading experts on disengagement. He has personally helped hundreds of young men and women withdraw from hate groups, prevented a terrorist attack on a Black Lives Matter march, and spoken to law enforcement agencies, civil rights organizations, and political officials across the world to warn of the dangers of white supremacy.[8]

Before Picciolini underwent his transformation, he and his cohorts stormed the south suburbs of Chicago—meeting in small apartments and dilapidated houses, seeking new recruits at punk rock shows throughout the area, and menacing, and on a few occasions even assaulting, Blacks and Latinos. White supremacists, and certainly racists, are everywhere, but it is significant that America's first skinhead gang, and one of its most populous, did not form in the Southern backwoods or even a large city in Alabama or Tennessee. It was the south suburbs of Chicago.

I asked Picciolini if he could explain the white power movement's success in the town immediately south of one of America's most diverse, cultured, and educated cities. Even as a lifelong resident of the area, I was curious if he could identify any unique traits, beyond garden-variety racism, that account for CASH's appeal in the 1980s and '90s. Recalling the images of decay prevalent in his own childhood, Picciolini said:

> Blue Island and Lansing, compared to nearby suburbs like
> Orland Park and Tinley Park or even Homewood's older white
> money, are lower middle–class towns. Many people who lived
> in these towns lost their jobs when the factories and plants left.
> The towns didn't keep pace with change, and businesses left.
> So, they fell into hard times. Hard times lend themselves to
> blame the "other" for those problems. Additionally, the towns
> themselves started to become more diverse. Cheaper prices
> allowed Black and brown folks to move in and, again, blame
> went around. People lost something and they blamed those

who "replaced" them instead of the greedy businesses who left, the politicians who sold them out, or themselves. Groups like CASH capitalized on people's frustrations, and their lost sense of identity, community, and purpose. It's the same way white supremacists pitch a return to glory—"Make America Great Again." But make no mistake, racism is everywhere, even in wealthy communities. The only difference is the sales pitch: "you've lost everything to these animals . . ." versus "you will lose everything to these animals . . ."

Picciolini telegraphs the dance between race and class but with a more sophisticated sense of movement than the average commentator attempting to alleviate a Trump voter of responsibility for their choices. The entanglement becomes even clearer as Picciolini examines how the origin of the suburbs themselves, far beyond his old stomping ground of the Chicagoland area, engineers a genesis of racial prejudice:

I think the suburbs provide a twisted sense of safety in a "white space" outside of urban areas that tend to be more Black or brown. I tend to think white people don't leave the city for the suburbs because of wealth or "more space to raise a family" as much as I think they leave the city for the suburbs to be among other whites in their own (or higher) financial class. It's escapism. When they are there, they then can control their situations by electing reps, judges, sheriffs, etc. It's essentially white separatism. You can look at Levittowns around the country for more evidence of that. Their covenants even excluded Black and brown people, and sometimes Jews. The suburbs are white enclaves. The minute non-whites enter, the whites flee further into exurbia.

Vladimir Lenin famously explained that the Bolshevik Revolution was not unpredictable or unprecedented to the trained political eye. "Power was lying in the street," he said. "We picked it up." A skinhead leader is a revolutionary in his dreams, and he must live according to the power of the street. Even if recruitment and terrorism take place in the outlaw domain, the agenda does not remain undercover. Picciolini has often explained that the long-term strategy of the white hate movement was to "trade boots for suits." He and his administrative brethren encouraged smarter and easily assimilable members to "invade positions with low barrier of entry," meaning police departments, corrections agencies, school boards, town councils, the military, and low-level local political offices. The plan, long in motion, is already succeeding.

The Brennan Center for Justice has reported on the alarming numbers of white supremacist sympathizers on the police force, Congress has held hearings on white extremism in the military, and thousands of far-right activists have become directly involved in country election boards, thus threatening to sink the foundation of electoral democracy. Similar agents of fascism have targeted school boards and library trustees, insisting on conformity to a narrow vision of the United States as a white, heterosexual, Christian homeland. The barriers of entry are much tougher to surmount in a city like Chicago, where a Democratic machine exercises tight control over most political activity, and a racially diverse population invested in social liberalism pulverizes the ambition of reactionary politicians.

The exodus into exurbia ensures that the dark revolution of white nationalist dreams is taking place in towns detached from Chicago and other cities. As Picciolini explains, the suburbs are no longer "safe" as white enclaves. The escape continues into the exurbs. The retreat from multiculturalism, shared power agreements, and democratic cooperation finds itself landing in towns like those that surround Valparaiso, towns like those that elect congressional representatives advancing a neofascist ideology, and towns like those that were the departure points for the insurrectionists of January 6, 2021.

As the recent example of the upper-middle-class town of Flossmoor, Illinois—where whites have left as Blacks have arrived—shows, the exodus is still here. Samuel Kye, a sociologist at Baylor University, conducted an extensive study of suburbs surrounding large metro areas in 2018. Inspecting the population shifts and changes of those counties, he found a disturbing but predictable pattern. As suburbs became more diverse, whites left in large numbers. Kye found that white flight was actually likelier to occur in suburban, middle-class communities, as opposed to poor or blue-collar towns in decline. His data indicate that much more than reduction in property values or loss of tax revenue, the influx of Black, Latino, and/or Asian residents was the "independent motivator" of white flight.[9] The movement of aggrieved suburban whites into more desolate exurban areas accounts for many of the so-called mysteries of the recent political cycle: a surge in "rural" votes for Trump, working-class counties flipping for Trump even if most working-class voters supported Democrats, the increasingly radical and hateful profile of Republicans in Congress, and state party platforms drawing on the desires of their isolated constituents rather than attempting to appeal to voters who share streets, schools, and public squares with Democrats from a variety of racial or religious backgrounds.

The electoral map of 2020 for the south suburbs of Chicago and the small towns of Northwest Indiana shows with perfect clarity that the Trump strongholds were the towns east and south of population density. An interesting divergence between the blue and red communities, with the notable exception of Crown Point, is the existence or lack of a walkable city center. My wife and I live within walking distance of the main street of our community, where we can meet the eclectic characters of the small commercial district, walk through farmers markets, and feel a genuine connection to the place where we've made our home. One of the most fascinating features of exurbia is its establishment of sprawl as a geographic and communal ethos. Most of the exurban towns in Northwest Indiana lack any visible city center or main street. Various residential plots surround a four-to-eight-lane busy street that cuts through life, prevents commuting by foot, and leads to almost nothing but multinational corporate chain stores and restaurants. As big businesses like Chick-fil-A or Home Depot arrive, the town must adjust with the installation of stoplights, creating an absurdity of heavy traffic and slow movement in a lightly populated area. Those who live in the newly built houses of exurbia enjoy a degree of isolation that would inspire galleries of Edward Hopper paintings, should the great realist painter find himself resurrected from the grave. The escape has gone to the extreme lengths of creating a silo where homeowners could conceivably have no interaction with fellow townspeople or even neighbors. A tour of an exurban residential plot will enhance the oddity through the revelation of an absence even stranger than the missing downtown: There are no sidewalks. The further an American moves from the city, the less likely he is to find a walkable path in a residential zone.

When Ed Ward, a friend of mine who is a Catholic priest, moved to a new parish assignment in an exurban section of Joliet, Illinois, he found his nightly routine of taking a leisurely stroll after dinner suddenly difficult. "I have to walk down the street, and if a car comes along, it starts honking at me." With the use of esoteric theological terminology, he asked, "What the hell?"

Anastasia Loukaitou-Sideris, a professor of urban planning at the University of California, Los Angeles, has an answer to Ed's rhetorical question: "There is this perception that if we have sidewalks, we're going to bring people who do not belong to our neighborhoods."[10] The same hope for exclusion extends to urban design without city centers. Political scientist Robert Putnam's classic treatise on the loss of community in American life has the title *Bowling Alone*. In the exurbs, Americans are walking, driving, and living alone. The politics of escape has left them isolated and increasingly paranoid. Donald Trump spun his supporters into a frenzy of terror with dramatic tales of rapist immigrants and vicious gangs of Mexicans stabbing random whites. Studies show that his hate speech resonated most with voters who live in counties "least likely to have immigrants" among the local population. It is easy to believe propaganda when you are sitting inside your living room in a neighborhood with no sidewalks, watching a maniac scream at you. Credulity hits the wall if you live next to the supposed rapists and drug dealers whose kids play in your son's Little League.

The splendid isolation of the right-wing movement is the consequence of the retreat from diversity and democracy that, in the trajectory I witnessed, took voters from marching the streets with Confederate flags far into the exurbs with low taxes and no public square. Chloe Maxmin, the youngest woman ever elected to the state senate in Maine, represented a Republican district as a social liberal whose primary political interest was the adoption of more aggressive policies to mitigate the effects of global warming. In an interview with Bill Maher, her interlocuter challenged her to answer, yes or no, if her white constituents who pledge fidelity to Trump and the far-right policies he champions are "racist." Maxmin managed to dodge his trap by referring to the complexity of the dynamic. They aren't necessarily racist, she insisted, but for a "variety of reasons" they have come to "believe racist things."[11]

Lee Atwater, one of the most malevolent and masterful Republican strategists, gave the game away in 1981 when he confessed:

> You start out in 1954 by saying, "Nigger, nigger, nigger." By
> 1968 you can't say "nigger"—that hurts you, backfires. So you
> say stuff like, uh, forced busing, states' rights, and all that
> stuff, and you're getting so abstract. Now, you're talking about

> cutting taxes, and all these things you're talking about are
> totally economic things and a byproduct of them is, blacks get
> hurt worse than whites . . . [12]

This Machiavellian operator, an advisor to Ronald Reagan and George H. W. Bush and former chairman of the Republican National Committee, reveals how economic language is often the disguise with which racists smuggle their ideas through customs. Donald Trump, not exactly the most delicate of political communicators, attempted a Lee Atwater move in the 2020 election, continually warning his audience, "You have this beautiful community in the suburbs, including women [*This is an actual quote, "including women" is not explained*]. I ended where they build low-income housing projects right in the middle of your neighborhood. If Biden goes in, he already said it's going to go at a much higher rate than before. They want low-income housing, and with that comes a lot of problems, including crime."

In a total fabrication, Trump claimed that Biden planned to appoint Cory Booker, the anodyne Black senator from New Jersey, "in charge of the suburbs." No such suburban czar exists, or has ever existed in American history, but Trump's hallucination projected a clear image to the voters he hoped to persuade: Blacks and Latinos would destroy the escapist enclave, bringing poverty, drug dependency, and criminal predation.

Because the escape is an attempt to flee significant percentages of the American people and the progress of American culture that began in the 1960s and, more or less, continues into the present for racial minorities, LGBTQ people, and women, the escapees have grown not only isolated but estranged. Estrangement from their country means an inability to understand its culture, and diminution of loyalty to its institutions. The presidency of Donald Trump, and the insurrection of January 6, despite all the weepiness over the flag and the "heroes of the military," is possible only when large masses of voters no longer respect the United States. They do not respect its diversity. They do not respect the expansion of freedom and opportunity to previously exiled groups, and they do not respect a democratic system that would challenge their stranglehold on power, authority, and resources.

The estrangement accounts for a few eccentricities among a group that is still the majority of one of the country's two major political parties. Republican voters routinely tell pollsters that the next election, regardless of the year, is the "last chance to save America" from impending doom. They also find themselves alienated from the energy and activity of American life. The counties that went for Joe Biden in 2020 are responsible for 71 percent of America's gross domestic product.[13]

Lansing illustrates the contrast between suburbia and exurbia. It is striking that for all the fear and forecasts of doom in the 1990s, not much has changed in the small town. The southern portions remain commercially vibrant and middle class, while the northern edge signals decay with empty storefronts and battered apartment buildings. The TFS football team is no longer the Rebels. It is the Red Wolves, and the school itself, with a predominantly Black student body, has high graduation and college placement rates. For the students without university ambition, it offers innovative trade programs in cosmetology and culinary arts. *Chicago* magazine recently named Lansing one of the best south suburbs for first-time home buyers.[14]

One of the most noticeable additions to Lansing is Fox Pointe—a midsize outdoor concert space in the heart of town. At a spring performance in 2022, Lauren Dukes, a singer with a pretty, big smile and a prettier and bigger voice, popular throughout the region, entertained a crowd with renditions of pop hits of recent decades and indelible classics from Motown Records. Teenage girls danced with hula hoops, a young Black boy devoured an ice-cream cone as if he had not eaten in weeks, and an elderly white couple held hands across their lawn chairs.

At an intermission in Dukes's show, a town official encouraged residents to return to Fox Pointe for upcoming summer events, classic car cruise nights, and, although it seemed like a long time away, the annual fall fest. A scene like Fox Pointe reduces even the most astute scholar of sociology and political theory to naivete. The only question one can ask is: What was everyone so afraid of?

*

"THE NIGHT THEY DROVE OLD DIXIE DOWN" BY THE Band is one of most moving elegies in the rock and roll canon. Despite its lament of Southern surrender in the Civil War, it captures universal feelings of loss, disappointment, and sorrow. Levon Helm's miraculously tender vocal makes the original version definitive, but decidedly non-Southern social liberals have covered it to beautiful effect, including Joan Baez and Jerry Garcia. Approaching the song's mournful conclusion, Helm declares with emotion pouring out of every pore of his body, "I swear by the mud below my feet / You can't raise a Caine back up / When he's in defeat."

Like protesters desperately clutching a Confederate banner until their knuckles turn pale, the voters who have taken flight to the exurbs are holding steadfast to an America that is gone. Hoping to have communion with a ghost, they are willing to kill the America that is.

GODZILLA JESUS

Every year of my childhood had two markers of anticipation and celebration. In the winter, Christian Advent season, my elementary school would gather one evening in December for a school- and churchwide Christmas service. The entire staff and student body of Trinity Lutheran in Lansing would devote weeks to choreography and rehearsal, preparing for an evening to mark the arrival of Christmas, the commencement of the holiday break from classes, and the birth of Jesus Christ. The number of students at the small, two-hallway institution of education would never rise above two hundred. Stretching from kindergarten to eighth grade, the intimacy of the school enabled nearly all the students to get to know each other well and the parents to form bonds of mutual interest, respect, and sympathy. The staff included the equivalent of Lutheran nuns—intimidating women who exerted tight control over the classroom and whose personalities made it impossible to imagine them having any life whatsoever outside the schoolhouse. The seventh-grade teacher and the second-grade teacher were married and equally docile, while the principal—a New Jersey transplant who, despite his piety, had an aggressive, loud East Coast attitude and attendant obsession with all things Springsteen—splashed vibrant colors around the lockers and water fountains with every step and forceful utterance. My best friend, Greg, was the son of lifelong Lansing residents who owned an independent automotive parts store. There were also children of doctors and dentists, and small boys and girls who wore the same clothes nearly every day, arriving in vehicles without mufflers. Trinity did not levy tuition fees against their families. It was a charitable and hospitable community. The weekly chapel service on Wednesday mornings collected offerings for children's hospitals, soup kitchens, or relief efforts to help families that recently suffered losses due to a nearby tornado. Even if everyone seemed fiercely devoted to the faith, there weren't any backward lessons on creationism or the apocalypse. Science courses taught evolutionary biology as an "instrument of God's plan" but also an empirical reality. The "end of the world" and "return of Jesus" would emerge in religious education with only vague reference as something that we kids should view as inevitable but not contemplate too frequently or intensely. Other than mock presidential elections in which students would impersonate candidates for office before tallying votes, politics was never a subject of discussion. I played Ross Perot in 1996, because I found his manner of speaking amusing. My enthusiastic and dramatic imitation earned the third-party candidate an unlikely victory.

The Christmas pageant unified everyone. From the eighth-grade teacher who hid a bottle of Jack Daniel's in his desk drawer and took smoking breaks in his pickup truck parked down the block to the beautiful young teacher from Kansas who most of the older boys desired in ways Martin Luther would disapprove, we all shared a sense of camaraderie on Christmas. The lighting of the Advent wreath candles, and the announcement of the coming of the Savior, was an exciting time, signaling hope and possibility.

Every summer, on the last day of school, Trinity would give us our second marker of the passage of time—the schoolwide summer picnic. If the weather permitted, the entire student body and staff would walk to a nearby park. The older boys would play baseball or basketball, the young children would experiment with a series of acrobatics on the playground equipment, and the older girls would sit on the grass, maintaining a seemingly endless conversation full of laughter and chewing gum. We would break at lunch for hot dogs, hamburgers, baked beans, potato chips, and ice-cream sandwiches. When our parents began to fill the diagonal parking spaces slicing into the edges of the park, we were disappointed that the picnic was over but ecstatic that we were entering the initial seconds of three months of freedom. During the time away from school grounds, most of the Trinity families regularly had fellowship, of the official variety in church but also at birthday parties, summer barbecues, and backyard Fourth of July gatherings. On occasion, the pastor of the church would even join these parties, imposing a dignified bearing on the festivities. The minister, a widower from Michigan who converted from Catholicism in his twenties, could just as easily discuss theories about the development of American theater and literature and the previous evening's baseball scores as he could the Bible. His mild manner would morph into fire and brimstone, not to condemn gays or abortion—even if he did have a reactionary attitude on those topics—but to upbraid America's inadequate interest in rectifying homelessness and child poverty.

My childhood years at Trinity were largely formative of how I believe a community should operate. Hospitality, charity, and compassion should govern institutional practice, whether it is a small-town church and school or federal government with trillions of dollars at its disposal. When I no longer counted myself among the religious, it wasn't due to the kind of childhood trauma that many lapsed Christians, Jews, or Muslims report. I was alarmed and shocked to learn, in the early 2000s when I first developed an interest in politics and history, that American Christianity had a wildly different personality from the quiet and kind piety of my Lutheran upbringing. One of the Bible verses that the minister and teachers of Trinity were most fond of sharing was from Matthew when Jesus instructs his disciples, "When you pray, do not be like the hypocrites, for they love to pray standing in the synagogues and on the street corners to be seen by men . . . but when you pray, go into your room, close the door and pray to your father who is unseen."[1]

The polar opposite of the image that Jesus sketched is the contemporary iteration of the religious right—routinely invoking God in speech as a bludgeon against their political enemies, using scripture to justify the persecution of gay and transgender Americans, and demanding the demolition of the wall separating church and state. The right-wing merger of Christianity and political extremism reached new heights of absurdity when Donald Trump used his authority as president to clear Lafayette Square in Washington, DC, of protesters, authorizing police to use gas and force, so that he could pose with a Bible in front of a historic church. Months later, a handful of insurrectionists would stand in the rotunda of the Capitol, loudly praying for God's blessing moments after assaulting police officers, vandalizing public property, and attempting to nullify the votes of eighty-one million people. One would hope that the events of January 6 represented the climax of Christian nationalism, not a preview. In historic terms, Trump's fascist maneuver and the insurrection are signs that the Christian schism of suburbia has settled. Stretching back decades, there was a cold war for hearts and minds between the churches like Trinity in Lansing and the churches that sent thousands of parishioners to carry crosses while chanting for the execution of the vice president of the United States.

*

FRED BOENIG, A GOLD STAR FATHER AND RADIO HOST in Emmaus, Pennsylvania, has remarked that one of the most "amazing continuities" of American history is the ubiquity of race. Nearly any aspect of the culture, good or bad, is traceable to racial antipathy or harmony. Contrary to popular belief, the rise of the religious right did not happen on a chariot of fire, nor did it transpire in reaction to the legalization of abortion or liberalization of gay rights. In fact, as Randall Balmer, a historian of American Christianity, has painstakingly documented, most Protestant churches, and most Republicans for that matter, including Ronald Reagan and George H. W. Bush, were pro-choice through the 1970s. They would later turn on a dime for reasons of political expediency, but not before the evangelical right became an influential electoral force. Evangelicals voted in large numbers for Jimmy Carter, because they viewed the devout Baptist as one of their own and admired how he broke with campaign convention by regularly providing testimony about the importance of his faith. When Carter ran for reelection, they viewed him as a traitor, a dangerous liberal who was part of the scheme to destroy traditional America. His offense against Americana and Christendom was to substantially increase the funds and personnel devoted to punishing "segregation academies" in the South—private Christian elementary and secondary schools that allowed white parents to circumvent *Brown v. Board of Education* by excluding Black, Latino, and Native American children from enrollment. Like the politics of escape at work in suburban white flight, institutional Christianity became a getaway car from social diversity and multiracial democracy.[2] Most evangelical Christians fell into the arms of Ronald Reagan, who made an early 1980 campaign appearance in Philadelphia, Mississippi, the site where the Ku Klux Klan, with the aid of local law enforcement, murdered three civil rights workers in 1964. The topic of Reagan's address was the importance of "states' rights."

It is an irony that most of the religious right would fail to appreciate, but Charles Darwin's words best capture the political constituency. He wrote that "man bears the stamp of his lowly origin." The "lowly origin" of racism and segregation eventually gave way to opposition to women's rights, organized hostility toward gay and transgender Americans, and reverence for Donald Trump.

✳

THE NUMBER OF CHURCHES WITHIN CLOSE RANGE of my home is staggering. It is difficult to refrain from wondering how so many Christian houses of worship manage to survive in such close proximity. Even after accounting for denominational differences—Catholic, Orthodox of various national origins, Protestants of various sectarian affiliations—it seems absurd that all of these churches could fill the pews, and collect offerings, week after week. There are a handful of churches within less than a mile of my home, even more within short driving distance. There is one next to the gym where my wife and I exercise. On some streets, there are churches directly across from or adjacent to one another. The ubiquity of Christian fellowship, or at least invitations for it, opens a window into a previous era of American life. Even in the 1990s, most families belonged to a church. Religion had influence over not only Americans' weekend schedules but also their beliefs and behavior. Many of the churches fell into the category of Trinity Lutheran, similar to what David Foster Wallace describes so well in his essay about his experience on September 11, 2001, in his then hometown of Bloomington—a midsize city in the rural region of central Illinois:

> The church I belong to is on the south side of Bloomington, near where I live. Most of the people I know well enough to ask if I can come over and watch their TV are members of my church. It's not one of those Protestant churches where people throw Jesus's name around or talk about the End Times, which is to say that it's not loony or vulgar, but it's

fairly serious, and people in the congregation get to know each
other well and to be pretty tight. Most of the congregants are
working-class or retirees; there are some small-business owners.
A fair number are veterans or have kids in the military or—
especially—the various Reserves, because for many of these
families that's simply what you do to pay for college.[3]

My friend Father Ed Ward has often said that the "best thing a church
does happens before and after the service." A trained philosopher and
amateur sociologist, Ward is referring to the communal utility of religion and, if asked for elaboration, will describe overhearing conversations between people who might otherwise never have had a chance
to meet about their children, careers, vacations, hobbies, parents, etc.
When Joe Biden ran for president in 2020, he often discussed the "war
for America's soul," infusing theological terms into his political rhetoric.
The election that Biden won was a uniquely critical one, but if there is
such a thing as a national soul, its identity and loyalty are always in contention. From the framers' debates about the Bill of Rights and slavery
to the weeks and months following the attacks that inspired Wallace's
essay, the United States is forever wrestling with its spiritual identity.
Although I was unaware of it as a child, an important part of that war
has taken place in American churches. It isn't that Jews, Muslims, people
of other faiths, and people of no faith are insignificant, but given that 60
percent of Americans are Christian, this particular group will continue
to exert a large influence on national culture and politics. Even higher
percentages of residents of suburbia and exurbia are Christian.

American Christianity, despite its comparably high number of
adherents, is diminishing. In the past fifteen years, the percentage of
Americans who identify as Christian has dropped by 15 percent while
the "religiously unaffiliated" has made a 14 percent jump and is now at
29 percent of the public. The unaffiliated, or "nones," as pollsters like

to call them, are even more populous among generations under the age of forty.[4] As American Christianity has shrunk, it has become more extreme, politically active, and strange. Young families that typically would have joined a church like Trinity or the one that Wallace describes are no longer interested, leaving the churches in the hands of the elderly and the true believers who are not merely looking for piety and community. Instead, like the white fliers of suburbia into exurbia, they are exercising a form of political and cultural estrangement, and the estrangement is morphing into belligerence.

As powerful as Jerry Falwell's Moral Majority, Ralph Reed's Christian Coalition, and other right-wing religious groups became in the Republican electorate throughout the 1980s and '90s, reactionary activists composed a minority of practicing Christians. Even Falwell and other leaders would regularly acknowledge their relatively small status. Francis Schaeffer, a conservative theologian, wrote something of a call to arms with his *A Christian Manifesto*, wringing his sweaty palms over the lack of political involvement from American churches. Christian historian Kristin Kobes Du Mez captures the conflict with the title of her book on the subject, *Jesus and John Wayne*. Through academic research and her own intimate familiarity with evangelical culture, she documents and describes how the "John Wayne side is winning the argument." "It's a very common theme in white evangelical writing on masculinity from the 1960s to the present," Du Mez explains, "that you need to have very tough, rugged men who can protect women and children, who can protect Christianity, and who can protect the American nation. And for the sake of protecting these vulnerable things, these precious things, the ends will justify the means."[5]

Many secular Beltway analysts continually treat record shattering evangelical fealty to Donald Trump as an improbably complex mystery. He is a thrice-married serial adulterer who publicly repudiates Biblical instruction on forgiveness. More significant than the cancer within his character is that he is the means to achieve certain ends. Du Mez recognizes that nothing about Trump and American Christianity is mysterious—"When Donald Trump was elected, white evangelicals were absolutely critical to his victory . . . It seemed like evangelicals had betrayed their values. But if you look at this longer history of evangelical masculinity and militarism, then you see that this wasn't a betrayal. There is this strong kind of justification for their vote for Donald Trump in terms of, he is a strongman. He is going to protect Christianity precisely because he is not constrained by traditional Christian virtues."

Because of the decline of Christianity, remaining members of the flock feel alienated and combative. As a consequence, traditional church membership is in decline. Studies show that Episcopalian, Lutheran, Methodist, Catholic, and Presbyterian churches have lost significant numbers of parishioners in the past twenty years, while another report finds that small to midsize churches are "hemorrhaging attendance."[6] Often the people who have stopped attending traditional church are not spending Sunday mornings reading Voltaire or listening to Slayer records. They are filling the stadium-style aisles of megachurches. Father Ed Ward has offered a loosely reliable method for identifying churches practicing a John Wayne theology: "A weird name is usually a giveaway."

Some of the most popular churches in Northwest Indiana are Life Point Church, Anthem Church, Faith Church, and Rise Church. Not far into the south suburbs of Illinois, a spiritual seeker could also find Family Harvest Church. These are megachurches, often with tens of thousands of members, that discard conventional liturgy and replace it with a slick entertainment aesthetic and presentation. Typically, they exercise very little charity, and instead have ministers who preach a right-wing political version of fire and brimstone or vaguely theological version of capitalistic motivation.

One of America's most famous pastors is Joel Osteen, who regularly instructs his tens of thousand of followers in Texas, and millions of viewers on television, that God wants them to be rich, and that they can acquire a life of luxury through positive thinking, prayer, and devotion to Christian behavioral doctrine. Osteen lives in a multimillion-dollar mansion, complete with two elevators, and flies on a private jet, but his house of worship, according to various watchdog reports, does next to nothing for the poor. Osteen is the most successful practitioner of the "prosperity gospel"—the perversion of Christian thought that somehow transforms Jesus Christ, who according to Biblical legend was born homeless, instructed his disciples to donate all their belongings to the poor, and died as a political prisoner, into an amalgamation of Milton Friedman and Tony Robbins.

Prosperity gospel megachurches are increasingly dominant in exurbia. Charity Carney, a historian specializing in religion and gender, writes that since the 1990s, 75 percent of megachurches were built in the suburbs, with most constructed in "distant suburbs and exurbs." Financial expediency is one reason for the exurban location of the megachurch. "Lack of zoning restrictions and the advantage of low taxes" make exurbs attractive to megachurch planners, but according to Carney there is also a cultural explanation: "Such areas also have access to the type of people most attracted to megachurches: consumer-oriented, willing to commute great distances, highly mobile and often displaced, with a traditional nuclear family structure."[7]

The self-engineered isolation of exurbia provides the perfect home for the megachurch. Combined with the entertainment ethos of American culture, which thoroughly rejects the staid old-time religion, and a theological baptism of greed and consumerism, the megachurch becomes a far-out amusement park for modern American Christians. Too often when mainline media reporters visit exurbia, or megachurches, they merely collect and repackage superficial observations and clichés. In 2005, however, a journalist for *The New York Times*, Jonathan Mahler, diagrammed a few points of accuracy. Visiting the exurb of Surprise,

Arizona, and attending a service at a megachurch, he wrote, "Exurban cities tend not to have immediately recognizable town squares, but many have some kind of big, new structure where newcomers go to discuss their lives and problems and hopes: the megachurch." He concluded that megachurches in desolate, detached villages "operate almost like surrogate governments, offering residents day care, athletic facilities, counseling, even schools."[8]

When I was a boy at Trinity Lutheran, every October to celebrate Reformation Day—the Lutheran holiday honoring when Martin Luther demanded change in the Catholic Church and initiated the Protestant reformation—a group of faculty would perform a surprisingly enjoyable play depicting Luther's struggle. One of the most dramatic moments was when the monk nailed ninety-five theses on the front door of the cathedral in Wittenberg, Germany—a midsize city south of Berlin, and where Luther is buried. Our teachers explained that in 1517, when Luther posted the theses, the church door functioned as the communal bulletin board, or, in modern parlance, one might say the town Twitter feed. Luther chastised the Catholic Church for the sale of indulgences and for prohibiting laypeople from reading scripture without the intermediary of a priest. Moments after he posted his revolutionary statements, the entire city, and soon all of the Catholic Church, was intensely debating whether Luther was a visionary, heretic, or combination of both. Similar to Ed Ward's positive appraisal of church, the religious institution was a social institution with close connections to the wider community. Trinity Lutheran had the same identity during my childhood years. It was its own community, and yet it made a significant contribution to the surrounding community. On my most recent drive past the Lansing church, its sign read, FREE MEAL ON MONDAY—ALL WELCOME!

Exurban megachurches take the traditional identity and utility of the church, for all its flaws, and walk it through a hall of funny mirrors. The typical megachurch of exurbia, having already succeeded in seeking out a location that lacks community and vibrant public institutions, further isolates its members, creating an internal community that is not complementary to the larger local or national one but substitutive. It is hardly a surprise that megachurches, with questionable constitutionality, have become essential infrastructure to the insurgent antidemocratic right-wing movement within the United States. Donald Trump makes regular appearances at megachurches in states like Florida, Texas, and Arizona. During his address to the latter, he referred to COVID-19 as the "kung flu," and the crowd went wild with laughter and applause. Trump uttered the racist joke at—remember Ward's warning about weird names—Dream City Church, where Charlie Kirk—right-wing radical and former chairman of Students for Trump, hailing from Arlington Heights, Illinois, a Chicago suburb—hosts a monthly event, Freedom Night. Dream City boasts that Freedom Night is "an effort to continue winning the American culture war." Predictable as always, they give an obligatory nod to "restoring America's traditional values." One of those traditional values, at the height of the COVID pandemic, was the "freedom" to violate mask mandates and reject vaccination. A minor debate stirred for months online over whether Tucker Carlson, the propaganda champion of the neofascist right, got the vaccine, because he refused to answer questions about it. How fitting that he announced his status as unvaccinated at a California megachurch. Like "kung flu," the admission provoked an uproarious response. Congregants at FloodGate Church in the Detroit exurb of Howell, Michigan, routinely cheer their minister when he tells them about how Joe Biden stole the election from Donald Trump, invites guest speakers who refer to Democrats as "evil," and makes mean-spirited jokes about "pregnant men" to disparage transgender people. FloodGate is the largest megachurch in Michigan, offering colorful illustration that Americans who still attend church are leaving traditional institutions for those with a minister who functions as Rush Limbaugh in a robe and collar.[9]

It isn't only aggrieved and hostile whites who are flocking to the exurban megachurch. Latinos, according to many studies, are leaving the Catholic Church and joining independent, weird-name evangelical megachurches. The Pew Research Center reports that Latinos are the fastest-growing group of evangelicals in the country. While there is intense scrutiny of Latino voting patterns, few political commentators offer an informed, coherent analysis of why Donald Trump won more Latino votes than Mitt Romney (Trump won vastly fewer than George W. Bush) despite his brazen hostility toward Mexican immigrants. Pundits tend to focus on fear of socialism, but that only applies to Cubans in Florida—the most consistently conservative voting bloc among American Latinos. Pundits also tend to ignore that Latinos still vote overwhelmingly in favor of Democrats, as they did for Joe Biden in 2020 and Democratic candidates in the 2022 midterms.

To explain the small minority of Latinos that have shifted to the right, religion, more than politics, offers a clue to solving the mystery. Latino Protestants are far likelier to vote Republican than their Catholic counterparts. Of all the variables determining Latino approval of Donald Trump's presidential performance, Protestant affiliation was the most significant. Mark Mulder, a sociologist who studies Latino culture and religious devotion in the United States, explains that Latino Catholic churches "emphasize social justice," while evangelical megachurches preach entrepreneurialism, social conservatism, and the development of a "personal relationship with Christ," which neatly aligns with right-wing notions of individualism.[10] A few pundits posited that Trump's brash machismo appealed to Latino men and immediately received condemnation as politically incorrect, but they were not entirely wrong. The Catholic Church is far from a bastion of feminism, but evangelical institutions more frequently exercise the John Wayne theology that Kristin Kobes Du Mez writes is crucial to the identity of the religious right. A paternalistic male protector who ignores pesky rules and ethical considerations to act in accordance with a larger goal is the profile that many evangelical ministers attempt to adopt. It is also the political personality that Trump projected to the electorate.

One common characteristic of the megachurch is its independence. A Catholic diocese, Lutheran synod, or national denominational organization restrains churches and pastors who venture too far out of the mainstream and risk sullying the reputation of the broader church. An institutional drama with the Southern Baptist Convention (SBC) typified the value of governing bodies in the aftermath of the Black Lives Matter rebellion that took place following the police murder of George Floyd. Moderate and liberal Baptists hoped to address systemic racism and aspire toward racial reconciliation, whereas right-wingers pressed the SBC to "denounce critical race theory" and distance itself from Black Lives Matter. At the SBC annual conference in Nashville in 2021, its members voted on a new president with the understanding that he would determine the direction of the church. With 52 percent of the votes, Ed Litton achieved victory. Litton is an influential member of the Pledge Group, a multiracial and ecumenical organization in Mobile, Alabama, dedicated to "promoting racial healing among people of faith." In his one-year term as president, Litton made headlines by championing an effort to publicize and rectify SBC's abysmal record of mishandling sex abuse claims from parishioners.[11]

Churches without organizational direction operate without theological constraints, often flying far off the rails of Christian convention. Just as exurban residents desire an escape from political restriction and democratic balance, congregants of large megachurches enjoy the odd perversion of freedom that has come to dictate much of American politics. A popular megachurch in Munster, Indiana, captures the dark side of megachurch theology and culture.

✳

FAMILY CHRISTIAN CENTER (FCC) OPENED THE doors to its massive, arena-like building in 1999. Its location, Munster, IN is a wealthy, predominantly white suburb immediately over the border of Illinois, and right next to Lansing. Full of many residential complexes of "old money" and luxurious homes, Munster also boasts one of the region's best public high schools. Parents will often downsize into tight apartment quarters to send their children to study in Munster. The high school borders a large community park and pool, Munster Community Hospital, and a sizable sports complex where traveling teams compete in baseball and softball, and tennis tournaments take place every summer.

Munster is also home to most of the small Jewish population of Northwest Indiana. It has two synagogues—one Orthodox and one Reform—and prominent Jewish families that support the local Democratic Party and programs for children. For three consecutive summers, I attended Sid Rothstein's tennis camp, where Munster high school tennis team members taught us how to serve, volley, and hit forehands with topspin. Rothstein used much of the money he procured from the camp to support services and activities for children with developmental disabilities. The teenage tennis instructors he employed included a Polish Catholic who later converted to Islam and acquired a PhD in political science, a beautiful Italian immigrant who made every adolescent heart swoon, and an aspiring singer-songwriter who imagined himself a heterosexual Elton John, his all-time favorite performer. Among my fellow campers there were Sikh siblings, Jewish kids, and a Macaulay Culkin circa *Home Alone* lookalike whose parents moved from a tony North Side of Chicago neighborhood. Equipped with a criminally expensive racquet, he won nearly every match, making him the designated villain of the camp. The park where the camp took place is the largest in the county and during the summer months offers free jazz performances, a local craft beer festival, and an assortment of rock and roll tribute band nights, ranging from Green Day to the Eagles. The jazz bands are consistently good, especially the region's best and only fusion quintet, Freek Johnson, while with the rock tribute bands quality varies.

As far as production values go, however, it would take the Rolling Stones to compete with the plays and pageants at Family Christian Center. Most famous for its elaborate theatrical shows, complete with professional actors, expertly trained musicians, and lighting and special effects that Broadway directors would envy, Family Christian Center takes religious entertainment to a new level. Plays depict Christ's crucifixion and resurrection, along with other Biblical tales, but most fascinating are the freshly written stories set in modern times. The descriptive advertisement for a Family Christian Center original production, *Heartbreak Hotel—Hotel Hallelujah*, informs buyers of $25 tickets that they are in for a "Las Vegas style production that will blow your mind." Attendees can expect "celebrity look-a-likes, mega dance acts, live animals, cars, motorcycles, and more on a 200 feet stage!" The only indication of the theological or philosophical substance of the performance, while not exactly competing with Thomas Aquinas in the area of intellectual heft, is the tagline, "We all have to make choices in life." The poster spotlights Pastor Steve Munsey preparing to do battle with a mace-wielding skeleton. Munsey is, typically, the star of the show, and there is truth in advertising with the identification of Las Vegas as inspirational, as long as one thinks of Sin City circa Wayne Newton, Liberace, and the weird combination of cheese and sleaze as depicted in Paul Verhoeven's 1995 film, *Showgirls*. The shows typically embed a vaguely Christian and conservative message in an action-packed melodrama. Villains are corrupt secular officials, and characters often go astray searching for independence, sexual pleasure, or knowledge beyond church sanction. The skeleton threatening Munsey with a mace is likely an exception, but villains are also often effeminate men, resurrecting the old Hollywood tactic of associating malevolence with hints of homosexuality.

Munsey makes for an odd hero. Rather than looking like Tom Cruise in *Top Gun*, he appears to have modeled his appearance on Donald Trump and post–plastic surgery Mickey Rourke. When not wearing flashy suits, the seventy-one-year-old Munsey is fond of skinny jeans, leather biker jackets, the kind of boots with high heels that Prince and Elvis Presley preferred, and bright, bulky jewelry.

Munsey makes occasional gestures toward liberalism in the interest of serving his racially diverse congregation, such as inviting Reverend Jesse Jackson to speak at the pulpit, but Family Christian Center leadership offered no public support for Black Lives Matter. Munsey's method of church management, despite occasional nods to diversity, like his prosperity gospel theology, exposes a pattern of greed, sociopolitical indifference, and deceit. It did not take long for Munsey to begin courting controversy after the doors of the gigantic Family Christian Center opened in Munster. After the 9/11 attacks, Munsey constructed a massive Last Supper mockup with life-size mannequins dressed as Jesus and the Disciples in one of FCC's windows. Behind them was an American flag covering the entire wall, making it appear as if Christ administered the first Eucharist at a suburban VFW. A few local Catholic priests objected to the display, explaining that while they were sympathetic to the patriotic impulse, especially in a time of national mourning, it was blasphemous to so closely associate the Christian savior with national identity. Money, more than theology, was the source of Munsey's more damaging scandals.

While researching her book *God's Profits: Faith, Fraud, and the Republican Crusade for Values Voters*, Sarah Posner became aware of Munsey. He was one of the featured ministers at the 2007 Praise-A-Thon, an annual fundraising program for the Trinity Broadcasting Network, the ESPN of televangelism. With his rap music video business suit, Munsey was giving a fiery delivery of his "Blessings of Passover" theory—the subject of one of his books. The Biblical story of Passover is about escape from slavery and governmental persecution. It remains an inspirational holiday to Jews all around the world and is also routinely the subject of Bible lessons in Christian schools and churches. In Munsey's hands, it is not an allegory of faith and freedom but only about dollar bills. For a monthly donation of $70 over the next ten months, Munsey insisted, viewers would "get back" everything that has "ever been stolen" from them. Reciting the greatest hits of the prosperity gospel, Munsey explained that "God is not moved by need" but "by faith." If the Christian sitting at home has sufficient faith to make the donation while expecting a bountiful return, "God will take that offering and magnify it in the Devil's face."[12] Munsey is like the casino. While the odds are against the donor, Munsey can't lose. If the Christian viewer parting with $700 subsequently experiences a windfall, Munsey looks like a true prophet. If their financial woes worsen, or even remain the same after writing the checks, maybe it was because they didn't really have enough faith to impress God. Those quiet moments of doubt, sneaking up on them in the middle of the night, prevented them from striking it rich.

Bill Berkowitz, a journalist covering the far right in the United States, noticed that Munsey upped the ante for Yom Kippur, the Jewish day of atonement that Christians do not celebrate but learn about in scriptural study. Appearing on the television program of "faith healer" Benny Hinn in 2015, Munsey told viewers, with the certainty of a scientist explaining photosynthesis to teenagers, that for a donation of $300 they would be "healed of cancer, get out of debt, and see their children return to the faith." With the proper dosage of belief, they would soon find themselves "unbelievably wealthy."[13]

It requires a special brand of iniquity to sell false hope to desperate people and, when those hopes collapse, allow them to believe that their poverty, disease, or estrangement from their children is due to their failure to please God with prayer and personal devotion. An essential element of the prosperity gospel swindle is the appearance of wealth and luxury. If God blesses the faithful with material abundance, the pastor pushing the con must demonstrate affluence. Otherwise, the racket would immediately appear inconsistent and dubious.

Steve Munsey and his wife, Melodye, live in Briar Ridge—a gated community, with its own private country club, in the exurb of Schererville, Indiana. It is one of two private and patrolled residential complexes in the county, but by far the most opulent and exclusive. Jerry Springer, the late reigning champion of trash television, had a mansion in Briar Ridge when he filmed his program in a Chicago studio. The phrase "Briar Ridge," throughout my childhood, communicated unfathomable levels of luxury. It was common for working- and middle-class locals to, if joking about winning the lottery, announce, "I'm going to buy a home in Briar Ridge." Most of the homes price in the low seven figures, but the neighborhood becomes much less interesting upon the realization, with age and maturity, that its residents are surgeons, successful business owners, and high-priced attorneys. As a child, especially after hearing the news about Jerry Springer, I imagined that beyond the security shack, Briar Ridge was chock-full of celebrities. Now that Springer is gone, its most famous homeowner is Munsey. The election results map indicates that the small precinct containing the gated community went for Trump in 2020 by a landslide margin of 25 percent.

Beyond the garishness and unfashionable hair, anyone with knowledge of Trump's deceptive financing, shady management of money, and bamboozlement of contractors, customers, and workers will find more recognizable similarities in Steve Munsey. In 2013, the *Northwest Indiana Times* reported that the Family Christian Center, despite having a weekly total attendance average at Sunday's two services of 15,235 people, and regularly selling out performances of its elaborate entertainment productions, was facing foreclosure. FCC owed over $700,000 in mortgage payments to the Evangelical Christian Credit Union (ECCU) in California, a lending institution specializing in, as its name would suggest, financing for evangelical churches, bookstores, and other enterprises. The ECCU, now AdelFi, has seen its profits skyrocket in the age of the megachurch. As of February 2022, according to *American Banker*, AdelFi managed over $582 million worth of assets. AdelFi donates 10 percent of its earnings to Christian charities, and claims its central mission is to "spread the gospel," but it still is a business and wasn't about to allow Family Christian Center to skate on nearly a million dollars of debt, especially considering the surrounding circumstances.[14]

In addition to the Munseys' gated community mansion, Pastor Steve owned a Mercedes with a bluebook value of $80,000, and, along with his wife, was part owner of a private plane. IRS records show that in 2011, two years before the foreclosure crisis hit the press and the pews, Steve Munsey collected a salary of $519,514, while the "first lady" of the church took home $201,607. From 2008 to 2011, their son enjoyed total compensation from the church to the tune of $914,886. As if that wasn't enough to prove God's favor to an audience of potential donors, the Munseys also took out a loan from Refuge Productions—the "nonprofit" they administer to produce the live-animal, mega-dance extravaganzas of local lore—for $183,934. God might work in mysterious ways, but Steve Munsey does not. He authorized the loan to himself in the same year that he and his wife purchased their $2.3 million house in Briar Ridge. All the while, FCC was delinquent on its mortgage, threatening the life of the church and whatever solace it provides its members.[15] Munsey said that he never brought the financial crisis to the attention of followers because he "put his trust in God."

Family Christian Center congregants trusted Munsey enough to bail out the church—most of them appearing not even to pause to consider why a humble "servant of God" has a wardrobe that costs more than the used car that the pastor of Trinity Lutheran drove when I was in confirmation class. Given that attendance rates have remained consistent, it also seems that most FCC members did not find anything suspicious in the details of the Munsey family's most disturbing scandal.

On May 29, 2015, eighteen-year-old Domonique "Nikki" Smith was babysitting Steve and Melodye Munsey's six-year-old granddaughter at the Briar Ridge residence. Steve was not home, but Melodye was upstairs. She claims that her granddaughter ran into the bedroom crying. Domonique Smith was face down in the family pool, and unresponsive. Although there were never any criminal charges, and Smith's parents' wrongful death suit was dismissed after several years of legal drama, the story of the teenage babysitter's death remains mysterious. Domonique Smith was a trained lifeguard, and the toxicology report indicated no drugs or alcohol in her system. The Lake County coroner ruled her death an accidental drowning, but could find no water in her lungs. Because Smith was an organ donor, authorities did not perform an autopsy. Compounding the alarming oddity of the death, Melodye Munsey allegedly admitted to Domonique Smith's mother, Vicki Walker, that she hesitated to call for an ambulance, waiting ten to fifteen minutes, because she saw Smith's "soul leave her body." Munsey would later claim that she did all that she could to summon help, but Walker and her attorney insist that she made the claim of witnessing spiritual ascension. Walker requested security camera footage from the night in question, and was initially encouraged when the Munseys cooperated. Her suspicions would only intensify upon viewing the tape. Fourteen minutes of footage were alleged to have been missing. Munsey's congregation never left his side throughout the credible allegations of financial malfeasance or the suspicions surrounding Domonique Smith's drowning.

Munsey can claim a dubious legal victory. A judge dismissed the Smiths' wrongful death suit, because Melodye Munsey could prove that she was unable to swim. No law, according to the presiding judge, requires a person to put herself at physical risk to provide aid to another.[16] The megachurch operates according to an explicitly antidemocratic, firmly autocratic model. The charismatic pastor is an authority figure outside the boundaries of supervision, scrutiny, or accountability. People believe what the pastor says because the pastor says it. The cult of Donald Trump, given its disproportionate number of Christian nationalists, is a political application of the authoritarian characteristic of the exurban megachurch.

✺

REFUSAL TO PROVIDE AID IS A CONSISTENT PATTERN among megachurches. As Steve Munsey phrased it himself, "God is not moved by need." Family Christian Center is not nearly as political as the average megachurch. It had a soft policy on COVID-19, opening rather early into the pandemic without enforcement of mask mandates, but unlike many prominent church leaders, the Munseys never discouraged vaccination or facial covering. FCC ministries avoid inflammatory topics, such as allegations of voter fraud in 2020, that other exurban arenas of worship dish out like communion wafers. The moderating influence of FCC is, undoubtedly, its nearly half Black membership. Martin Luther King famously said that "eleven o'clock on Sunday morning is one of the most segregated hours . . . in Christian America." While King's exhortation of the racial divide in American Christendom remains true, it does not apply to the Family Christian Center. Munsey has to proceed with caution in going beyond garden-variety social conservatism when addressing national politics. Rather than illustrating the antisocial, antidemocratic right's capture of Heartland churches, FCC typifies what Mike Lofgren, a former high-level Senate aide to the Republican Party who now dedicates himself to denouncing the right wing, identifies as the proliferation of gullible cynics.[17] The gullible cynic reflexively rejects scientific evidence, public health protocols, logical argument, and the "official story" of any major event, from the

January 6 insurrection to Russia's invasion of Ukraine, but maintains a "faith-based view." The faith-based view, which is another way of saying absence of evidence, covers not only creationism and the power of prayer but also critical contemporary issues, like global warming, educational policy, and transgenderism. In the prosperity gospel context, it also dictates indifference to poverty and systemic failure to address extreme inequality or potential improvements to the social welfare state. If God cares not for need, why should anyone else? Democratic proposals to raise the minimum wage, provide for easier and more affordable access to health care, and subsidize essential services, like childcare and paid family leave, bounce off tin ears.

Christianity is certainly in decline in the United States, and the share of evangelical Christians consistently lands between 20 and 25 percent of the public. Fewer than one in four might seem like a small minority, but it is a minority that, in the words of one journalist, "holds unchallenged dominance within the GOP."[18] Forty-six percent of Trump's voters in the 2016 election were white evangelical Christians. The religious right is the most crucial constituency within the national Republican coalition. If a Republican candidate for president alienates the masses flocking to exurban megachurches, they have written their own political obituary. Many political analysts have attempted to understand the increasingly volatile extremity of the contemporary Republican Party, but few identify the most combustible ingredient in America's political recipe for disaster—apocalyptic Christian nationalism. Family Christian Center might not dive fully into the sewage of far-right politics, but it is an exponent of "End Times" preaching. Steve Munsey gives sermons forecasting inevitable Armageddon, when Christ will return to Earth, plunging all the nonbelievers into an eternal inferno of torture and ushering his worshippers into a celestial paradise. Because social convention in the United States considers criticism of people's religious faith impolite, most journalists avoid stating the obvious: if you combine apocalyptic preaching of a violent end to the universe with the brand of reactionary politics that evangelicals routinely exercise, you will not only end up with dangerous beliefs but also destructive behavior.

Most coverage of the January 6 insurrection concentrates on the ordinary profile of the average insurrectionist, the organization of domestic terrorist groups, like the Proud Boys, Oath Keepers, and Three Percenters, and the influence of neo-Nazis, along with other outspoken anti-Semites. There is a noticeable and unforgivable oddity even in much of the best coverage of the insurrection: an absence of sustained attention on the most common ideology and iconography among the mob—Christian nationalism. Researcher Teddy Wilson examined 850 of the Capitol riot defendants and found that "Christian nationalism, more than any other ideological belief, has played the most significant role in the motivations of the defendants."[19] Even a cursory glance at photos from the event itself reveals a consistency of crosses, Christian flags, signs with Bible verses and references to Jesus, and weird apparel, such as a baseball cap promoting "God, Guns, and Trump."

Mikey Weinstein, a Jewish attorney and former Air Force officer, is one of the few Americans sounding an alarm about the danger of Christian nationalism, both within the military and throughout civilian society. When in the Air Force, Weinstein regularly witnessed and endured attempts from fellow airmen, including superior officers, to convert entire units to fundamentalist evangelical Christianity. When he not only rejected conversion but also challenged the religiosity of the Air Force on constitutional grounds, he was harassed with anti-Semitic slurs and, eventually, beaten so severely that his injuries required treatment in a hospital. According to research from the advocacy organization that he helped create, Military Religious Freedom Foundation, between 28 and 35 percent of active duty military personnel are Christian nationalists. Weinstein makes it clear that, unlike his persecutors, he has no desire to convert anyone to a different faith. There are many Christians on his staff. They join Weinstein in warning that if the United States does not aggressively address the threat of Christian nationalism, it will experience "blood in the streets." Nearly one in five defendants in cases against Capitol insurrectionists served in the armed forces. Weinstein submits that the disproportionate percentage of veterans among the January 6 mob is due to Christian nationalism that manifests in the violence that he observed and suffered while wearing the uniform.[20]

The dangerous myth that the United States is a "Christian nation" in which the Bible supersedes the Constitution, and that democratic means of negotiation, compromise, and power sharing are obstacles in the way of America's divinely destined status of glory, motivated many insurrectionists and scaffolds the entire far-right project of neofascism. Charlie Kirk, who has made the megachurch his recruitment staging ground, told his radio audience in 2022 that "There is no separation of church and state. It's a fabrication . . . made up by secular humanists."

Philip Gorski, a professor of sociology and religious studies at Yale University, and coauthor of the book *The Flag and the Cross: White Christian Nationalism and the Threat to American Democracy*, insists that Christian nationalism is the most lethal threat facing the future of American civil society, particularly one that includes and franchises non-Christians, LGBTQ people, and women as citizens with equal rights and opportunities as men. Gorski worries that "the secular left in the country is highly underestimating how strong these forces are."[21]

One reason for the underestimation is isolation. I recall a pleasant evening, full of great sushi and stiff drinks, with friends in the heavily gay and assertively liberal Chicago neighborhood of Andersonville, less than a mile from my friends' home. Situated on the far north side of the city, Andersonville combines the charm of a small-town neighborhood, with its walkable "main street" commercial district and historic bars with regulars occupying the stools and booths, and the cosmopolitan politics of a major city. Lori Lightfoot, Chicago's first Black woman

and first gay mayor, launched her campaign from Andersonville. The
neighborhood, paying homage to its history of Swiss immigration, has
a variety of Swiss-owned restaurants and cafés, along with prominent
Swiss flags. It is also home of the Women and Children First bookstore,
where its "trans-inclusive feminist" owners boast of a mission to not only
promote great literature but to help "realize the dream of an inclusive
feminist future." Sitting a few doors down from Women and Children
First, I casually remarked to my friends—a retired high school Spanish
teacher and his wife, who works in television production—how the majority of the American people are Christian. The retired teacher did not
offer much of an audible reply, but his spouse's initial reaction was vehe-
ment disagreement, arguing that I was wildly misguided in my perception. After displaying polling data on my phone, her disposition turned
to surprise. By her own admission, she has no friends who are practicing
Christians, which made it difficult for her to imagine that her immediate circle was so far removed from the American mainstream. While this
anecdote might seem like a parody of progressive detachment straight
from a Fox News script, a similar quality characterized the mainline
media coverage, and general Democratic reaction, to widespread evangelical support for Donald Trump. It was so common as to become cliché to hear baffled and indignant inquiries regarding how church-going
Christians could support a man who, to select one example at random,
committed adultery with a pornographic film actress while his wife was
home taking care of their newborn child, and then instructed his lawyer
to bribe said actress into silence so as not to threaten his marriage or
presidential ambitions. One will notice that these expressions of bafflement over the Grand Canyon separating Christian doctrine and the
habitual action of the evangelical political idol often come from reporters and commentators who live and work in the New York–DC nexus,
have Ivy League degrees, and confuse Twitter for an accurate gauge of
American values.

Proximity to exurban megachurches, along with the academic literature on the subject, shows that the religious right has not fundamentally changed since its entrance into politics when it organized to violate multiracial democracy. It has only become more radical, insurgent, and violent. Analysts confused over the contradiction between Christian doctrine and Trump's behavior should understand that Christian nationalists do not petition the political system to advance pious personal values of sexual restraint and moral austerity. They confront the political system to impose a theocracy. When America's triumvirate system of democracy works to its advantage, they celebrate the results; most infamously, in 2022, when the Supreme Court revoked *Roe v. Wade*. When the system fails their narrow, reactionary agenda, they seek to radically transform, topple, upend, or destroy it.

Katherine Stewart, a journalist who studies the religious right, explains that when well-intentioned observers complain that Christian fundamentalists are "breaking democracy," they should recognize that the destruction they lament is not an unintended side effect of the religious right's political design. It is "the point of the project."[22] One of the reasons that Mike Lofgren left the Republican Party was, as he recalls from his years on the Hill, the Christian nationalist "infiltration and subversion of the Party of Lincoln." He shares Stewart's diagnosis of the danger but also posits that Christian fundamentalists are eager to form alliances with groups that do not share their personal values or lifestyle choices if they have common cause in "breaking democracy": white nationalists, armed militias, and extreme libertarians.

Journalists, academics, and left-wing Christians who attend services at exurban megachurches in the Heartland, Sun Belt, and Deep South consistently report that ministers compare liberals, and even moderate Democrats, to "wolves," "demons," and "terrorists," while presenting nearly every item in the far-right agenda, from nativist border policies to denial of global warming, as dogma of the faith. Scholarship demonstrates that 28 percent of Americans believe that "the federal government should declare the United States a Christian nation." Advocates of an American jihad are clearly not pining for a country obedient to Biblical laws prohibiting banks from charging interest on loans or restaurants from serving shellfish. They desire a country where women are subordinate to men, gay and transgender citizens have few protections outside the closet, and any belief system alternative to Christianity is unworthy of respect.[23]

The politics of fight or flight manifest in exurban growth. Jason Luger, a political geographer, offers an ethnographic study of an unnamed Southern exurb, finding that the right-wing community is self-selecting and self-perpetuating. As its megachurches became more popular, they acted as a magnet for far-right voters and activists. Many of them even moved to the town or a nearby exurb, making the area their permanent home. The creation of an unofficial commune enables exurban Christian nationalists to develop "powerful bonds of trust," but even more significantly, "perpetuate infrastructures of faith" by voting for "evangelical-Christian and Christian-nationalist local, county, state, and federal elected officials, who fill municipal positions, school boards, courts, law enforcement institutions and planning/zoning committees."[24]

Bill Bishop, a Texas journalist, famously warned that the "big sort" would threaten American civility and cohesion, reporting on how many Americans are living in ideological enclaves, whether an evangelical exurb or the Andersonville neighborhood of Chicago, having almost no contact with people who disagree with their opinions. Both sides are not equal, however. While the consequence of isolation in Andersonville is underestimation of Christians in the United States, the effect of the exurban enclave is much more dangerous. For example, when someone announces that he is going to participate in a "stop the steal" rally at the US Capitol to prevent the certification of the presidential election, he will receive the encouragement of an enthusiastic group of supporters.

The suburbs of Northwest Indiana do not exemplify the big sort.

Proximity to Chicago, along with the history of midsize cities, like Gary, ensure a reliable amount of sociopolitical diversity. The exurbs are another story. St. John, Indiana, a small town about forty miles south of Chicago, showcases exactly what Bishop describes. Its exurban profile attracted right-wing voters, and now the dominance of those voters repels suburban liberals. Spotlighting the sorting dynamic was the 2022 news that John Kass, a former longtime columnist for the *Chicago Tribune*, purchased a home in St. John. Chicago's most prestigious newspaper employed Kass through a series of shameful episodes, including his use of the derogation "feral" to describe inner-city Black youth, a slur that Evan F. Moore, former Chicago journalist and current press secretary for the Chicago public school system, compared to Ku Klux Klan propaganda of the 1920s.[25] He also wrote in anti-Semitic code about the evil influence of George Soros and other wealthy "globalists," all of whom just happened to be Jewish. Kass, the most prominent and obnoxious proponent for the far right, Donald Trump, and the thinly veiled racism of the Republican Party in Chicago, likely received a hero's welcome in St. John—a township where most precincts voted for Trump in 2020 by a margin greater than 30 percent. Even if Kass won't wave hello to visitors from the side of the road at the town welcome sign, St. John does have an effective advertisement of Christian nationalism.

ROUTE 41, ALSO KNOWN AS INDIANAPOLIS BOULE-vard, is the artery running north and south through Northwest Indiana. The "main road," as many locals like to call it, stretches all the way from Munster to Terre Haute, Indiana—home of Indiana State University, Larry Bird's alma mater. Driving south toward the center of the state through the suburbs where I live provides a pretty ordinary scene—national chains, strip malls, and public facilities, like schools and libraries.

The surroundings become sparser as one enters St. John—more space between businesses, a large veterinary hospital, a public high school, and some undeveloped land. Then, emerging from out of the sky like Godzilla, there is a silver-colored statue of the Virgin Mary. With her arms outstretched, she towers over the community, threatening to come alive like when the Statue of Liberty begins to walk through New York in *Ghostbusters 2*. At Mary's gigantic feet, there is a gift shop and entrance to the Shrine of Christ's Passion. The shrine, in the words of its website, is a "multi-media interactive, half-mile winding prayer trail," featuring forty bronze statues of Christ, each one weighing between three hundred and seven hundred pounds, that depict the last days of his life. The shrine calls these statues "life-size," but many of them are far bigger than the average man. They present Christ with the bodily proportions of Shaquille O'Neal. In addition to Christ's passion, the shrine also pays massive statue tribute to Moses at Mt. Sinai—the site where God gave him the Ten Commandments to share with the Israelites. Covering thirty acres of land, the shrine cost $10 million to create and attracts 250,000 tourists every year. Bill Kurtis, a highly regarded Chicago television journalist, narrates the audio tour guide that visitors can play on their journey.

The shrine is the brainchild, and one might say passion project, of Frank and Shirley Schilling, an elderly St. John couple who made millions of dollars as real estate developers and proprietors of a home improvement business.[26] Although they are committed Catholics, and have received many Catholic honors for the shrine, they strive to ensure that the Christian tourist attraction remains nondenominational in language, aesthetic, and spirit. Its politics are easier to identify. A few steps past the main entrance, visitors will see the "Sanctity of Life Shrine." There is a gravestone with the engraved text, DEDICATED TO THE SANCTITY OF LIFE. IN LOVING MEMORY OF THE INNOCENT VICTIMS OF ABORTION. A statue of Jesus on his knees, with a sorrowful facial expression, rests before the headstone. It gives the impression that Christ mourns for aborted embryos and fetuses and, unlike Amy Coney Barrett and Brett Kavanaugh, is powerless to intervene. The Schillings are not politically outspoken. In interviews, their concentration of personal piety, and vague references to social conservatism, imply a set of reactionary politics, but they are admirably charitable on a number of fronts—making large donations to not only "right to life" groups but also food banks, homeless shelters, and the Special Olympics. It is all the more curious an act of political exposure, then, to spotlight abortion as injustice, but nothing else. There is no shrine for the innocent victims of war, poverty, racism, or environmental destruction.

The Schillings, along with the employees of the shrine, will insist that they are offering an ecumenical and apolitical devotional experience, but evidently see no contradiction in greeting every tourist with a message that might anger and unnerve the 61 percent of Americans who oppose the Supreme Court's decision to revoke *Roe v. Wade*. One could imagine the controversy that might ensue if the shrine did indeed have a memorial for civilian casualties of war or those who suffer the ill effects of poverty. Any mention of racism would create a firestorm. And yet abortion is so thoroughly and deftly embedded into the posture of Catholicism and evangelical Christianity that its explicit mention does not qualify as "political." Even scholars no longer think of abortion as a subject of debate or activism within the confines of Christian theology. James S. Bielo, an anthropologist from Ohio, visited the shrine and noted that the "Station treats the liturgy in personal, devotional terms," also observing that there is "not an engagement with liberation theology," referring to the Catholic teaching, once popular throughout South America, that claims God has a "preferential option for the poor," demanding involvement with issues of economic and social injustice.[27] The Sanctity of Life Shrine signals the influence of megachurch evangelicalism on traditional denominations.

Father Ed Ward has often commented that no one thinks of church work in terms of business and marketing, but economic standards and ambitions are inseparable from any large institution. As megachurches fill the seats, churches with empty pews begin to take notice, and, with the hopes of retaining their dwindling membership and attracting new exurban arrivals, adopt more right-wing positions and priorities. In 2022, the Orthodox Church in America decreed that their various institutions were to allow no debate on the matters of same-sex attraction, gay marriage, and transgenderism; they are "disordered." The US Catholic Bishops routinely denounce abortion, and discuss denying communion to Democratic politicians who favor reproductive rights. Rarely, if ever, do they issue similar decrees on poverty, the cost of health care, global warming, capital punishment, or the federal budget's prioritization of the military over social services. After a gunman murdered nineteen children and two teachers at an elementary school in Uvalde, Texas, a San Antonio priest demanded that the bishops uniformly call for stronger gun control measures. In response, four bishops cosigned a letter to Congress expressing support for a ban on assault rifles, provoking the obvious question: Where were the other 256 bishops? One Catholic writer wondered, "Catholic bishops support gun control. Why don't we hear about it?"[28]

The reason for the silence is that it is a good marketing decision. Abortion is about "protecting the unborn," whereas gun control risks opposition from the "freedom" fanatics who equate even minor restrictions on firearms with "tyranny." The future of American Christianity is in the megachurch. Multiple reports confirm that in recent years megachurches have grown, while the size of the more generic church has diminished. A journalist with *Religion Dispatches* summarizes the data by juxtaposing two different styles of church: the rock and roll, prosperity gospel, and often nationalist megachurch, and the "dying small-town church, complete with elderly pastor and greying (mostly female) congregation."[29]

The graying and dying small-town church is Trinity Lutheran—the church where I spent much of my childhood, witnessing and learning the virtues of thrift, respectfulness, modesty, and charity. In 2017, Trinity closed the doors of its school. It could no longer draw a sufficient number of families or students to make payroll. Four years later, St. Ann School in Lansing also closed. Family Christian Center, along with similar megachurches, show no signs of slowing down.

THE STREETSIDE CAFÉ THAT TREATS NEARBY PEDEStrians with the tearful sound of Jerry Garcia's guitar has the appropriate name of Sip. Its Highland location, although larger than the original, opened several years after Sip began enticing customers with "Fire on the Mountain" and "Sugar Magnolia" in Crown Point. Its menu offers a delicious variety of sweets in addition to artisanal sandwiches and a staggering range of specialty coffee beverages—all of which are well worth trying. Their cold to-go drinks come in plastic cups from the coffee company Uncommon Ground. The cup displays a rainbow flag as part of its design with the slogan, "Roasted with Pride." Saturday and Sunday evenings, especially in the warmer months, the handful of tables outside the coffeehouse, along with the sidewalk on which they rest and the neighboring parking lot, overflow with teenagers. Smoking cigarettes, vaping, or sneaking non-tobacco but smokable products, the eclectic assembly of local youth talk and idle well beyond the nine o'clock hour when Sip shuts its doors. The towns of Northwest Indiana have their large share of jocks, aspiring jocks, and effervescent cheerleaders, but a different crowd meets at Sip on the weekends. There is a Black high school senior, thin as a rail, who wears tight purple pants and heeled boots. There are pairs of young women who hold hands, and there are long-haired wallflowers whose T-shirts advertise punk rock and heavy metal bands, some with names I've never heard and others like Metallica and the Misfits. One of Sip's teenage employees, tongue in cheek, is fond of claiming she is a vampire, while another is friendly to customers, but as soon as she has a moment of freedom, she crosses her nylon-clad legs on the nearest park bench, dangles a combat boot with a slight bob at the ankle, and smokes American Spirits while scrolling through her phone. Equally as colorful as the weekend customers are the walls that surround Sip. Highland hired local artists to paint murals throughout its downtown streets. Some of them showcase the blue heron, a beautiful bird common throughout the area, while others are more abstract. They are all bright—flashing pink, purple, sky blue, and a wide range of colors with names from a Crayola box.

It is the proudly eccentric Sip customer base that is responsible for the bumper stickers on street lamps near the café, the library, and a local bar reading, GENDER IS OVER (IF YOU WANT IT). The update of John Lennon's anti-war slogan and song does not feel or appear utopian at Sip on a Sunday evening as teenagers gather, laugh, converse, and snap photographs without regard for role or label. When Highland had a small business and local crafts fair in the commercial center during the spring of 2022, a teenage rock band, against all the cultural odds and peer pressure, presented itself as a replacement to the Runaways. The loud, aggressive, and emphatic female trio blasted and banged away on their drums, bass, and guitar, with rinky-dink amplification, as they shouted. The vocal delivery never wavered or varied no matter the topic—teenage romance, anti-authority sentiment, or, believe it or not, cat food. Sip sponsored the performance, and in its parking lot, a motley congregation of adolescents and burgeoning adults danced, jumped up and down with fists in the air, and moshed, but not in a way that resembled any of the borderline assaults that take place at a Slayer show. It was a playful, affectionate excuse to collide and create friction with their bodies.

The sociologist Ray Oldenburg studied and wrote about the essentiality of the "Third Place"—somewhere that isn't home and isn't work, and enables people to "relax in public," enjoy the camaraderie of "familiar faces," and form new friendships. The Third Place is a "home away from home" with a "playful mood" and unspoken ethics of equal acceptance. Socioeconomic status should not influence a patron's reception.[30] Maybe the guy in the Misfits shirt lives in a cramped apartment with his single mom and two siblings, and maybe the androgynous young Black person in high-heeled boots is the son of a doctor. At Sip, they are both paying customers, members of the same social set, and potential friends. As Oldenburg convincingly argues, the Third Place is important everywhere—whether in the heart of New York City or a small town in Indiana. David Mamet wrote that there are few experiences as pleasurable as walking into a favorite diner or bar and hearing as a greeting, "The usual?"[31]

Third Places are not always beneficial to individuals or the communities where they reside. The megachurch is a Third Place for millions of Americans who derive comfort and social capital from religious institutions that reinforce harmful prejudices, undermine opportunities for democratic collaboration, and encourage estrangement from progressive values. Where the megachurch thrives, it is essential for alternative Third Places to provide a home for anyone whose identity and ambition cannot conform with the restrictive dogmas broadcasting from the evangelical pulpit.

Familiarity and hospitality in a home away from home can only gain importance for teenagers and young adults who hear in the national news stories of state legislators and governors seeking to prohibit discussion of LGBTQ history and ban novels with gay or transgender protagonists from school libraries, especially if those teens realize that their parents are supportive of censorship, suppression, and exclusion by way of contemporary puritanism. The stakes are high for many young people when performing an act as simple as buying a cup of coffee. One of those young men is Holden Voyles. With the encouragement of his mother, Katie, he became the youngest member of PFLAG, after coming out as gay at the age of eleven. Katie describes the comfort and solidarity that PFLAG offers as "absolutely crucial."[32] The local chapter of PFLAG is located in Crown Point, and in 2019 it partnered with LGBTQ Northwest Indiana to organize and host the county's first Pride Festival in the community center of Highland. With the sponsorship and support of several local businesses, the Pride Festival included food, drink, live music, poetry readings, seminars on LGBTQ suicide prevention, and a same-sex wedding.

Holden's future is likelier to include self-respect and self-confidence because of the work of PFLAG, the organic camaraderie of Sip, and the love of his mother. The scene around Sip offers patrons and passersby a snapshot of hope; an indication of how the expansion and enlargement of freedom, legal protection, and democratic participation is not merely a political theory but a lifesaving mechanism for millions of people.

Americans longing for freedom live under a threatening shadow. Godzilla Jesus can come alive at any moment to smash buildings, crush the fleeing masses, and radically redesign the political architecture of any neighborhood in its path. Instead of projectile fire as its weapon, it has state and local governments, right-wing propagandists, and the Supreme Court of the United States. Cheering in orgiastic delight from below will be the exurbanites, huddling in their megachurches with the belief that the destruction of progress is an answer to prayer.

In the first Godzilla movie, scientists develop an "oxygen destroyer weapon" to defeat the ruinous monster. The oxygen destroyer vaporizes all oxygen surrounding Godzilla, causing him to suffocate and collapse. Scientific truth and free inquiry, at the movies and on the ground, often prevail.

A POLITICAL TRAFFIC JAM

An astute observer might notice that the two most dominant right-wing issues driving the fight-or-flight politics of exurbia aren't exactly political. Racist aversion to Black and Latino people and Christian fundamentalism are not political issues as much as they are social pathologies with political effects. Aristotle defined "politics" as matters related to the city, meaning the collective community, and asserted that the entire point of any community is to make life happier for its inhabitants.[1] A private citizen who chooses to leave a neighborhood if Blacks, Latinos, or Asians move down the block is merely exercising a personal preference, albeit a bigoted and potentially harmful one. In isolation, he will have relatively no influence. If dozens of his neighbors join him, and city governments, lending institutions, and candidates for national office begin to adopt rhetoric and policies that protect, encourage, and promote the runaway's prejudice, the private preference morphs into a public problem. The same goes for adherence to Christian dogma. If an exurban man maintains a quiet belief that Christ will soon return to smite his heretic acquaintances, he might make unpleasant company. When the Republican Party campaigns and governs according to his "faith," he becomes a member of a dangerous insurgency. The United States is wrestling with the calamity of the Christian nationalist–white flight coupling. Reactionary politics can no longer promise safe flight, because the "threats" of demographic diversity, multiculturalism, secularism, and sexual liberalism have gone national. As the election of Donald Trump, his enablement in the US Congress, and the events of January 6, 2021, have demonstrated, flight has turned to fight.

In the Midwest, there was always an element of right-wing fight. The state of Indiana was a KKK stronghold, and one of the most gruesome photographs of a lynching captures a racist mob murder of two Black men in the Indiana town of Marion. Not too far north of Marion, Richard Daley presided as Chicago's mayor from 1955 to '76. When the "city of big shoulders" erupted into riots after the assassination of Martin Luther King, Daley gave police a "shoot to kill" order for anyone suspected of arson, and a "shoot to maim" order for looters. To Chicago's north, travelers will find Wisconsin—a delightful state, where visitors can enjoy a weekend in the underrated city of Milwaukee, ski in the northern hills, explore Madison, one of the country's best college towns, tour Lambeau Field, and sample a shockingly large variety of cheeses. They can also learn about Joseph McCarthy, who was one of Wisconsin's US Senators from 1947 until 1957, the year of his death. Those three ghastly examples of reactionary persecution of the American people are far from alone, but the popularity of flight did allow for the maintenance of civility throughout the culture, as long as civility was on the terms of the powerful majority. Acting in opposition to Aristotle's original, and still most clarifying, definition of community, flight engineered pain, poverty, and disenfranchisement for millions of Blacks, Latinos, Asians, Jews, gays, transgender people, and women who were not content to retire from the workforce at age twenty-two, bear children, and submit to their husbands' household rules. As the United States transformed into a national community re-sembling the "land of the free," and made genuine progress toward the democratic endowment of its entire polity, the fight instinct became more dominant on the right. Now it is all that the right, including one of the country's two major political parties, can offer.

Journalist and political analyst Steve Benen writes in his aptly ti-tled book, *The Impostors: How Republicans Quit Governing and Seized American Politics*, that the "nihilistic" GOP is "indifferent to the sub-stance of governing. It is disdainful of expertise and analysis. It is hostile toward evidence and arithmetic. It is tethered to few, if any, meaningful policy preferences. It does not know, and does not care, about how com-peting proposals should be crafted, scrutinized, or implemented." Benen quotes John Dilulio, a University of Pennsylvania political scientist who resigned from the George W. Bush administration in disgust over their disinterest in governance, as calling Republican officials, advisors, and campaign strategists "Mayberry Machiavellis."[2]

Mayberry, a reference to the lovable town of *The Andy Griffith Show*, is a romanticized and fun version of something that no longer exists in American life but many Republican voters believe they can recreate in the desolation of exurbia. Pushing the buttons of unrealistic nostalgia helps to explain how "the impostors" so often succeed in state and na-tional elections when they not only fail to propose solutions to pervasive environmental, social, and economic problems but also often refuse to even acknowledge the reality of those problems. How does a party that offers nothing to the American people on the issues of financial pre-carity, ecological destruction, educational attainment, and health care access—to name a few—actually win elections? And why do its most extreme and obstinate messengers carry the day in exurban districts?

✳

GEOGRAPHICAL PRECISION IS NECESSARY TO UNDER-
stand the locational headquarters of the fascist movement within the
United States. Too often the national press depicts and debates developments in "the suburbs" as if suburbia is one giant monolith. The 2016
and 2020 presidential elections showed that what I've observed in "Illiana" generalizes across the country. Republicans are losing ground in
the nearby suburbs of large metro areas. There are exceptions, but typically the closer one gets to Chicago, the likelier it is that the suburb is
blue. The pattern holds for Philadelphia, Washington, DC, Atlanta, and
even the towns to the north, east, and west of Indianapolis. South of
Indianapolis, a traveler begins to enter the region colloquially known
as "Kentuckiana"—the setting of John Mellencamp's hometown—the
"small town" of Seymour—and a vicious brand of reactionary politics
unlike those of the singer. Much to Mellencamp's chagrin, and the consternation of anyone interested in strengthening American democracy,
the Republican Party, especially its most hateful members, are becoming
dominant in small metro suburbia, gaining victories in the towns that
neighbor midsize cities like Youngstown, Ohio; Grand Rapids, Michigan; and Peoria, Illinois. Exurbia, most consequentially in the swing
states of Michigan, Arizona, and North Carolina, is almost entirely
right-wing—a breeding and stomping ground for militia mania, threats
to school board members and election officials, and the empty-headed
and destructive politics of "Mayberry Machiavellis."

I asked Mike Lofgren—a former GOP aide to the US Senate who
left his party during the Obama tenure, presciently denouncing it as
a "nihilistic death cult"—to draw on his years in the boiler room of
Republican politics and explain how the shifting colors of the electoral
map read to him. "It is important to never forget that the Democratic
suburban vote is diluted by gerrymandering," Lofgren said. "So, it isn't
just a sociological thing. It's structural." Republicans have excelled at gerrymandering in ways that put the Democrats' paltry efforts in Illinois,

a state infamous for Congressional districts with askew and jagged borders, to shame. In 2018, Republicans in Ohio redrew the congressional map with technique more creative than Jackson Pollock. Several civic activist groups, including the League of Women Voters, challenged the legality of the map, taking the case all the way to the state supreme court. In a 4–3 decision, the Ohio Supreme Court ruled that the Republican-drawn map violated the state constitution.[3] No such intervention occurred in North Carolina, where the 2020 House district map gave Republicans eight out of thirteen seats with only 49.9 percent of the vote.[4] There is a similar violation of the will of the electorate in Michigan, where Republicans only recently lost control of the state legislature despite consistently earning fewer statewide votes.

Republican saboteurs triumph in Georgia and Texas, where, according to the ACLU, state leaders "stack and pack" Black, Latino, and/or progressive voters into as few districts as possible, stripping their electoral power, and undermining their influence.[5] Combined with various tactics of voter suppression, including shutting down polling sites in Black and Latino precincts, understocking voting machines so as to increase wait times and discourage participation in poor neighborhoods, and moving ballot boxes off college campuses, partisan redistricting has helped Republicans flip formerly Democratic states. Given that Black, Latino, and Native American voters are most often the targets of disenfranchisement tactics, John Mellencamp's 2007 lyric that refers to Jim Crow "changing his name" but refusing to alter his behavior is a poetic summation.

As Lofgren suggests, the problem is not entirely structural. There is a sociocultural disease spreading throughout small metro suburbia and exurbia. Its symptoms include childlike conceptions of freedom that value assault rifles over health care, religious-like faith in the veracity of conspiracy theories, even those that originated in white supremacist circles, and a perpetual state of petulant aggrievement. The disease is particularly virulent in the Midwest—a region that Lofgren explains has "kept the Republicans nationally competitive."

Iowa, Missouri, and Ohio were swing states as recently as 2008, but they have since moved "decisively in the direction of the GOP." Michigan and Wisconsin now fall into the battleground category, while in 2012 they were part of a seemingly indestructible "blue wall." Barack Obama had unique gifts and appeal as a presidential contender that rendered his initial candidacy beyond recent compare. It is still significant that he handily won the state of Indiana in 2008. Four years later, he lost Indiana by nearly three hundred thousand votes, and in subsequent elections, Hoosiers have moved even further to the right. The electoral map is shifting. George W. Bush won Colorado, without much difficulty, in 2000 and 2004. Now it is a Democratic stronghold. Obama lost Arizona in 2012, Hillary Clinton hoped to win there in 2016, and Biden pulled it off in 2020. In the same year, Georgia flipped to the Democrats' favor for the first time since Bill Clinton was on the ballot. Despite the rearrangement of national schematics, the Midwestern story is heartbreaking for any liberal or leftist who came of age in the region and associated it with political and artistic figures like Abraham Lincoln, Carl Sandburg, Kurt Vonnegut, and Jesse Jackson and with movements such as "sewer socialism" in Milwaukee and the Chicago Freedom Movement for civil rights and fair and affordable housing.

Mike Lofgren was born and raised in Akron, Ohio. Reflecting on his formative years, as well as his career in Washington, DC, he explains that the loss of manufacturing and the erosion of family farming created a new class of economic aliens in the global market. "Somehow the victims of those policies"—most of which were from the Republican brain trust—"latched on to the diversionary politics of the culture wars." Family farmers voted overwhelmingly for Trump, despite the agricultural tariffs of the Trump administration that bankrupted them, and the mainstream media made heavy weather out of displaced factory workers flocking to Trump in Rust Belt outposts like Anderson, Indiana, and Sheboygan, Wisconsin. The decline of union membership left most of these workers dazed and confused, with no political guidance other than the hysterical and demagogic voices shrieking at them through car radio speakers and televisions tuned to Fox News. While these white workers, especially in rural stretches of the Heartland states, were an important part of the Trump coalition, they were far from representative. Political scientists at Duke University and Vanderbilt University found that only 30 percent of Trump's voters were "working class." Even if a majority of "white working class" voters supported Trump, they did so at a rate consistent with a pattern of Caucasian blue-collar support for the Republican Party that dates back decades.

Even beyond the Vanderbilt and Duke study, there is the dubious nature of the "working class" definition prominent throughout popular reportage and commentary.[6] Typically, the same socially isolated pundits take it to mean merely income earners without college degrees. Adjunct instructors at universities, social workers, ministers, and elementary school teachers often have advanced degrees but earn tens of thousands less in annual income than electricians, plumbers, and other workers in the trades. Hardly anyone in the mainstream press would consider a lecturer in English literature or a Lutheran pastor "working class," which leaves the average reader of *The New York Times* with the impression that a construction crew supervisor earning $90,000 per year and chanting "Build the Wall!" is a cautionary tale regarding the evils and misery of "globalism."

The truth is that polling data, voting patterns, and political science research routinely show that, except in moments of inflation or recession, the average voter does not cast a ballot for economic reasons. Far from a story of scarcity or precarity, the emergence of a neofascist right in the United States is a revolution of cultural militancy. Lofgren attributes much of the cultural militancy to the "growth of Christian fundamentalism," observing how moderate Protestant sects are in decline and megachurches have become dominant of the theological terrain. "Missouri is like a citadel of Pentecostalism," Lofgren said, "and it makes people susceptible to authoritarian appeal and magical thinking."

"Why does the Midwest vote like the South?" Lofgren asked in the middle of our conversation before answering, "Because they've become like the South. They've adopted Southern culture—pickup trucks, Confederate flags, corporately synthesized country music." The communities of Lofgren's Ohio childhood were similar to those of mine in Illinois and Indiana—to use his words, "village green with white picket fences." In much of the Midwest there is now a pseudo-Southern attitude and aesthetic, not only in the cultural amenities Lofgren identifies but also, among the men, a macho swagger, bellicose bravado, and obsession with guns. Bikers, military vets, and barroom tough guys reject cultural liberalism because of its insistence on civil restraint and cultural sophistication. Along with the bad music and dumb vehicles, Midwestern good ol' boys have adopted Southern politics. They fly "Don't Tread on Me" flags, despise the federal government, and look upon any political or cultural movement to enlarge the democratic possibilities for Blacks, women, or gay and transgender people with suspicion.

Exurbia enhances the neo-Confederate culture, functioning, regardless of state locale, as a Southern hamlet. It is in the exurbs where right-wing activists disrupt school board meetings in order to object to Black history and LGBTQ-friendly curricula, threaten election officials and poll workers, and join the ranks of dangerous, anti-government militia groups. Gerrymandering, in states like Ohio, Michigan, and Missouri, protects the political future of congressional representatives who need only appeal to the most extreme constituency. Without the civilizing mechanism of a district where many Democrats live, or any Republicans to the left of Attila the Hun, Representatives like Ohio's Jim Jordan and

Michigan's Tim Walberg—both "stop the steal" zealots who make light of the January 6 insurrection—are free to run wild.

"Karl Marx called it the 'idiocy of rural life,'" Mike Lofgren said when I asked why exurbia has become the launching pad of American fascism. There is an organic dynamic in pastoral precincts rendering it reactionary in both the United States and Europe. The United States differs only in that middle-class and upper-middle-class families are migrating into exurbs, where there is an interplay between the preexisting reflexive conservatism of the region and the political priorities of the new arrivals. The mix strengthens the right-wing ingredients, and dulls any remnants of liberalism.

In her book *Suburban Warriors: The Origins of the New American Right*, historian Lisa McGirr studies the "conservative counterrevolution" that emerged in defiance against liberal progression on civil rights, feminism, environmentalism, and gay rights in the 1960s and '70s. Placing the suburbs of Orange County, California, under a magnifying glass, she describes "ordinary men and women—engineers, physicians, dentists, and housewives—forging the nucleus of grassroots conservatism."[7] Not unlike most of the Trump cult, they were financially secure homeowners operating according to an ideological anchor "that was a fusion of Christian fundamentalism, xenophobic nationalism, and western Libertarianism." Throughout the 1970s and '80s, Republican campaign strategy and right-wing propaganda located the heart and soul of America in the suburbs; the "village green" of Lofgren's youth and my childhood, arguing that stay-at-home moms, small business owners, and the beat cop were the last line of defense against the encroaching menaces of multiculturalism, sexual permissiveness, and something—nobody is quite sure what—resembling socialism.

The cultural emphasis shifted in the 1990s. It was then that Republican politicos and reactionary media personalities noticed that much of their constituents were moving to exurbia. "That was the origin of the 'real

America' stuff Sarah Palin was saying, ten or twelve years later—the claim that 'real values' are concentrated in a mythical, white America in some exurban, rural town. Republican political strategy moved away from the archetypal suburban housewife, and it got more rural," Lofgren said when I asked for his recollection of how Republicans in Congress changed campaign tactics and political rhetoric during the 1990s.

As the Republicans were attempting to convince the electorate that all that was pure in American history and life was discoverable in a village of exurbia reaching back into the 1950s, they found their perfect foils.

✻

"ENTER THE CLINTONS," SIDNEY BLUMENTHAL, JOUR-nalist, historian, and former aide to President Bill Clinton, said early when I interviewed him over the phone. "They were a modern couple of the baby boomer generation. Bill Clinton was a mainstream person who knew and worked with all sorts of people in Arkansas but was very much a man of his generation. He had not served in the US military, he opposed the Vietnam War, he was liberal, and he was married to an outspoken feminist. That was enough to stigmatize him, from the beginning, as the enemy of the new culture war right."

Blumenthal, the author of *The Clinton Wars* and *The Rise of the Counter-Establishment: The Conservative Ascent to Political Power*, explained that in the late 1970s, the right wing had made a strategic recalculation in how it would create and prosecute a culture war that would animate their voters and distract the larger electorate from disapproval of their narrow economic agenda. Richard Nixon's cultural appeal emanated out of paranoia regarding drugs and urban crime, and subtle projections of the Black threat to white security. While these elements have never completely vanished from Republican tactical command, and racist smears certainly roared back with Trump's amplification, Blumenthal delineates how in the late 1970s, the right wing discovered new strings to pull, attached to a new bloc of voters—namely, the religious right that ascended into the political sky to oppose racial integration in their private academies.

"In the late 1970s and early '80s," Blumenthal continued, "the right's culture war became oppositional to women's rights. The religious right then joined the anti-women's rights cause by changing, fundamentally, the theology of the Southern Baptist Convention. The Southern Baptists had not been opposed to abortion. They changed their theology, and they did it in conjunction with operatives working out of the Reagan White House. The far right's goal was to ally the religious constituency in a new culture war with other constituencies to form a new Republican coalition. The new coalition included suburbanites who had fled the cities as responsive to Nixon's appeal against Blacks, and the idea that crime had made the cities unlivable."

The religious right's increasing presence, and thereby influence, over Republican Party politics also manifested in homophobic hysteria. During the 1970s, agents of anti-gay hatred succeeded in convincing several states, including Florida and Oklahoma, to pass ordinances banning gays from positions of public employment. When tens of thousands of gay and bisexual men were dying of HIV/AIDS in the 1980s, President Reagan refused to publicly address the endemic and authorized only minimal funding for HIV research in the Centers for Disease Control and National Institutes of Health. Clinton's cultural battle as president commenced after he told a journalist that he intended to lift the ban on gays openly serving in the armed forces. After Colin Powell and the Joint Chiefs of Staff issued a statement in favor of the ban, Clinton negotiated a compromise with the Republican Party, the "Don't Ask, Don't Tell" policy. Meanwhile, Hillary Clinton's feminist posture and unprecedented policymaking role as first lady provoked the right wing to depict the young couple, and the first Democrats to live in the White House in thirteen years, as Luciferian foes of family values, Biblical living, and basic decency. Rush Limbaugh, and other far-right demagogues, even circulated a rumor that Hillary Clinton intended to decorate the White House Christmas tree with condoms.

"The hatred for the Clintons, as the target of the new, culture war right, carried all the way through from his candidacy to the end of his presidency," Blumenthal said. Beginning with bizarre outrage over Hillary Clinton's comments that, as first lady, she would not merely "bake cookies," and spiking with every phony scandal and false accusation, ranging from fraud to murder, a dark and imaginative obsession with the Clintons dominated discourse on the right, poisoning debate in the mainstream. The irrational conspiracy theories, deranged accusations, and vulgar hatred that form the lingua franca of the authoritarian right originated as opposition to President Bill Clinton. With the bluster of Rush Limbaugh and the leadership of Newt Gingrich, the antidemocratic genesis of the Republican Party went far beyond rhetoric. It also included extraconstitutional tactics of voter nullification and electoral subversion. The right-wing willingness to work outside the political system in an attempt to overtake the system had an ideological scaffold that would later become even more dangerous.

"When Clinton took office," Blumenthal summarized, "he faced intense opposition. He was regarded by many Republicans similarly to the way Barack Obama was, not because he was Black, but because he was a politically potent Democrat who could change things. Robert Bartley, the editorial page editor of *The Wall Street Journal*, said that Clinton was an 'illegitimate' president. That feeling was widespread among Republicans, and certainly among the right wing. They sought to advance that idea, even if they did not genuinely believe it. That idea of illegitimacy has been applied to the two subsequent Democratic presidents—Barack Obama and Joe Biden."

The popularity of Clinton led Republicans to desperately search for a "scandal" that could demolish his political future. When various investigations of financial impropriety failed to produce anything immoral, much less illegal, Ken Starr, the corrupt special prosecutor inspecting every aspect of the Clintons' lives, hit paydirt with the Monica Lewinsky affair. From Brett Kavanaugh, working as a Starr staffer, to Ann Coulter, writing hallucinogenic and strident polemics against the Clintons, many right-wingers made their bones by smearing the president and first lady. More significantly, the Republican Party attempted to disqualify the will of the public, using well-documented techniques of blackmail, entrapment, and deception to attempt to remove a sitting president from office on the basis of sexual indiscretion. Previewing the "impostor" status of Republican governance, senators and congressional representatives spent more time talking about the lurid details of Lewinsky and Clinton's trysts than issues like public safety, health care, and environmental conservation.

Meanwhile, violent militias saw their membership rolls grow exponentially, while the newly emergent right-wing media portrayed Clinton as a demonic threat to their lives. Timothy McVeigh bombed Oklahoma City, murdering hundreds of people in the largest domestic terrorist attack in US history, claiming that he was "fighting a war" for freedom against the evils of "big government," "socialism," and "gun confiscation." McVeigh's demented and volatile ravings now resemble the speeches of Republican officials and the nightly monologues of Fox News talk show hosts.

"The Republicans forced two constitutional crises during the Clinton period," Blumenthal said. "The first was the events that led to Clinton's impeachment, which was unconstitutional not least because they refused to specify the constitutional grounds for impeachment. It had nothing to do with his public conduct in office. It was fanatically driven and involved a conspiracy of right-wing lawyers to work with Ken Starr and the office of the independent counsel to widen the probe after Starr was conclusively advised that there was no illegal activity in the Clintons' financial history."

The growth of militias, culminating in the Oklahoma City bombing, and the dubious impeachment of Clinton offer catastrophic and absurd glimpses into an American right that would eventually worship a former president who celebrates and collaborates with violent extremist groups even after failing to honor the the peaceful transfer of power, which is the bedrock of democracy.

Clinton was the first president to enter into political combat with a new breed of Republican: members of Congress, to use Blumenthal's words, "infused with radicalism of a violent populist movement." Most of the hazardous officials, including then Speaker of the House Newt Gingrich, represented suburban and exurban districts. As historian Kevin Kruse concludes in his book *White Flight: Atlanta and the Making of Modern Conservatism*:

> By the 1990s, the political power of suburbs was evident
> across the country . . . As postsecession suburbanites emerged
> from their isolation and took the lead in national life, they
> would shape the course of politics and reshape the country
> itself. The trend was evident across the country, but nowhere
> more so than the suburbs around Atlanta. Indeed, for much
> of that decade, the city's northern suburbs were represented
> by the most influential conservative politicians in the nation.
> The northwestern expanse, which included western Cobb
> County and beyond, was represented by Congressman Bob
> Barr, an archconservative Republican who emerged as the
> earliest congressional advocate of President Bill Clinton's
> impeachment. The northeastern suburbs, meanwhile, elected
> Congressman John Linder, head of the Republican National
> Congressional Committee. While both were powerful

representatives of the Sunbelt South and key figures in the Republican Party, they were surpassed on both counts by a colleague who represented the suburban enclave between their districts, Speaker of the House Newt Gingrich. More than anyone else in the 1990s, Gingrich embodied the politics of the suburban Sunbelt, especially suburban conservatives' embrace of privatization, free enterprise, and local autonomy, as well as their antipathy to the federal government, public services, and the tax policies designed to support both.[8]

Among the other most prominent and influential Republicans in Congress during the 1990s were Henry Hyde, the impeachment trial manager who represented the northwest suburbs of Chicago, and Dennis Hastert, a representative of Illinois exurbs who would become House Speaker in 1999. As they attempted to destroy the Clintons, and vanquish the desire of the electorate, congressional Republicans, arriving to the Capitol on the fuel of suburban and exurban estrangement, also aimed to dismantle the workings of government.

Bruce Bartlett, who was a domestic advisor to President Ronald Reagan and an official in the Treasury Department under President George H. W. Bush, told me that as Speaker, Newt Gingrich "did everything he could to scale back Congress."

"Some of the most damaging stuff he did," Bartlett elaborated, "was abolish three thousand Congressional staff positions. So, the majority staff suddenly had the staff of the minority party, and the minority party staff was reduced to a fraction of its size. Gingrich also cut the budgets of the Congressional Budget Office and the Government Accountability Office. He abolished the Advisory Commission on Intergovernmental Relations. He abolished the Office of Technology Assessment, which did studies on things like pandemics. The Republicans went to war with the Congressional Research Service, and they scaled back their activities as a consequence."

Gingrich's intention was, in the words of Bartlett, to "make Congress bad at its job." Chief among the items on his strategy, attendant to his demolition of congressional offices, was "making the committee system irrelevant." "He would have someone introduce a bill and send it straight to the rules committee, rather than the jurisdictional committee"—such as the Education and Labor Committee or the Ethics Committee—"to be made available for voting, literally, the next day. People were voting on bills that Gingrich cooked up, and they had no idea what was in them." Dennis Hastert, during his reign as Speaker, imposed what journalists labeled the "Hastert Rule"—allowing only bills that a majority of Republicans supported to reach the floor for a vote. Political scientist Norman Ornstein has written that Hastert, following the Gingrich example, "blew up the House's order," taking an institution that was already partisan to a "new, more tribalized plane."[9]

In opposition to a mutated species of the Republican breed, hell-bent on devastating the functionality and efficacy of government, the Clinton administration managed to accumulate a record of staggering achievements. It was not merely Clinton as a person that the Republicans hated, but Clinton's ambition and efficacy as president. "Clinton understood and worked through what happened in the 1960s, '70s, and '80s to discredit the entire project of democratic liberalism," Sidney Blumenthal explained during our conversation, "He then understood that what was required was kind of a political agility to try to recreate it—not to restore it, which could not be done, because you can never restore the past. Nostalgia was never the basis of Clinton's politics. He attempted to revive liberalism in a new political, social, economic, and global world where the old truisms no longer held."

There is a widespread illiteracy on the left when it comes to interpreting the Clinton years, casting him as a corporate sellout whose policies helped to usher into American life a new era of inequality. Reality is uncooperative with ideological disparagement of the Clinton

presidency. The record shows that the Clinton policies enabled working-class and middle-class mobility and progress while exercising fis-
cal responsibility. In 1993, Clinton signed the largest extension of the
earned income tax credit in American history—a move that a wide
variety of economists attribute to lifting four million people out of
poverty. The Clinton White House's work to balance the budget, and
create a federal surplus, led to a dramatic reduction in interest rates,
causing business investment to boom and homeownership rates, particularly for first-time buyers, to skyrocket. Unprecedented investments in education resulted in record-breaking numbers of college
enrollment and graduation, while targeted programs to spur economic
growth increased wages for members of all income strata, especially
those making below $100,000. Poverty declined at historic rates, and
GDP increased without interruption. In 1997, Clinton signed the
Children's Health Insurance Program (CHIP) into law—at the time
the most significant expansion of health care services since Medicaid.
Millions of children and pregnant women receive medical treatment
through CHIP. He also steered into law a ban on assault rifles and
universal background checks on all purchases of firearms—lifesaving
reforms that Republicans either reversed or allowed to expire in later
years. Before Republican sabotage, crime rates reached record lows,
and mass shootings were far from regular occurrences. Like any presidency, Clinton's is not without failures. In his book *My Life*, Clinton
himself admits that there were unintended consequences to his massive crime bill, and that his failure to regulate derivative investments
on Wall Street produced economic blowback. It is still undeniable and
meaningful, especially considering that it receives little attention, that
under the leadership of Bill Clinton in the 1990s every single indicator
of national life was moving in the right direction. The revival of liberalism was succeeding, and despite Clinton's reckless act of adultery, he
left office with a high approval rating.[10]

The second constitutional crisis that Sidney Blumenthal identified as the product of Republican extremity is the presidency of George W. Bush. In 2000, at the height of the election turmoil, A "Brooks Brothers riot," involving young white men in expensive suits acting on the command of Trump confidant Roger Stone, busted into the offices of Miami-Dade County, forcibly stopping the counting of votes in the most populous and liberal precincts of Florida. A brazenly biased Supreme Court then ruled that Florida could not continue its recount, giving Bush the presidency over Al Gore by a mere 537 votes. Gore would have continued and enhanced the Clinton policies, escalating the economic prosperity of the previous decade. A decades-long obsession with climate change would have given his administration a moral and environmental mission, and it is highly unlikely that he would have made the catastrophic errors of the Bush administration—ignoring memos warning of the 9/11 attack, launching a preemptive war on Iraq, undercutting disaster management with horrific results in New Orleans during Hurricane Katrina, and removing the regulatory bodyguards from Wall Street that could have prevented the financial crash of 2008.

President Obama made historic gains in health care as president, and managed to correct some of the fatal missteps of the Bush administration, but by the time he took the oath of office, the culture war right had already sharpened its knives and organized its forces. The Gingrich and Hastert–style Republican had become dominant and, by party leadership's own admission, more committed to politically harming the first Black president than making the country more just, safe, and prosperous. Conspiracy theories involving Obama's foreign birth and secret agenda of Islamic terrorism became obsessions on the right. Voters in the suburbs of small cities, and the evangelical white flight paradise of exurbia, became increasingly radical. The ranks of militia organizations and hate groups started to swell, while dangerous new organizations, like the Proud Boys, made their debut with threats of violence and hostile demands. Donald Trump, seeing the kindling and lighter fluid unguarded in the middle of a forest, threw a match. He became the neofascist cult leader during his first presidential campaign, in part by appealing to the old, obsessive hatred of Hillary Clinton.

When Biden won in 2020, partially because he tallied high percentages of voters in the suburbs of Milwaukee, Detroit, Pittsburgh, Philadelphia, Atlanta, and Phoenix, right-wing strategists, including former Trump advisor Steve Bannon, sought to recapture suburban territory by imposing inflammatory national debates on local races. Journalists report that Republicans in sections of suburbia and exurbia hope they can triumph if they distance themselves from Trump's loathsome comportment and sell a decaffeinated version of toxic brew. They are telling middle-class families of the same variety that benefitted from Clinton's revival of liberalism that their worst fears are educational curricula involving America's history of systemic racism, and schoolwide acceptance of gay and transgender students, teachers, and neighbors. The American Library Association reports that one of the largest book banning campaigns in the country's history occurred in 2022.[11] Most of the books that right-wing activists targeted for censorship featured Black, gay, or transgender protagonists. A small suburb of Grand Rapids, Michigan, even voted to shut down their entire library when librarians refused to remove books about LGBTQ history from the shelves.[12]

The politics of fight or flight have manifested in tragic dimensions throughout exurbia, and they threaten to reverse Democratic victories in suburbia. Promising an escape from the changing racial demographics of the United States, sexual liberalism, and shared investment in solving the country's problems, the fight-or-flight instinct reverses one of Clinton's maxims. During the 1996 presidential election, Bill Clinton ran on a highly detailed policy platform, declaring in his nomination acceptance speech his vision of "opportunity for all, responsibility from all." The reactionary suburban and exurban voters who elect conspiracy theorists, racists, and anti-Semites to Congress seek to deny opportunities and evade responsibilities. When Democrats offer substantive remedies for the escalating crises of climate change, poverty, gun violence, and access to health care, Republicans counter with propaganda that tells their estranged and isolated constituents that, enjoying the detachment of exurbia, they need only worry about "socialist" and "secular" encroachment.

At best, cultural warfare will merely slow down political progress. In the first two years of his presidency, Joe Biden was able to sign historic measures on gun violence, health care, infrastructure, and climate change. Commenting on the latter, Al Gore credited Biden and the Democrats with passing the "most significant climate change initiative in the history of the world."[13] Even still, the Biden promises of childcare subsidies for the working poor, tuition-free community college, and lowering the entry age for Medicare could not survive the obstinance of Republican opposition. The worst-case scenario is one that, after four years of Donald Trump's subversion of government, appears all the more likely and scary. As historian Richard Hofstadter warned in 1965: "It is conceivable that a highly organized, vocal, active, and well-financed minority could create a political climate in which the rational pursuit of our well-being and safety could become impossible."[14]

Referring to a declaration that Bill Clinton made early in his presidency, Sidney Blumenthal remarked, "When Clinton said, 'this country doesn't need a culture war,' he knew what he was talking about."

BUSTED ON A BAD BEAT

Michael Jackson died on June 25, 2009. A close friend and I had previously made plans to have dinner at a restaurant near my friend's home in Crown Point. Breaking news of the King of Pop's demise insisted on an immediate alteration. Roger, my friend and former teacher at Thornton Fractional South, grew up in Gary, Indiana—the hometown of not only Michael Jackson but his sister Janet and all his brothers of Jackson 5 fame. Knowing exactly where to go without a map, Roger drove us to the Jackson childhood home—a ramshackle white house so tiny that it seems as if it would require an engineering degree to determine how Joe and Katherine Jackson raised their nine children within its walls. Roger and I quickly learned that we were far from alone in our spur-of-the-moment desire to visit the site where a recently deceased legend of music spent his formative years. The block was full of Black locals dancing to the instantly recognizable sounds of "Beat It" and "Bad" emanating out of car radios and boom boxes. Not long after the closing notes of "Billie Jean" did more white tourists arrive. Following the suburbanites came news vans from Chicago television stations, radio reporters, and print journalists working on deadlines for local newspapers. Crying white teenagers and elderly Black women alike dropped flowers and handwritten notes at the doorstep where Michael Jackson shuffled his feet long before he could moonwalk.

Growing thirsty on a hot summer night, Roger and I attempted to locate a nearby bar—a challenge that proved daunting after observing that most buildings that resembled a place of business were long empty and abandoned. Finally, on our way out of town, we saw flashing lights in a Gary tavern with an odd moniker, the Cave. Greeting us at the entrance was a Gary police officer in a Kevlar vest. He patted us down, and directed our attention to the sign bearing the rules of the establishment. In addition to the standard "No Shirt, No Shoes, No Service," there were admonitions against gang colors, bandanas, visible jewelry, the flashing of gang signs, and weapons of any kind. The bartender, a flamboyantly gay Black man, welcomed us like old friends—taking our drink orders and immediately bonding with Roger when he referred to his Gary childhood. The only other patron was a middle-aged woman who also joined in the conversation, playfully ribbing my friend because he, unlike her, graduated from Gary's "inferior" high school. We were soon surrounded by Gary residents and visitors, and it wasn't too long until the dance floor was full with patrons of various sizes and hues dancing along to Michael Jackson's greatest hits. Because we skipped dinner, Roger and I were beginning to fight off hunger pangs. As we settled with the bartender to leave, he thanked us for stopping by and added with a sardonic grin, "If Michael Jackson could die every night, the bar wouldn't be in trouble."

Gary's troubles began long before Michael Jackson's fatal drug addiction. When Jackson first learned he could sing and dance, and when my friend Roger came of age, in the 1960s, Gary was thriving—a representation of America's postwar powerhouse status of industry. John Mellencamp pays rollicking tribute to the kind of men who broke a sweat, and their backs, in Gary's mills, even naming the city in "Minutes to Memories," a song about an elderly man sharing with his son the hard-won wisdom of family, thrift, and work. Because Gary became a mecca of the steel industry, it promised stability and prosperity for many families throughout not only Indiana and Illinois but also the Deep South. Many Black Americans escaping the terror of Jim Crow and lynching, and seeking suitable employment, migrated to Gary. It was an emblematic epicenter of a secure middle class, resting comfortably on a scaffold of American hegemony, trade unionism, and manufacturing. At the height of Gary's success in the 1960s, boosters, local politicians, and cooperative journalists actually dubbed the industrial center "Magic City."

Merely two decades later, Gary took on the appearance of a small town in the weeks after a bombing raid. Magic City turned into a cruel joke, giving way to other descriptions in the press: "the murder capital of the world," "the most miserable city in America," and "ghost town." In 1970, approximately 175,000 people lived in Gary. Now it is home to 66,000 residents—most of them poor.[1] Few families, professionals, or entrepreneurs have any reason to live in Gary, especially when considering the proliferation of poverty, crime, and smog. Few people even have reason to visit. In 1993, after watching the city crumble and capture headlines for all of the wrong reasons, a celebrity with bags of money to throw around toured Gary, making promises and raising hopes. His name was Donald Trump.

"WHAT YOU HAD WAS A SLICK BUSINESS DEALER COMing in," a former Gary city council member said in reference to Donald Trump when the casino mogul was first running for president in the Republican primary. "He got as much as he could and then he pulled

up and left."[2] At precisely the moment when Trump promised to resuscitate dying cities and suburbs in the Midwest, the United States
could have avoided disaster had its voters only paid close attention to
an allegory from a dying city in the Rust Belt.

Trump's campaign thrived on two forms of fuel: white nationalism and pie-in-the-sky promises of economic resurrection. Much of
the mass media acted as if these two appeals stood in distinction and
attempted to limit Trump's appeal to one or the other. Stunningly
ill-equipped to analyze a flimflam fascist like Trump, mainstream
commentators would have done well to read the late Italian historian,
philosopher, and novelist Umberto Eco's essay on the fourteen key
characteristics of fascism. Number six suggests that fascism "derives
from individual and social frustration." It "appeals to a frustrated
middle class," Eco explains, "a class suffering from an economic crisis
or feelings of political humiliation, and frightened by the pressure of
lower social groups."[3] Postindustrial cities throughout the Midwest,
such as Youngstown, Ohio, and Erie, Pennsylvania, did not entirely
flip Republican in 2016, but the Trump-led party made enough
gains to capture their respective states, leading to the collapse of the
"blue wall." Voters longing for a return to past eras of glory accepted
Trump's pledge to "bring your jobs back." Viewing him as a business
genius who could leverage his skills of manipulation to their advantage,
they believed that the crude and ruthless strongman would triumph
on their behalf, unlike leading figures of the so-called "establishment."
Hillary Clinton identified half of Trump supporters as "deplorables,"
but said of the other half, "They are people who feel that government
has let them down, nobody cares about them, nobody worries about
what happens to their lives and their futures, and they are just desperate for change. It doesn't really even matter where it comes from.
They don't buy everything he says but he seems to hold out some hope
that their lives will be different. They won't wake up and see their jobs

disappear, lose a kid to heroin, feel like they're in a dead-end. Those are people we have to understand and empathize with as well."

One of the questions that mainstream media refused to explore, and that well-intended politicians, like Bernie Sanders, never seemed to grasp when waxing poetic about the "white working class," is why only whites were gullible enough to buy wholesale the fantasies of Trump. Black workers in Gary voted overwhelmingly for Clinton, one of them saying bluntly, "Is Trump a racist? Of course, he is. And he can't bring jobs back, because the jobs are gone to automation."[4] Gary, in stark contrast to other Rust Belt towns, never fell for the Trump trap because its residents understand the dangers of racism, and because they know him.

In 1993, Trump flew his private jet into the impoverished city, launching a campaign to acquire a casino operating license from the state of Indiana. Seeing a business opportunity outside of Chicago, he claimed that a Trump gambling operation would lead to "beautiful" and "unbelievably good" jobs, culminating in a replay of yesteryear. Gary would morph back into Magic City—a Las Vegas of the Midwest. Only three years earlier, Trump, while operating a failing casino in Atlantic City and fearing competition, told the *Chicago Tribune* that a casino in Gary would be "very bad." It would "empty the pockets of the people," and do nothing to improve living conditions in "the slums." As is customary with Trump, he radically changed his position when he thought it could benefit his bank account and "brand." The Gary mayor and city council weren't eager marks. Aware of his string of bankruptcies in the 1980s, his reputation for bilking contractors, and his myriad tabloid scandals, Gary leadership saw Trump as an unnecessary gamble, especially in comparison to the more stable, reputable, and local Black businessmen who were also vying for gaming licenses. Unable to take no for an answer, Trump parlayed his notoriety, requesting to meet directly with the Indiana Gaming Commission. He presented himself as a corporate Jesus, offering to perform a variety of miracles for the beleaguered townspeople of Gary. He promised to pour millions of dollars into reno-vating an old, dilapidated, and long inoperative Sheraton hotel across the street from city hall. He would include local investors, even if they could not put money down immediately by initiating a loan payout sys-tem. After the casino opened, according to Trump's loftiest pledge, a foundation of local civic, religious, and business leaders would direct 7.5 percent of all profits into the coffers of Indiana charities. He also prom-ised to personally fund college scholarships for qualifying high school seniors in Gary. The Indiana Gaming Commission sang hosanna, and soon even Gary's skeptics issued statements of support.

Trump Casino wasn't as catastrophic as Trump White House, but similarly, it advanced a series of lies, broken promises, and betrayals. Immediately after acquiring the operating license, Trump dissolved the investment agreement with local businessmen, his lawyers claiming that it was merely "verbal," and nonbinding. The future president did not spend one dime on restoring the old Sheraton hotel. He never even seemed to give it a second look. Although open for business until 2004, when the parent company—Trump Hotel & Casino Resorts Inc.—folded, none of the profits went to charity, and the foundation that Trump promised to create never had a single meeting. Conned and fleeced, a few of the "business partners" sued Trump and initially won $1.3 million. A federal appeals panel later revoked the verdict by declaring that Trump's "verbal agreement" defense was legally correct, even if morally reprehensible.[5] As far as Gary is concerned, the warnings of Donald Trump himself proved prescient. The embattled Rust Belt town is currently host to the recently opened Hard Rock Casino. Within the surrounding area, there is the Blue Chip Casino in Michigan City, Indiana, the Horseshoe Casino in Hammond, and Ameristar Casino in East Chicago, Indiana. Northwest Indiana's four gambling halls have to compete with two casinos in Joliet, Illinois—a mere thirty-five miles away—and, an hour's drive east on the highway, the gigantic Four Winds Casino in New Buffalo, Michigan. As

Trump predicted, the casinos have done little to improve the standard of living, business prospects, or property values in their respective host cities. They are not the scourge that critics who expected increases in street crime, drunk driving, and compulsive gambling argued, but neither are they messianic. Instead, they are massive monuments to state-sponsored fantasies. With the exception of New Buffalo—a charming and luxurious lakeside town popular with wealthy weekenders and recreational tourists—all of the cities hosting Illiana casinos are suffering through economic decline, cultural decay, and social instability. They have in ways literal and figurative placed a bet on betting as their ticket to recapturing former greatness.

Father Ed Ward came of age in Joliet in the late 1950s and early to mid-1960s. He recalls the small downtown area bustling with commerce and communication on almost a daily basis, but especially on the weekends. Diners and shoppers could find department stores, clothing shops, boutiques, bars, restaurants, and ice-cream parlors on every inch of pavement surrounding the courthouse and the "crown jewel of Joliet," the two-thousand-seat Rialto Square Theatre. Photographs of John Kennedy campaigning for president in downtown Joliet in 1960 display not only the charisma and glamour of the candidate but also the vitality of his surroundings. Neon lights, business facades, and bedroom lamps in condominium windows illuminate the dark skies behind the future president and the adoring masses clamoring for a handshake. By the 1990s, the streets were mostly empty, save for the clients and attorneys coming and going from the courthouse by day and the prostitutes, drug dealers, and homeless working them by night.

The impact of the casinos opening in Joliet in the 1990s was forceful and instant, particularly the Harrah's in the downtown city center. Substantial gains in tax revenue allowed the city to repair infrastructure and hire more police officers to patrol the area. Millions of dollars funded neighborhood improvement projects, school rehabilitation efforts, and reductions in property taxes. As the city council went into full self-congratulation mode, popping champagne bottles to celebrate its own brilliance, Earl L. Grinols, an economist then at the University of Illinois who studies the influence of legalized gambling in his home state, warned, "The net gain will be virtually zero . . . . There is a job lost or a job not created for every job you see in a casino," he added, "There's very little economic growth going on in riverboat areas."[6]

Subsequent studies of casino economics and local communities in Illinois, Iowa, and the urban Northeast bear out Grinols's prediction, as does even a short drive through Gary, Hammond, or the impoverished east side of Joliet (the midsize town's west side is suburban and mostly middle-class). There is a short burst of growth and development following a casino's establishment, but the long-term effect is minimal. While the city and state collect tax revenues, local entrepreneurs have to compete with corporate conglomerates that can entice customers with a variety of bargains. Those corporations then take their profits back to their headquarters, doling them out among executive staff and shareholders. There is a similar draining dynamic between the gamblers themselves and their hometowns. A dollar spent at the craps table is a dollar not spent at the neighborhood bar or donated to Father Ward's parish.

A character in Fyodor Dostoevsky's novella *The Gambler* confesses that the pull of the roulette wheel is irresistible, because it offers the hope that "in a couple of hours, one may grow rich without doing any work." Reflecting on the Russian novelist's exploration of gambling, theologian H. David Baer writes, "the prospect of a windfall is a quick fix to life's intractable problems." The personal delusion becomes public policy when, as Baer argues, a casino can "raise revenue without raising taxes." Legal gambling "allows citizens to enjoy public goods without shouldering the burden of paying for them." "A society which fills its public coffers with gambling revenue," Baer concludes, "has figured out how to get something for nothing."[7]

The illusion and enticement of the painless, profitable quick fix, after suffering through years of privation and population retreat, leaves small towns and cities susceptible to the self-serving deceit of grifters like Donald Trump and the grandiose but unrealistic claims of the multinational corporations looking for another satellite business opportunity. As Dostoevsky would have appreciated, it is yet another resurrection and iteration of the politics of escape. Pennsylvania, Ohio, Michigan, and Wisconsin, like Indiana and Illinois, have opened casinos and allowed for video gambling in bars in and near towns that once thrived due to manufacturing. As Chloe Taft, author of *From Steel to Slots: Casino Capitalism in the Postindustrial City* summarizes, "Since the waves of deindustrialization in the 1970s, Rust Belt cities increasingly have looked for service- and entertainment-based "new economy" replacements . . . .The casino model of urban development seems particularly attuned to these regions' sense of desperation, where even a business model premised on the vast majority of players losing their money sparks hope for new beginnings ."[8] Governors, mayors, city council members, and many of their voters, like a gambler who just knows that with the next pull of the lever or the dealer's next run of cards he'll hit it big, believe that, with construction of the next casino, they can escape the complicated realities of a changing, global economy and the consequences of poverty, austerity, and dying ecology. In poker slang, "busted on a bad beat" refers to when a player loses a substantial sum of money on a hand that looked like a winner. The suburbs that once counted their success according to the sounds of furnaces blazing, assembly lines moving, and heavy machinery banging away are busted on a bad beat. Any gambling addiction therapist worth her fee would explain the importance of determining what brought the gambler to the table in the first place.

*

MY GRANDFATHER, NICK BRUICH, WAS A SECOND-
generation American. His grandparents immigrated to the United
States from the former Yugoslavia and settled into an ethnic enclave
in the South Side neighborhood aptly called South Chicago. Occupying a row house on a block full of Serbs, they had an Orthodox church
in close proximity and relatives and friends who shared their cultural
and religious rituals, preferences, and habits. Every May, they celebrated
Slava, a familial and spiritual feast honoring the family's patron saint.
For days, a host family opens their doors and offers a smorgasbord of
Serbian dishes and pastries to all visitors. There is also an open bar that
rivals any small tavern. The tradition continues to the present even if my
great-grandparents, and their children, are no longer with us. Christmas
festivities commence not on December 25 but January 7. When I was
a child, I would look forward to entering the doors of an aunt's home—
old men playing tambouras (Serbian string instruments that sound like
a cross between an acoustic guitar and mandolin) and drinking vodka
would fill the air with song and laughter. A stuffed pig would rest on top
of the dinner table, where hay—a symbol of harvest and good luck—lay
underneath. Before everyone sat down to dine, the oldest and youngest
members present would spin a loaf of bread while reciting the Lord's
Prayer. Tucked inside the bread was a dime. The recipient of the dime
slice would, according to legend, enjoy a year of blessings. One year I had
the honor of turning the bread with my own grandfather. My mother's
eyes overflowed with tears.

Nick's family moved to the small suburb of Thornton, Illinois, when
he was a baby. Their house was close enough to the train tracks that, as
my grandfather told it, they could feel its bones rattle when a freight
train rumbled through town. He played football in high school, but the
battle of the gridiron gave way to combat of much higher stakes. After
graduation, the United States Army drafted him to fight in the Second
World War. The sole survivor of a plane crash, he received decorations,

a couple of months residence in a military hospital, and an honorable discharge. He never talked about the war but had a lifelong hatred of violence and steely political opposition to anyone who made it. When his wounds healed, his best option was clear: to work in the Material Service Quarry in Thornton. The limestone quarry cuts, crushes, and supplies rock for delivery around the world, producing more than seven million tons of rock products every year. By the 1980s, when I was born, it employed over three thousand people.[9] Most of the workers, ranking high and low, belonged to a union. Organized labor shaped my grandfather's sense of loyalty and politics. He joined picket lines and, although not outspoken, would register succinct comments when reading a story about worker-management disputes in the newspaper; something along the lines of, "They're trying to hurt the workers again."

The quarry was hard work. My mother has told me that on more than one occasion my grandfather broke bones in his hands, and he often showed fatigue on his face and in his posture when returning home for dinner, accompanied by a small glass of beer. But the benefits of the union allowed him to make a mortgage on a small Thornton home and provide for his wife and daughter on a single salary. For social and monetary reasons, he would supplement his income by occasionally bartending at a corner bar within walking distance, the Pit. The Pit brought different men together in recreational communion, and it too solidified certain loyalties. Years later, my grandfather would organize a town can collection for the neighborhood drunk who walked the streets with a half pint of Jack Daniel's in his back pocket, picking up whatever cans he could find. The can collector was a fellow World War II veteran with undiagnosed PTSD. He lived in the above-garage studio apartment at a generous cousin's house. My grandfather also drove a local man with developmental disabilities to the grocery store once a week, buying the items that his food stamps would not cover. He spent time with the next-door neighbor—an elderly man who the local gossips believed was gay—keeping him company while waiting for the arrival of Meals on Wheels—a food delivery charity for the poor and disabled.

When my grandfather's only child, a daughter named Pearl, got married, there was a loose connection of labor between the father of the bride and the groom. My father, Lou, worked in trucking as a dispatcher. Around the same time that my grandfather retired, my father and a friend would start their own trucking company. My father's company was small, with offices and a truckyard in South Holland, Illinois—a town right next to Thornton. He and his dozen employees became like family. As a child, I played basketball and watched pro wrestling with his secretary's sons, attended performances by the country cover band for which one of his driver's sang, and knew the other drivers by name when I would visit Dad in the office. I beamed with pride when my father made an appearance at my elementary school on "career day," giving a talk about running a trucking business, and describing how he contracted the transportation of equipment and supplies to the World Trade Center after it was bombed in 1993. Disaster relief wasn't the bread and butter of my father's company. Instead, he derived most of his income from working with the nearby steel mills of Gary and the exurb Portage, Indiana, and moving equipment from plants and warehouses throughout the south suburbs. Even though he put in long hours—often going to the office on Saturday mornings and staying into the evening on weeknights—he never missed one of my Little League games, plays, or birthday parties. His company was far from alone in the area. He had plenty of competition, but there was always enough work to go around.

There is the observable irony that the suburbs, particularly those of the middle class, would not exist if not for massive government expenditure, subsidy, and infrastructural support. The history of suburban development vanishes into a cacophony of slogans regarding liberty, rugged individualism, and the free market. After their birth, however, they were able to maintain prosperity and grow, especially in areas like Illiana, because of industry. My grandfather and my father are two men among massive crowds who earned their pay, fed their families, and contributed to their communities by making and moving things. When Gary was home to 175,000 residents, 32,000 were steelworkers.[10] An entire network of industry formed around the steel mills, including trucking and transport, and not everyone was going to live in Gary itself. The suburbs that developed in close proximity often did so simply because workers needed somewhere to live with a close commute to the furnace or factory floor. Those workers also needed to send their children to school, have options for dining, entertainment, and recreation, and stores to buy everything from booze to basic necessities. Construction and commerce became inevitable, and as long as the mills, quarries, plants, and truckyards were still operative, unstoppable. People like my grandfather and father, my friend's parents who owned a truck part and supply shop, or my cousin, a Serbian immigrant who worked in a Gary steel mill, had seemingly stable sources of income, along with the pride and satisfaction that derived from knowing that they were making a beneficial contribution to the infrastructure, commercial success, and triumphant identity of their country. As Walt Whitman wrote in his paean to workers, "I hear America singing . . ."

One of the most powerful emotional forces in American suburbia and exurbia, injected into national discourse, is nostalgia. Even people too young to remember the glory days of industry articulate a longing for yesteryear; when smokestacks reached into the skies creating their own clouds, promising a bountiful rain for workers and neighbors on the streets below. Nostalgia, when it comes in the simple form of reflecting with affection on bygone times, is relatively harmless. As a weapon of politics, it is often deadly. Rachel B. Gross, a professor of Jewish studies, assesses the role of nostalgia in politics as permitting "the absence of critical thinking and the abdication of personal responsibility."[11] Because political nostalgia must find someone, typically of different national origin, race, or religious belief, to blame for the demolition of past greatness, it often complements, produces, or supports fascism. In his study of political violence, Albert Camus warned that nostalgia, as an irrational substitution for a coherent political program, will inevitably lead to violence. Aching for "order" that never truly existed in an unstable, complex world, the terrorist or fascist revolutionary imagines himself a "romantic hero," and will "consider himself compelled to do evil for an unrealizable good."[12]

When Donald Trump incited hatred to adoring crowds across the United States—many in the audience wearing hats that express the nostalgic demand to "Make America Great Again"—he denigrated various "undesirable" groups of people responsible for the decline of "order" and "prosperity" in American society—Latino immigrants, the indolent poor, journalists, intellectuals, and corrupt liberal elites. He also promised the resurrection of industry. Much like his unrealistic and insincere pledge to the desperate officials and townspeople of Gary, Trump's claim that he could "bring the jobs back," in reference to manufacturing, mining, and family farming, never had a chance of becoming real. They differed, however, from the xenophobic and racial hatred in the reaction they provoked from the most powerful media outlets and high-ranking officials of both major parties. From profiles of displaced factory workers in *The New York Times* and *The Washington Post* to cloying segments on *60 Minutes* and CNN, there was a widespread exercise to understand the aggrievement of the industrial worker who claimed to find hope in Trump's pipe dreams. Almost without exception, the profiles and television stories had the setting of a blown-out midsize city or an adjacent suburb. The timing was, to put it mildly, strange.

*

MY CHILDHOOD SEEMED ORDINARY. AS A YOUNG
boy, I had no reason to think that the economic ecology of the Chicago
suburbs and the small towns of Northern Indiana, along with the culture it created, was not eternal. It was to my surprise and confusion that
my grandfather told me otherwise.

Sitting in his favorite diner in Lansing, where he stopped for coffee
and breakfast or a sandwich and Coca-Cola on a daily basis, enjoying
warm conversation with the owner and his favorite waitresses, I said in
my ten-year-old's voice, "When I grow up, I want to be like you and work
in the quarry."

"No, you don't," my grandfather spoke softly back. "Those kinds of
jobs are going away. You are a smart boy, and you should do something
that allows you to use your mind."

According to the current inanities of American political culture,
my grandfather—himself a World War II veteran and retired industry
worker—was an "elitist," because he recognized reality and refused to indulge in bizarre fantasy. He knew, like anyone paying even fleeting attention, that manufacturing was in decline. The decline began in the 1970s,
deepened in the 1980s, and showed no signs of abatement. Although
political leaders largely ignored the loss of industry until it became too
late to do anything to mitigate its adverse effects, various works of art
amplified the testimony of struggling workers when Ronald Reagan declared "morning in America."

Bruce Springsteen's records of the 1970s and '80s are replete with
songs of unemployed auto workers, small suburbs wrestling with poverty in the shadows of shut-down textile mills, and Vietnam veterans
who resort to petty crime when they fail to find work with a living wage.
One of the country's finest writers, Richard Russo, wrote his early novels in the 1980s, depicting life in an economically stagnant upstate New
York town floundering after the closure of a glove factory. Russo's work
brilliantly chronicles socioeconomic transition with humor and pathos,

but also maintains a progressive sensibility and keeps pace with cultural change. *Nobody's Fool* depicts a small town in New York under the gun of postindustrial threat. Decades later, its sequel, *Everybody's Fool*, features characters foolishly blaming Latino immigrants for their problems. By 2023, the third installment of the stellar triology, *Somebody's Fool*, describes characters who are happy to keep taxes, social spending, and infrastructural investment low as long as the "potholes and second-rate schools kept . . . degenerates, atheists, and Starbucks out." It is a subtle, and yet precise delineation of the devolution of the reactionary, exurban mentality.

One of the most popular television shows of the late 1980s and early '90s was *Roseanne*, comedian Roseanne Barr's amusing and emotional look at the personal drama and financial precarity of a working-class family in an Illinois exurb. Dan Conner, played by John Goodman, cannot hold steady employment, as manufacturers and small businesses are constantly closing or relocating. His wife Roseanne works at a diner, barely adding to the inadequate household income as they raise three children. A rock and roll singer, a novelist, and a stand-up comic demonstrated more awareness of the changing economic situation in the United States than most of the country's public officials.

As president, Bill Clinton, promoted education as a necessary alternative to industry, but by the 2000s progressive visions for the future, no matter how sensible or helpful, could not compete with nostalgia. Clinton, in an odd turn, became a scapegoat for the weakening of manufacturing, even though it began decades before he took the oath of office. Instead of consulting the actual record, and dealing with the confluence of factors that demolished long-term, stable manufacturing employment in the United States, the nationalist right and progressive left settled on a convenient culprit: free trade. If not for the North Atlantic Free Trade Agreement (NAFTA) and the admission of China into the World Trade Organization (WTO), the odd pair of Donald Trump and Bernie

Sanders would have the public believe that tens of thousands of young men would graduate high school every year and immediately find suitable employment at the factory. The story resonates among the general public, because it reinforces the essential instinct of American life: escapism. Rearing its snarling face and flashing its fangs again, the politics of escape animates the provincialism of the public. Both parties, along with the major institutions of the media, cooperate, telling Americans that, when it comes to jobs and trade, the real crisis is interaction with the rest of the world. The American mutation of nationalism differs from its Polish, Russian, or Italian counterparts, because the United States enjoys the separation of two oceans from much of the planet. Fight or flight takes hold in right-wing rhetoric and delusions, and even in some left-wing circles, offering equally false diagnosis and comfort: Because the United States did not take flight from the global economy, it must now isolate and adopt a hostile posture against Mexico, in the form of draconian immigration policy; China, with bellicose speechmaking and idle threats; and NATO and the European Union, with extortionary threats to exit postwar peace agreements.

The continual obsession with trade, mills, and factories obscures the real issues at the heart of a transforming and, in some ways, decaying economy. While manufacturing employment continues to decline, home health care workers grow by the millions. The fast-food chain Arby's, currently employs more Americans than the entire coal industry. Millions of young Americans, including seven hundred thousand part-time college instructors, struggle to stay afloat in a freelance "gig economy." The growing ranks of the marginal, low-wage workforce need access to public goods and services, higher wages, dependable benefits, and affordable education—not pipe dreams about the resurrection of the 1940s. Blaming free trade for the economic afflictions and alterations of the Midwest Rust Belt ignores politically neutral realities while giving cover to the real culprits of communal destruction. The

Center for Business and Economic Research at Ball State University found that, since 2000, 85 percent of job losses in the manufacturing sector were "attributable to technological change."[13] A similar study of Ohio from the Carnegie Endowment for International Peace discovered that the Buckeye state lost 750,000 "good paying manufacturing jobs" between 1969 and 2009, and that over two-thirds of the losses occurred as a result of automation.[14] Advancements in technology have not only eliminated the need for thousands of workers in the manufacture of everything from cars to steel bearings. They have also destroyed entire industries. When countless consumers bought cameras and developed film, Kodak employed 145,000 Americans. It now has 4,500 employees.[15] Nothing short of a Luddite revolution will reverse the inevitable triumph of computer engineering and digital programming over the smokestacks.

At the same time that technology began to transform industries and flip small towns and suburbs throughout the Midwest, regulations on the corporate capture of small businesses and major markets, both of the legal and unwritten, ethical variety, vanished. With the disappearance of checks and balances on the ability of multinational corporations to dominate markets and exploit workers and customers, the economic arrangement lost all symmetry, allowing for extreme inequality. Because the federal government pulled the security guard off duty, raiders and plunderers made a score comparable to a jewel thief who finds an unmanned, expensive shop with an open door and unlocked case.

✳

TERRY STEAGALL'S LAUGHTER IS THE MOST IMPOSing force in nearly any room. Steagall, a large and gregarious man with encyclopedic knowledge of nearly any topic related to local politics, has worked in the Northwest Indiana steel mills for over thirty years.

Doubling his labor, he also spent years as a union organizer and volunteer for political organizations and campaigns ranging from Tony Mazzocchi's efforts to coalesce the labor and environmental movements to Jesse Jackson's presidential run of 1988. Sitting across from me in a Highland bar on a Wednesday night, when cheeseburgers cost only $6, he is punctuating his booming voice with a range of soft hand gestures. Pausing only to pull on the brim of his Chicago Cubs cap or take a bite out of the "All Day Burger," which weighs in heavily with its bacon and fried egg toppings, he is on a tear over the "economics that most people don't understand."

"NAFTA had some good things in it and some bad things," he explains, "But the real problems began in the 1980s during the so called 'Reagan Revolution.'" Unlike Trump, who presented a monstrous face to sell murderous policies, Reagan managed to swindle the United States with what musician Warren Haynes refers to as a "carny smile." Reagan declared "morning in America," and spoke of national triumph and superiority but busted unions, most infamously the air traffic control workers, deregulated industry, and changed corporate laws to enable stock buybacks—a devastating instrument of greed that encourages management to use profits to enrich themselves rather than strengthen the company and improve conditions for workers. "Then, the raider and pirate types crashed the party, took over major companies, and strip-mined them, selling them piece by piece," Terry said, his voice rising to compete with the Aerosmith song blasting from the jukebox.

The Oliver Stone film *Wall Street* gives viewers an easily comprehensible, dramatic version of the economic transformation that Terry described, worked, and organized against. Gordon Gekko, an investor and corporate raider inspired by real-life trader Ivan Boesky, who was imprisoned for insider trading, and played brilliantly by Michael Douglas, convinces a naive admirer to assist him in the acquisition of a small airline. The apprentice's father is one of the union bosses of the airline. He alone sees the writing on the wall, warning his son against the deal and attempting, in vain, to convince his workers to vote in opposition. As soon as Gekko takes ownership of the airline, he breaks his promise to enlarge it and instead dumps it onto the market.

When his devastated and outraged squire asks, "Why do you need to wreck this company?" Gekko answers back, without a second of hesitation or scintilla of remorse, "Because it's wreckable."

Nihilistic and sociopathic, Gekko boils his philosophy down to its infected bones during a speech to the shareholders of a paper company he has also acquired and plans to strip for parts: "Greed is good." Oliver Stone expressed personal horror, and worried that he failed as a filmmaker, when he learned that millions of young men across the United States idolized Gekko, adopted his lethal motto as their own amoral vision for wealth and glamour, and began voting Republican.

"Greed is good" functions as an explanation for the demolition of the social compact that provided for the poor, regulated business practice, and largely contributed to the prosperity of small businesses, such as my father's, that interlocked to form the backbone of suburbia. It not only authorized destructive public policy, mainly the restructuring of corporate and finance law to make the shareholders royal while casting customers, contractors, and workers into the roles of the peasantry, but also shifted the culture underneath the feet of entrepreneurs.

My father explained that when he started his trucking company there was an "unwritten, gentlemen's agreement" forbidding "back solicitation"—that is, according to one legal definition, the "practice where a delivering carrier or interline carrier obtains the freight business through another carrier, logistics company or broker and then uses the information obtained from this party to determine who the customer is and then solicits the business of the customer." It is a dishonest practice in which a transportation company that learns of a customer through a dispatcher directly outbids the dispatching company, undercutting the middleman and, in the process, creating an increasingly predatory commercial landscape. Back solicitation not only steals a lucrative contract but destroys the relationship that birthed it. My father sustained his business through a relational network of similar businesspeople, regularly transporting goods and equipment for them. In the early 2000s, large trucking companies brazenly violated "business ethics" by back soliciting their way into myriad contracts—offering services at prices they knew that smaller companies, such as my father's, could not match. The owner of S&J Stereo, a record store that opened its doors in Highland in the 1990s and later moved to neighboring Griffith, explained that a similar practice forever damaged his store and countless stores like it. When music listeners still purchased CDs prior to the advent of streaming, big-box retailers, like Best Buy and Walmart, would entice customers into their doors by offering the new album from Beyoncé or Bon Jovi—anything guaranteed to sell—at below wholesale cost. They would accept the loss on the CD, expecting the customer to purchase other items in store. Big agribusinesses, running factory farms, would do the same with their produce, fully aware that the family farmer had no chance to compete.

Nostalgia is a current that runs through many suburbs, powering the move into exurbs, because the degradation that American culture and community have suffered is most plainly visible within their borders. It was relatively recent that an entirely different universe existed in small villages like my wife's hometown of Park Forest, Illinois. During the 1980s, the racially diverse town located thirty-five miles south of Chicago, had a large city center full of booming businesses selling everything from flowers to coffee, secure middle-class subdivisions, and its own entertainment venue. Freedom Hall not only hosted performances by jazz and rock bands, symphony orchestras, and theater troupes but also gave its stage to high-profile speakers, like Studs Terkel and Gwendolyn Brooks. Pulitzer Prize–winning playwright David Mamet landed his first paid writing job as a sports reporter for the Park

Forest *Star*. Park Forest now looks like the set of a dystopian television series. The city center is empty, Freedom Hall rarely books events, the newspaper is long defunct, and many of the formerly professional neighborhoods now feature homes with boarded windows, wild lawns, and sunken rooftops. The town no longer even has a grocery store.

A short drive from Park Forest is all that is necessary to reach Thornton, where my grandfather worked the quarry, tended bar, and operated his own unofficial social work agency. Most of the restaurants, bars, and shops that my mother knew as a child are now empty and unreplaced. When I was a boy riding a bicycle around the suburbs, it was typical to see more family-owned businesses than corporate chains, and it was common to meet people who earned a middle-class salary according to their own initiative. I could buy an ice-cream cone at the dairy bar that my high school classmate's parents owned, help my mom carry a Christmas tree out the doors of Holiday World—a novelty store under the ownership of a Trinity Lutheran Church family, and buy CDs from S&J Stereo. People with their own small businesses felt invested in their communities and helped supply the stability for local churches, civic organizations, and venues of recreation, like bowling alleys, pool halls, and arcades. Cynics might dismiss suburban community as Hallmark Channel naivete, but it was real, and its endangerment distorts reality for those who miss it or never experienced it but long for it.

As my grandfather understood and explained when I told him I wanted a job like his, working in a quarry or factory is hard. It takes a toll on the body—stretching muscles to the lengths of pain, crushing the bones underneath them, and tearing at the edges of the joints. When he was in his seventies, my grandfather labored to lift himself off the furniture, bouncing up and down on the couch cushion to build sufficient momentum to act as a spring as he struggled to his feet. The hand that he broke twice while cutting stone appeared permanently swollen—as if he inflated it like a balloon every morning after breakfast. The artists who depicted blue-collar labor won acclaim and attracted large audiences not for glorification but for demonstrating an understanding of its agony. In the song, "Factory," Bruce Springsteen sings about a man who loses his hearing, and workers leaving the plant with "death in their eyes." Loretta Lynn declared that she is "proud to be a coal miner's daughter," not because of the beneficence of the coal mine but because her family gave her a loving and joyful home despite the miseries of their work. Jim Harrison's brilliant novel *Sundog* leads readers through the rich life of a foreman who built dams and bridges; his happiness arrives in moments of beauty that balance the aches and pains of his labor. One of the everyday laborers Studs Terkel interviewed for his legendary oral history *Working* said, "I think most of us are looking for a calling, not a job. Most of us, like the assembly-line worker, have jobs that are too small for our spirit." Another interview subject, a steel worker, explained that he despises the "highly educated snobs" who "look down" on him but hopes that his son becomes one of them.[16]

Psychologists explain that human beings have a natural tendency toward sublimation. Stripping away the pathological elements of sublimation, it is the deflection of instinctual urges onto noninstinctual, concrete endeavors. The bizarre fixation on industry, despite its attendant agonies, is an act of national sublimation. The only reason that manufacturing employment ever seemed desirable was because of the organization and advocacy of unions that won high wages and generous benefits. Unions have largely vanished from the American economy, given that only 9 percent of workers belong to one. More significantly, the mill, factory, and quarry have become emblematic of a lifestyle, both individual and communal, that, depending on the location, is either dead or on a respirator.

The fixation is also a consequence of inadequate public policy, showcasing the failures that derive from individualism and escapism. In Western European countries and Canada, organized labor, representing different companies throughout a wide range of fields, coalesced to practice "social unionism," which is various trade unions joining forces to advocate for universal regulatory and welfare policies. It is one of the chief reasons why Canada and countries throughout Europe have national health care systems, paid family leave programs, and high minimum wages. In the United States, labor, generally, worked in isolation, practicing rigid "business unionism." As evident by the name, it is when a trade union advocates strictly for its own members in its own industrial sector (the United Auto Workers was a notable exception). The Teamsters, the Chicago Teachers Union, and even the Screen Actors Guild have outstanding medical insurance, and yet the United States is still without a national public health care program. Canadian and European unions moderated and civilized the free market, while their American counterparts were content to merely secure their escape.[17]

Nostalgia for the bygone days when a town's life turned around the plant goes beyond even health care, wages, and other material benefits. When young men could easily find suitable employment after graduating high school, parents could acquire goods and services from their neighbors, and locals could swap stories and share opinions at the nearest dive, the town, the country, and the world seemed solid. Solidity is exactly what the late Polish sociologist Zygmunt Bauman explained is missing from modern life. Because it is missing, modernity's inhabitants have a vague notion that something is wrong. No longer living in predictable and stable times and cultures, most people are now occupants of what Bauman called, "liquid modernity."[18] When something is liquid it is unreliable, ephemeral, unlikely to last, and always under threat. Bauman likened living in liquid modernity to walking through a minefield—you know something will explode, but you don't know exactly when or where. The liquid quality of modern life quickly destroys and replaces industries and technology, often to the accompaniment of media praise for the responsible "disruptors." The liquid state of modern culture is evident when workers feel compelled to change jobs and companies every few years, a far cry from employees of previous generations who remained with the same business or organization for the duration of their careers. Perhaps most palpable is the liquid characteristic of contemporary communities, especially small suburbs.

No longer can families rely on a network of neighbors for social support, patronize their friend's business for decades, and see genera- tions change hands on the same roads, with the same values, in the same institutions. The proliferation of niche markets, entertainment options, and digital communication forums has even melted the once solid national culture into liquid form. Americans in the 1980s and '90s largely watched the same television programs, obtained news and opinion from the same sources, and reacted to the same events with a shared vocabulary. Professional sports is all that remains within the universal culture of broad appeal and understanding. Now Americans of different ages, classes, educational attainment levels, religions, and political persuasions often speak in oppositional dialects about individuated, contradictory perceptions of reality. Meanwhile, in the rapidly changing, liquid society, the men whose fathers and grandfathers enjoyed the solidity, whether their spouses did or not, of bringing home their weekly pay to a subordinate wife are struggling to compete against educated, independent women in the job market. The same women might not give them a second look on a Friday night. Women's emancipation has created a culture of regressive and resentful manhood. The irrational and fantastical longing for the resurrection of a manufacturing economy doubles as the articulation of a petro-masculine vision of a society where the extraction of fossil fuels and the pollution from industry continues without consequence. Men rule the roads and make the rules of the house.

Reactionary politics of nostalgia offer an escape from time, history, and reality itself. Demagogic promises to "bring the jobs back" function as an entrance into an intellectual time machine, transporting the roused rabble to an era when the foundation of ice didn't show a crack. In the present, the political project of nostalgia, resting on a scaffold of romanticization of the smokestack decades of the twentieth century, is the equivalent of removing bottles of Budweiser from a cooler hours after the ice has melted on a scorching summer afternoon and placing them in the refrigerator with hopes for revival. The beer is skunked. The party is over.

MEN AT WAR

Menacing the suburban and exurban road on any given day, like a battalion of the Chinese People's Liberation Army in Tiananmen Square, is a steady march of massive pickup trucks. Transforming the grocery store parking lot and afternoon school dismissal scene into a Fallujah battleground, behemoth pickups dominate the small-town streets. In 2021, five of the top ten bestselling vehicles in the United States were pickup trucks. Forty percent of pickup trucks were sold in suburbia, 39 percent in exurbia—and not only pickup trucks, but "heavy-duty" models; the kind that Ford, Chevy, and GMC advertise on television with slick depictions of heroic drivers steering their trucks up mountain terrain, or speeding off road through a rocky desert. Reality is a little less romantic. Given that heavy-duty pickup trucks, most of them costing between $35,000 and $50,000, are most popular in the suburbs and exurbs, the roughest obstacle the average driver will have to overcome is a strip mall speed bump. No matter how many times one shares a narrow avenue with one of these monsters, a sense of shock remains at the sheer size and scale. Even after several years of noticing the ubiquity of heavy duties, my wife and I will still comment on their unavoidable presence. It is as if the average suburban family is driving a tank to Sunday morning church service or to *pick up* a pizza for dinner. Much more than a particularly hideous aesthetic blight, research indicates that large pickup trucks are dangerous to anyone in their surroundings. Because the driver's sightlines are so poor, heavy-duty pickup trucks threaten pedestrians, pets, and even economy cars. The grille of the GMC Sierra, to name one of many examples, stands at nearly six feet—far taller than children, domestic animals, and most adults. The limited visibility is an especially sweet feature given that studies also validate what anyone with a scintilla of reason would assume: the heavier the vehicle the likelier it is to kill a pedestrian, and the heavier the vehicle the likelier it is to render a collision fatal. Pickup trucks now regularly exceed four thousand pounds, having grown more than 24 percent since 2000.[1]

I drive a Honda Civic. Even my automobile is no match for the battering ram on wheels behind me at the stoplight. The most popular pickup trucks have grilles that reach almost equal height to the roof of my car. Any accident will resemble a monster truck rally. Many publications, such as *Consumer Reports* and *Slate*, have reported on the lethality of heavy-duty trucks, while some consumer safety advocates have all but begged the federal government to regulate the weight and height of pickup trucks available to the average commuter. There are already requirements in place limiting who can drive a semitruck to those who pass the prerequisite written exams and road tests to attain a commercial driver's license (CDL). It is only logical, not to mention responsible, that some restrictions should apply to the vehicles available at the average dealership. As the automakers hit pay dirt on pickup truck sales, the regulation discussion can barely rise above a whisper. The typical driver and pedestrian are now conscripted into a game of Russian roulette. A short drive across town to see the dentist might turn into the day that an exurban warrior in the equivalent of a Humvee crushes your

Camry with you inside of it. The menace is hardly theoretical. Statistics reveal that most of the victims of "frontover deaths," which, according to journalist Dan Kois means, "when a pedestrian in a front blind spot is struck and killed," are children. Kois's research also shows that 80 percent of frontover deaths since 1990 involved a truck, van, or SUV. In a collision, a pickup truck is 159 percent likelier than other vehicles to kill the other driver. Clearly, none of this rates as a priority to the suburban or exurban parent when considering what automobile to buy. Driving a lethal weapon, and placing children, economy car passengers, and pets in jeopardy, is an American rite of personal liberty. It is exactly what Jefferson and Lincoln fantasized about when they trudged along in horse and buggy.

Lest one thinks this is a form of liberal snobbery manifesting in disdain toward the much vaunted "working class," it is a fact that most heavy-duty drivers have no practical purpose for their vehicles. The automotive research firm Strategic Vision found that 75 percent of heavy-duty truck owners never use their towing capacity and only 30 percent drive off road even once a year. Most significantly, 35 percent of truck owners never haul anything, and most that do report that it is only the occasional personal purchase. It has nothing to do with their occupation. Only 11 percent of truck owners work in the trades, and a piddly 1 percent are farmers. Taking a quick glance at most heavy-duty trucks is typically enough to assume what Strategic Vision confirms.[2] One will observe that the newer models of trucks advertising a $50,000 to $60,000 price tag (not exactly a "working-class" market) have suspiciously small beds. Even the most creative driver couldn't fit much lumber, furniture, or sizable equipment in the space that the monster truck makes available. When I lower the back seat of my Civic, and open the trunk, my hauling space is around equal, at least in width and length, to the average heavy-duty truck. One out of every six new vehicles sold in the United States is a large pickup, transforming the inevitable protests surrounding gas prices whenever there is even a moderate increase at the pump into an exercise in absurdity. Many of the people complaining about the cost of fuel are agreeing to major monthly payments on vehicles with the worst gas mileage on the road. And why do they do it if not for labor purposes or affordability?

Alexander Edwards, the president of Strategic Vision, offers the following summary: "Truck owners oversample in [reasons for purchasing] like: the ability to outperform others, to look good while driving, to present a tough image, to have their car act as extension of their personality, and to stand out in a crowd." Strategic Vision has also reported that the heavy-duty pickup truck is the most popular vehicle among drivers strongly identifying as Republican. It is the least popular among Democrats.

In order to look and feel tough, far-right heavy-duty drivers are willing to pollute the environment, pay higher gas prices (and then blame whatever Democrat is in power), and endanger nearby children, commuters, and dogs and cats. The heavy-duty pickup truck, weighing in at four thousand pounds and towering above its highway company at well-over six feet tall, is an American mascot. It symbolizes a perverse notion of freedom that places a premium on exaggerated individual whims over the common interest and general welfare of society. It is also emblematic of a new form of malevolent politics taking hold of the American right throughout the suburbs and exurbs.

Mark Metzler Sawin, a historian at Eastern Mennonite University who has studied the cultural importance of the pickup truck in the United States, notes with irony that the soaring increase in pickup truck sales commenced precisely when family farms began to go bankrupt and factories started to close, reduce their workforces with automation, or relocate overseas.[3] The pickup truck, especially as it bloats, is not practical for the overwhelming majority of drivers but representative and metaphorical—an exhaust fume–pumping souvenir of a lost age. A bygone era not so much of labor practice, manufacturing employment, or locally owned agriculture but of masculine dominance. Sawin told a reporter for *The Washington Post* that once the automobile industry realized that the traditional market for pickup trucks was shrinking, and that they could not expect much gains in rural America, where there are fewer people and higher concentrations of poverty, they shifted their sales strategy to a wealthier demographic: "suburban white men."

White men in the suburbs and exurbs provide an essential consumer base, and political constituency, for a product that is even deadlier than the heavy-duty pickup truck—guns, particularly the AR-15 assault rifle. While gun ownership rates are highest in rural counties, data and trends indicate that firearm use is also prevalent throughout suburbia and exurbia. Studies show that even though white men account for only 30 percent of the American public, they own 61 percent of guns.[4] They also dominate the "gun rights" activist sphere of the National Rifle Association and other organizations dedicated to obliterating even the mildest restrictions on gun manufacture and acquisition. Gun owners are 50 percent likelier to vote Republican than their unarmed neighbors.[5] Despite political placement firmly on the right, Democratic officials will often argue—correctly—that most American gun owners support universal background checks on gun purchases, limits on assault weapons, and "red flag" laws that allow police departments to confiscate the firearms of anyone whose behavior indicates danger to themselves or others. The political mystery that emerges, with profound pain, after massacres in schools, grocery stores, synagogues, or LGBTQ bars is why gun control has, aside from the flimsiest measures, become all but impossible on the federal level if a clear majority of both parties' voters support it. Many journalists and political scientists place the blame solely on the NRA, depicting the political lobby as a monstrous force in Washington, DC. The NRA theory ignores the source of the NRA's strength. If it were not for its most dedicated members, who coalesce to form an essential bulk of the Republican base, the organization could not succeed in threatening Republican representatives and senators to do its bidding. If an aspiring GOP politico alienates the gun absolutists within the electorate, he will have no hope of winning elected office. With a few well-timed advertisements, membership emails, and social media posts, the NRA can drive voters away from a candidate, almost instantly transforming him from hero to villain.

Sociologists at Baylor University conducted a revelatory study on not only gun owners but gun owners with significant emotional and moral attachment to guns—not the worried father who buys a single handgun and tucks it away in a drawer on the off chance that a burglar might break a window at two in the morning, or even the outdoorsman who enjoys weekends in the woods hunting for deer, but the bizarre fetishist who stockpiles an arsenal and comes to view the lethal weapon as central to his identity as a human being. Among this extreme iteration of the gun owner, 77 percent are white and 65 percent are male. The authors of the study conclude that these gunowners, especially the men, wrestle with feelings of economic and cultural insecurity. In their hands, the gun becomes a "symbol of power and independence." They also long for inclusion in a "hero narrative." Owning multiple guns activates their imagination, enabling them to cast themselves in patriotic roles of "saving the country" from foreign and domestic threats.[6] These threats almost always operate with racial codes—Latino invaders transgressing the southern border, Muslim terrorists hateful of "American values," and Black criminals prowling otherwise safe streets.

After conducting years of field research attending and interviewing participants at NRA conferences and gun shows, sociologist Christine Allen wrote that the gun rights movement thrives on an "apocalyptic narrative." It is a story that begins with a personal apocalypse—"criminals will break into my home and murder my family," which although statistically unlikely to occur is a legitimate concern—and then enlarges into a national and political Armageddon: the globalist and leftist plot, staffed with minorities, will soon revoke the Bill of Rights, impose tyrannical oppression, and destroy the country. The reason that gun sales skyrocket whenever a Democrat is president, most dramatically during the Obama years, is because an enemy presence in the White House fuels conspiracy theory and paranoia, making the apocalyptic threat feel much more real and immediate.[7]

Paranoid racism, outlandish conspiracy theories, and the impulse to satiate insecurity with an accessory of heroic posture interlocked with irony to make the United States much more dangerous. Ryan Busse, a former gun industry insider who earned distinction as one of its leading salesmen, writes in his expose, *Gunfight,* that when President Bill Clinton signed the assault weapons ban in 1994, everyone within the gun world expressed opposition. Within company offices, however, there was little panic. Assault rifles sold at such low rates that many leading manufactures, including his employer, Kimber, did not even produce them. It was a more responsible and measured time within the gun movement and broader political culture; several industry leaders cautioned against widespread promotion of assault rifles prior to Clinton's ban, predicting the chaos and carnage that now fills the headlines with gruesome tales of mass shootings on a monthly, if not weekly, basis. In 2004, Republicans in Congress and President George W. Bush allowed the assault weapons ban to expire, opening a new market for a then floundering industry. The AR-15, according to Busse, transformed from novelty item prior to Clinton's ban to, after Bush's change in policy, "America's rifle"—the country's top-selling gun. The metamorphosis transpired not so much due to legalities but culture.

While America was waging two wars in the "sandbox"—the gun world's derogatory term for the Middle East—millions of gun owners aspired to identify with the soldiers and Marines fighting in Iraq and Afghanistan. The NRA, in a clever marketing ploy, began to equate gun ownership with patriotism and "support for the troops." It was a sales pitch that culminated with the direct marketing of military weaponry to consumers. Gun companies began enlisting special forces veterans of the post-9/11 wars to speak at conventions, appear in advertisements, and host glossy and exciting online videos, all with the express purpose of selling the AR-15. Muscle-bound bearded men straight out of central casting regaled audiences with their combat stories and offered the opportunity for their admirers to feel exactly like they did on the battlefield by owning and operating their weapon of choice. According to Busse's account, gun industry insiders, including the combat vets, adopted a condescending term for their marks: "couch commandos." Couch commandos, in the words of one former soldier who became a gun spokesperson, "are people out there that couldn't serve for whatever reason, but they want to put on the body armor, run down the range with their AR, and do a fuckin' transition drill."[8]

Manufactures began selling AR-15s by the millions. Its most popular model had a desert camouflage finish. The proliferation of the AR-15 has transformed every public gathering in the United States into a potential bloodbath. Giving an amateur the capacity to spray bullets, it has created deadly scenarios where even armed police fear to tread. In Uvalde, Texas, dozens of officers stood idle while a school shooter murdered nineteen children and two teachers. A few years earlier in Parkland, Florida, an armed security guard cowered safely outside a schoolhouse while a killer stalked his victims. There are now twenty million AR-15 rifles legally in circulation throughout the United States. Even the catastrophe of massacred children could not inspire political progress or slow down the explosive market for every mass shooter's favorite instrument of death. What began as a dark and sad impulse to access the emotion of war from the comfortable confines of the shooting range has devolved into the destruction of public space.

The AR-15 bears an odd similarity to the heavy-duty pickup truck.

They are both consequences of the collapse of a social compact and communal ethos. The driver of the heavy duty and, to a much worse extent, the owner of the AR-15 places more import on an egocentric feeling of power than on the lives of their compatriots. Given that millions of these predominantly white men populate suburbia and exurbia, there is also a need to inquire into the existential crisis facing American manhood and the women who tolerate or even participate in bizarre and destructive impulses. How did it happen that millions of middle-class Americans are no longer content to play football with their sons, drink beers with their friends, and enjoy intimacy with their wives; instead they must envision themselves as Hollywood warriors, accessorizing as couch commandos to place themselves at the center of a hero's journey in which they valiantly battle against cosmic forces of evil lurking behind every shadow?

THROUGHOUT THE SUMMER AND FALL OF 2020, I BE-gan to notice something peculiar in Northwest Indiana and the south suburbs of Chicago. A strange sign of menace was prevalent as if those brandishing it were acting according to an overarching script. Driving on the two-lane roads past churches, gas stations, and grocery stores and speeding down the highway, an increasingly large number of vehicles, often heavy duty pickup trucks, had bumper stickers that went beyond conventional political expression and difference. First, the Punisher skull became ubiquitous, nearly always with red, white, and blue coloration. The Punisher is a comic book antihero who, after witnessing the murder of his wife and children, becomes a violent vigilante. Resorting to extra-constitutional measures and acting as judge, jury, and executioner for anyone he merely suspects of criminality, he is equally courageous and villainous. The character's creators have discussed how they never intended a reaction of reverence from their audience but instead a nuanced and contradictory examination of the law, rough justice, and violence. Chris Kyle, the pathological liar who claimed to hold the distinction as the military's most effective sniper in Iraq and Afghanistan, wrote in his memoir that Marines and soldiers adopted the skull as a symbol of intimidation during those respective wars. The war appeared to come home when couch commandos began advertising the Punisher skull on their vehicles, subtly threatening anyone who entered their line of vision. Various police departments also attempted to brand their squad cars with the skull until sufficient complaints prevented it from becoming an official insignia. Meanwhile, sales of Punisher apparel soared.[9]

Simultaneous with the popularity of the Punisher skull, bumper stickers with then unfamiliar logos became prominent. The roman numeral for "three" surrounded by stars was suddenly everywhere on the road. My sister-in-law's next-door neighbor had a sign with the same logo in his front window. A quick Google search revealed that the emblem promoted the Three Percenters—a far-right antigovernment militia that the Anti-Defamation League and Southern Poverty Law Center list among known hate groups. The Canadian government has declared the Three Percenters a domestic terrorism outfit. During the Obama and Trump presidencies, the Three Percenters routinely posted racist speech and graphics to their social media pages. Worse yet, its members had connections to several hate crimes and terrorist plots, including the plan to kidnap and kill Michigan governor Gretchen Whitmer as retaliation against her enforcement of COVID-19 public health protocols. Its members also "provided security" for Unite the Right neo-Nazi leaders at the Charlottesville rally of 2017 and had connections to the bombing of an Islamic center in Bloomington, Minnesota. Brazen white supremacy, intentions to murder innocent people, and the attempted assassination of an elected official did not prevent many Republicans from advertising support for the Three Percenters. It did not even make them bashful. Dozens of Republican officials, including Congresswomen

Marjorie Taylor Greene and Lauren Boebert, boast of their ties to the Three Percent militia.[10]

Before and during the immediate months following the 2020 election, I also observed a rise in bumper stickers and signs bearing the phrase "Oath Keepers." Like the Three Percenters, the Oath Keepers are a violent and seditious militia that openly declares war on Democrats, political liberals, and any law enforcement official who "breaks his oath to the Constitution" by executing orders of the state. The founder of the Oath Keepers, Stewart Rhodes, was a regular guest on right-wing media, often making appearances on Fox News. Rhodes's hope to violently overthrow the United States government did not dim his star in the right-wing cosmos. He no longer appears on Fox News, likely because he was convicted on charges of seditious conspiracy and sentenced to eighteen years in prison for his role in the planning of the January 6 attack on the Capitol.

In the same six-month period, it became common to see American flags washed out in black flying from suburban and exurban homes. Several newspapers began reporting on the black American flag, offering their readers insight into what it signifies about those who would proudly wave it. According to experts on the militia movement in the United States, it means "no quarter given," and implies a willingness to use violence against political enemies. Amy Cooter, a sociologist at Middlebury Instute of Interntaional Studies who spent three years embedded with a Michigan militia and whose concerns were largely ignored by mainstream media and broader political culture, cautions that the flag is a "warning sign" of "radicalization."[11]

Carl Hoffman, travel journalist and author of *Liar's Circus*, a journalistic account of dozens of Donald Trump rallies that he personally attended, sounds a similar alarm. He writes that the Proud Boys, Oath Keepers, and Three Percenters were a small presence at Trump's fascist extravaganzas but that, without exception, they received applause and enthusiastic cheers from the Trump supporters surrounding them. Many seemingly ordinary Republicans would greet militia members as celebrities, requesting selfies and autographs as mentally healthy people would with movie stars or professional athletes.[12] What might appear to the untrained eye as bizarre but ultimately benign behavior from immature men who fall asleep to fantasies of G.I. Joe is actually a disturbing augury for a society seemingly on the precipice of political disaster.

Rachel Kleinfeld, a senior fellow at the Carnegie Endowment for International Peace and the founder of the Truman National Security Project, writes that in unstable banana republics that operate according to perpetual conflict, such as Iraq, Nigeria, and Colombia, authoritarian regimes and insurgent parties "outsource violence to specialists in the trade, just as they hire consultants for robocalls and direct mail." Articulating an observation unthinkable since the early twentieth century when municipal and state governments in the Deep South coordinated efforts of terrorism with the Ku Klux Klan, Kleinfeld adds that the United States should fall into the political violence classification: "Militias have been embraced by GOP leaders at the national, state, and local level." Barely scratching the surface of evidentiary examples, she cites alarming incidents, within recent years and taking place in every region of the country, where Republican officials have appeared alongside militia leaders, brazenly expressed support for their participation in the political process, or refused to condemn them even after violent acts of assault or intimidation against protesters. In Oregon, Michigan, Colorado, and Texas, Republican officials have enlisted the "security services" of militia groups, including those like the Proud Boys that express an ideology hateful toward racial minorities, women, and/or gay and transgender Americans. The chairman of Wyoming's Republican Party is a member of the Oath Keepers, and several Proud Boys now sit on the central committee for the Republican Party of Miami-Dade, the most populous county in Florida. While the celebration of tactical gear and weaponry might appease the dreams of Hollywood heroism floating through otherwise dull minds, the Republican Party is using violence, in the words of Kleinfeld, "as a campaign tactic."[13]

Death threats have already succeeded in causing the resignation of hundreds of librarians, school board members, election officials, and poll workers, particularly in the battleground states that tipped the 2020 election in Joe Biden's favor. Sane Republicans, such as former congressman Anthony Gonzalez, have confessed to exiting politics due to fears for their families' safety. Gonzalez, a lifelong "conservative" from Ohio, faced an avalanche of death threats after voting to impeach Donald Trump as punishment for his attempt to blackmail Ukraine president Volodymyr Zelensky into making damaging allegations against Joe Biden.[14]

The United States military defines terrorism as the use or threat of violence to achieve political or religious objectives. Given the official meaning of the term, it is almost a banality to conclude that America is currently living in an age of terror. Anyone who studies terrorism, such as Rachel Kleinfeld, will explain that in order for a terrorist movement to function it must have support, or at least sympathy, among a significant section of the general public. The sympathizers are ill equipped or unwilling to commit acts of violence themselves, but they will tolerate, if not outright applaud, the use of force from outlaw parties that share their political agenda. In the aftermath of the January 6 insurrection, former president Donald Trump, several influential Republican congressmen and senators, and a few of the most popular right-wing media personalities screamed more derision toward apostate Liz Cheney and other members of the January 6 congressional investigative committee than they've ever expressed against the insurrectionists themselves. Others have even commended criminal convicts within the January 6 mob. At the Conservative Political Action Conference (CPAC), which functions as an annual Woodstock for the racist, fascist right, a performance artist cried and prayed within a makeshift cage, depicting the trauma and per-secution of an imprisoned January 6 terrorist. Attendees offered their tears, blessings, and sympathy card sentiments of consolation.

Months before a fascist mob stormed the Capitol, threatening to murder elected officials and defecating on the floor, bad feelings were growing more ominous among those paying attention to advertisements of political violence on truck decals and celebrations of hate crimes in right wing media. As Bruce Springsteen sings in the opening line of "Badlands," "Lights out tonight / Trouble in the heartland."

KENOSHA, WISCONSIN, IS AT THE CENTER OF THE Northern Chicago suburbs and the suburbs to the south of Milwaukee. While not following a downward trajectory as catastrophic as cities like Gary and Youngstown, Kenosha is one of many cities within the Mid-western Rust Belt—formerly thriving due to a manufacturing economic base, but long suffering from decline after significant erosion. It even-tually bore resemblance in the national consciousness to another Mid-western town—Ferguson, Missouri. Its Black residents, comprising 11 percent of the total population, often make claims of police persecution and additional racist practices within city limits. The claims turned to protest, and subsequently to riot, in August of 2020. With the country already experiencing explosions of political rebellion following then po-lice officer Derek Chauvin's sadistic murder of George Floyd in Minne-apolis, another law enforcement shooting from another heartland state started dominating headlines. A video surfaced that appeared to capture a police officer shooting an unarmed Black man four times in the back outside of a Kenosha home. The immediate reaction from the public, es-pecially activists within the Black Lives Matter movement, was outrage. Investigative details would soon separate the case from the modern-day

lynching of George Floyd. The man shot in the video, Jacob Blake, had
a warrant for his arrest on sexual assault charges, and the police arrived
at the scene due to frantic calls from the mother of his child claiming
that he was threatening to beat her and kidnap their son. Blake, armed
with a knife, refused to drop the weapon, placed one police officer in a
headlock, and was moving toward the child in the back seat when the
police opened fire.

Long before the details of the case emerged, protesters filled the
streets of typically quiet Kenosha. When those protests transformed
into riots, many business owners saw their shops, restaurants, and offices
vandalized and set on fire. The entire story is an American tragedy—taking fragments of poverty, racial segregation, violence against women and
children, police force, and the rage of the electorate and mixing them
together with the hard consistency of coagulated blood. It would turn
even more disastrous.

Kyle Rittenhouse was born and raised in Antioch, Illinois, an exurb
of Chicago. Home to only about fifteen thousand residents, it is predominantly white and a mix of working- and middle-class families. While in
high school, Rittenhouse expressed interest in becoming a police officer;
he participated in an explorers program, which is a law enforcement activity camp for youth, and filled his social media pages with expressions
of support for Donald Trump and Blue Lives Matter campaigns that
not only countered Black Lives Matter protests of police profiling and
brutality but often dovetailed into far-right, authoritarian politics. Gun
ownership in the Rittenhouse home was a patriotic and masculine ideal.
When Kenosha, merely twenty miles away from Rittenhouse, descended
into bedlam, he likely viewed it as an opportunity to make his dreams
come true. He could stalk the streets, heavily armed, protecting car
dealerships and coffeehouses from the leftist menace, joining the ranks
of the all-American heroes already on the scene: the Kenosha Guard, a
militia that posted an open invitation for all armed citizens to join them

in their protest patrol. The deranged and rabid *Infowars*—the flagship publication of conspiracy theorist Alex Jones—shared the invitation on its social media accounts.

Rittenhouse accepted the call to glory, telling interviewers at the protest, "I consider myself militia," and declaring that it was his job to protect private property with his AR-15. The night did not go according to plan. It is difficult to speculate what dreamlike visions of order or violence fill the mind of a teenager whose idea of a party is to prowl a protest with an assault rifle twenty miles away from home. An investigation and criminal trial attempted to determine the details of the destruction that transpired, but what is inarguable is that Rittenhouse shot three Black Lives Matter protesters, killing two of them. Rittenhouse claims that the protesters, in two separate incidents, attacked him, and that he fired his weapon only in self-defense. The protesters insist that he provoked the violent confrontations by issuing verbal threats and conducting himself in a menacing manner. Rittenhouse was arrested and charged with murder in addition to several other crimes, but a jury found him not guilty on all counts. The jury could not consider an undisputable weapons violation, because the judge threw it out. The same judge left his cell phone on during courtroom proceedings one day, and when he received a call, everyone could hear that his ring tone was Lee Greenwood's country hit "God Bless the U.S.A.," one of the preferred entrance songs for Donald Trump at campaign events. It is entirely reasonable to suspect that the trial suffered from judicial nullification. Among all the legal and ethical debates that surrounded the case, it remained undeniable according to the immutable laws of physics that Rittenhouse would have shot no one, and therefore no one would have died, if he did not travel to the protest and if he did not carry a gun. Even if one agrees with the acquittal, dubious as it was, decency and average intelligence would silence any celebration of Rittenhouse as a hero.

Before, during, and after the Rittenhouse trial, leading figures of Republican politics, including Donald Trump, various members of Congress, and Tucker Carlson, treated Rittenhouse as if he was Captain America—a red, white, and blue costumed crusader for justice, sweeping the suburban streets clean of evil marauders. Trump posed for pictures with Rittenhouse at Mar-a-Lago, congressman Matt Gaetz expressed interest in giving him an internship, and several right-wing organizations, including Turning Point USA, featured him as a celebrity speaker at conventions. At Turning Point's confab, Rittenhouse made a pro wrestler–like entrance to lasers, pulsating music, and deafening cheers. It is important to remember that the teenage vigilante has done nothing of distinction other than shooting three Black Lives Matter protesters, two of whom died as a result. Ryan Busse, the former gun industry leader, warns that the fawning praise for Rittenhouse is a clear warning that the "shock troops" will soon arrive onto the political scene, threatening leftist protest activity, free and fair elections, and previously mundane public procedures like school board meetings and library trustee discussions.[15]

Merely two months after Rittenhouse shot three protesters, the FBI announced the arrest of thirteen members of the Wolverine Watchmen militia for an intercepted and disrupted plot to abduct and assassinate the Democratic governor of Michigan, Gretchen Whitmer. Most of the aspiring terrorists had participated in the storming of the Michigan capitol building, which functioned as an eerie preview of the January 6 insurrection, to "protest" Whitmer's implementation of public health and safety protocols during the early months of the COVID-19 pandemic. Armed reactionaries screamed in the faces of police officers, shouted threats of violence toward Democrats, and promised to "take their country back." The Watchmen's original intention was to execute Whitmer and Democratic legislators during the capitol breach, but as it was impossible to get within close proximity of any elected official, they regrouped to form a second, and equally diabolical, plan.

As president, Donald Trump gave them all the encouragement they required to move from the realm of fantasy into the world of action. Similar to his compliments of neo-Nazis as "very fine people" after the Charlottsville travesty, and preceding his order that the Proud Boys "stand by," Trump tweeted commands to "LIBERATE MICHIGAN." During his rallies, he would also consistently target Whitmer as a "tyrant," provoking the rabid audience to chant "Lock her up!" while he smiled as if he was auditioning for the role of the Joker.

The Wolverine Watchmen, a gaggle of anti-government radicals in the suburbs and exurbs surrounding Grand Rapids, regularly met in a vacuum repair shop to discuss how they could exercise a "citizen's arrest" of Whitmer by snatching her from the governor's mansion in Lansing. After taking her into their custody, they planned to broadcast a mock trial for treason, find her guilty, and issue punishment by execution live on the internet. They stockpiled weapons and ammunition. Then they cased the governor's mansion multiple times, making dry runs and learning the lay of the land. An undercover FBI informant gained the trust of the Watchmen and reported their plans to his superiors, allowing law enforcement to apprehend the potential terrorists before they could initiate a violent confrontation with Whitmer's security and perhaps even the governor herself. Whitmer has expressed indignation at the media's insistence on describing the terrorist scheme as a "plot to kidnap" when the ultimate intention was to assassinate her.[16] "They weren't planning on holding me for ransom," the governor told an interviewer. While Whitmer's criticism of the characteristically tepid mainstream media reportage on right-wing violence is correct, the greater offense against the peaceful transfer of power, the stability of constitutional democracy, and human decency takes place within the locus of Republican Party politics.

At a hate rally in Lansing, Trump, in reference to the plot, said, "Maybe it was a problem, maybe it wasn't." The audience erupted in wild applause. Tudor Dixon, Whitmer's Republican opponent in the 2022 gubernatorial race, joked, "For someone so worried about being kidnapped, Gretchen Whitmer sure is good at taking businesses hostage." She refused to apologize for the remarks. Treating terrorism and murder as fodder for humor provides sufficient indication of the absence of ethics and presence of hatred within the ideological corridors of the right, but many analysts further erased logic and humanity from the discourse by advancing an incoherent defense of the criminals. Contrary to all available evidence, leading pundits on Fox News, Republican officials in Michigan, and "libertarian" analysts argued that the case was nothing more than "FBI entrapment." According to the factually dubious claim, the Wolverine Watchmen were guilty of nothing more than entertaining outlandish fantasies and without the encouragement of the embedded informant would have never put their plan into action. It was not only bloviators on the right who got down on all fours to crawl around the sewer with white supremacist maniacs. A few influential commentators of the nihilist left joined them. Glenn Greenwald, Briahna Joy Gray, and writers at *The Intercept*, making haste to condemn the "national security state," accepted and articulated the entrapment defense. Those who provided rhetorical excuses for terrorism had to ignore the stockpiling of weapons in preparation for the plot, the casing of the governor's mansion, and, most significantly, the testimony of two Wolverine Watchmen members who pled guilty to the charge of "conspiracy to commit kidnapping." In their interrogations with law enforcement and their time on the stand in the trials of other militia criminals, they explained that the FBI informant within their ranks did not conceive of the assassination plan, nor did he provide any encouragement beyond asking questions and offering generic statements of support. A recording taken during one of the vacuum shop summits demonstrates that the genuine Watchmen were leading the discussion, while the informant was far in the conversational background. Javed Ali, a former

FBI agent and Department of Homeland Security staffer who currently teaches at the University of Michigan, told me before the first trial for the Watchmen that the evidence was "overwhelming," and explained that it was one of the most "open-and-shut" cases for a conviction that he has seen in his three decades of anti-terrorism work with the US government and academia.

Shortly after the announcement of the verdicts of the first trial facing the Whitmer plotters, I emailed Ali. He was "stunned." Jurors acquitted two of the Watchmen on all charges, and in the case of the third, a ringleader, surrendered as a hung jury. Similar to the Rittenhouse case, commentary on the outcome of the trial ignored the most obvious factor: jury nullification. The acquittal of the Watchmen on the indisputable charge of owning an unregistered destructive device demonstrates sympathy for the militia and even their plot. Authorities found explosive material in their possession. The defense did not even attempt to argue against that charge. Early in the trial, the judge dismissed a woman from the jury for "flirting" with one of the defendants—consistently smiling in his direction, making subtle hand gestures.[17] Of the jurors that remained, several owned assault rifles, and one had a husband with a collection of multiple guns. Another juror who admitted to owning a gun criticized Whitmer for her enforcement of public health measures during the early months of the pandemic.[18] Giving more credence to the jury nullification theory is the federal trial of the ringleader on whose charges the Michigan jury deadlocked. He was convicted and sentenced to prison for nearly twenty years. Federal trials resulted in the conviction of four of the other Watchmen involved the assassination scheme.

The Watchmen resided in the Grand Rapids suburbs and exurbs. Most of the jurors in the first trial also resided in Michigan suburbia and exurbia. Kyle Rittenhouse spent his formative years in a small Illinois exurb and faced jurors from the suburbs and exurbs of southern Wisconsin. The Wolverine Watchmen and Rittenhouse, who announced that he "considered himself militia" and would later pose for photographs in a bar with members of the Proud Boys flashing a white power sign, acted as soldiers in a war of their own imagination.[19] Patrolling the streets of a protest with a high-powered weapon seemed reasonable to a teenage boy, and, evidently, his parents, while to the Wolverine Watchmen, the adoption of policies to protect the public from a lethal virus was tantamount to treason. The suburban and exurban jurors of Michigan and Wisconsin signaled more sympathy for the defendants than the victims and targets. Acquittal on the undeniable weapons charges showcases contempt for the laws of society and, in the case of Whitmer, the executor of those laws. It also indicates belief in the NRA fantasy of living in a state of permanent warfare—teenagers owning and carrying assault rifles and militia members possessing bomb-making material falls underneath the umbrella of patriotism; a noble defense against governmental interference in the lives of free citizens. One never knows when "they" might commence combat against the liberty of "real Americans," whether "they" refers to elected officials with dreams of despotism or Blacks and leftists seeking to transform suburban stability into anarchy. Gore Vidal titled a collection of essays *Perpetual War for Perpetual Peace.* The ironic phrase applies to the paranoid mindset of the suburban and exurban couch commando who has transformed from a fringe joke into a crucial marketing demographic and, finally, into a mainstream threat against the institutions of American society. If matters of criminal justice cannot proceed under the guise of fairness, honesty, and objectivity in exurban, suburban, and small metro districts, law enforcement will have little ability to bring criminals, and even terrorists, to justice. The culture war and anti-government iteration of right-wing politics will render Lady Justice not only blind, but deaf, dumb, and immobile.

✳

SUBURBAN AND EXURBAN WHITE MEN OVER THE age of forty, and the patriarchy participants who support them, have a warlike <u>mentality</u> and posture because they rightly detect that <u>their ideology is under siege.</u> As a compensatory device for their paranoia and sense of persecution, they refuse to accept that the United States has grown more socially liberal, racially diverse, and philosophically secular as the organic consequence of popular movements throughout the twentieth and twenty-first centuries. Blacks are no longer content to ride on the back of the transportational, cultural, or institutional bus, women of all colors are not going to dutifully comply with orders from their fathers, husbands, or chauvinist bosses, gay and transgender people will not cower in the closet according to a belief of imposed inferiority, immigrants from Latin America and Asia will no longer settle for menial roles within colleges and companies, and atheists and agnostics will not wear a scarlet "A" in shame, acting as if they are demonic for their lack of "religious faith." The transformation is visible throughout American society, even in the suburbia of *Pleasantville* and *Stepford Wives* lore of yesteryear. Highland, Indiana, recently elected a Black woman to the town council for the first time, other officials like chiefs of police and administrators such as school principals are increasingly diverse, and, meanwhile, the churches have more and more empty pews.

Due to ingesting the toxic stew of entitlement, exceptionalism, and ethnocentrism, suburban and exurban whites, especially those in older generations, are susceptible to believing that the changes taking place all around them, with particular immediacy among their children, grandchildren, nieces, and nephews, are the achievements of a grand conspiracy. According to the paranoid perspective, audible nightly on Fox News, universities do not aspire to educate their students or prepare them for professional careers but aim to indoctrinate them into the destructive ethos of "cultural Marxism." Gay and transgender teachers and librarians are not attempting to serve their communities. They want to "groom"

children into a lifestyle of lawless hedonism. Racial diversity, especially the form that manifests in Black, Latino, Asian, and Native American public officials, corporate executives, college administrators, and celebrity spokespeople, is not an ongoing accomplishment of the civil rights movement; rather it is a concerted campaign to inflict financial, emotional, and spiritual damage on the purity and power of white America.

The most lethal iteration of right-wing paranoia is "Great Replacement Theory." Originally the province of Klan rallies, terrorists like Timothy McVeigh, and street corner eccentrics, the racist conspiracy theory has infiltrated the mainstream of Republican politics and right-wing discourse. It is the belief that "globalists" (most often Jews, with the liberal financier George Soros's name acting as the dog whistle) are striving to subvert the racial demographics of the United States by ushering massive numbers of illegal immigrants across the southern border and funding treasonous movements like Black Lives Matter. White liberal politicians who cooperate with the great replacement, such as Nancy Pelosi and Joe Biden, are either useful idiots or part of the plan. Polling data shows that 68 percent of Republicans accept Great Replacement Theory as valid political science.[20] The recently elected senator in Ohio, *Hillbilly Elegy* author, J. D. Vance, told an interviewer during the 2020 campaign that Democrats "have decided that they can't win unless they bring a large number of new voters to replace the voters that are already here."[21] Like Donald Trump, Tucker Carlson, and most right-wing officials and media personalities, he referred to increased migration as an "immigrant invasion."

"Invasion" is a term of war. Any victim of aggression, from Poland in 1939 to Ukraine in 2022, recognizes there is no negotiation, compromise, or appeasement with an invading army. The only choices are to surrender to the aggressor's terms or fight. The insurrection of January 6 was one battle of historical importance in the ongoing war that estranged reactionaries have imposed upon politics and culture.

Anthony DiMaggio, a political scientist at Lehigh University, commissioned a set of survey questions with Harris polling examining the attitudes of the general public surrounding the storming of the Capitol. The study reveals that nearly half of the 1,200 Americans polled, 62 percent of whom were white, had sympathy for the insurrectionists, indicating agreement with the assertion that the mob had "legitimate concerns" regarding "election fraud." Sixty-two percent of those who believe that the "US should protect its European culture against those who would diminish it" articulated some level of support for the insurrection of January 6.

DiMaggio concludes, "January 6th, as a mass phenomenon, should be understood as fundamentally linked to white supremacy." The political scientist finds that belief in Great Replacement was widespread among the rioters, but cautions against siphoning them off as outliers from American culture. Susceptibility to white supremacy features throughout the United States—polling data, with questions similar to those DiMaggio presented his participants, demonstrates that tens of millions of Americans at least flirt with ideologies of hate and hierarchical exclusion.[22] Most of the men who believe in Great Replacement Theory are heavily armed as well as hopped up on the hallucinogenic narcotic of rage. They carve out time every day to indulge their addiction, pumping the drug into their veins from Fox News, deranged YouTube rant machines, and "alternative media" hosts like Alex Jones. University of Chicago specialist on terrorism Robert Pape learned through his extensive research that the most common characteristic of a January 6 insurrectionist was residency in exurbs that have recently experienced a spike in their non-white populations. Similarly, Arie Perliger, a criminologist and the author of *American Zealots: Inside Right-Wing Domestic Terrorism*, reports that spontaneous hate crimes occur with the greatest frequency in exurban communities with growing immigrant populations.[23]

Wrestling against the diversification of the United States and the increasingly liberal mores of younger generations is as likely to succeed as attempts to hasten down the wind. The "war" that the American zealots imagine has a predetermined outcome unless they can reverse the tidal sweep of history through violence, intimidation, and the steady construction of a legal apparatus, ranging from the Rittenhouse and Michigan Watchmen juries to a far-right Supreme Court, that will dilute democracy and concentrate white power, Christian nationalism, and minority rule. The most painful consequences are the human beings—the real-life "collateral damage"—that occupy the curvature in the arc as it waits to bend: the protesters that Rittenhouse killed and the Proud Boys target for beatings, the gay and transgender students under psychological assault in public schools, and the casualties of hate crimes across the country.

ALADDIN PITA PROVIDES CULTURE AND QUALITY IN an otherwise dank strip mall along Route 30 in Merrillville, Indiana. Since its opening in 2000, Aladdin Pita has served customers delicious Middle Eastern cuisine. At the building's entrance is a Mediterranean grocery store. Past the Turkish coffee and jars of hummus is the cash register and the entrance for the dining area, where traditional Arabic music fills the air along with the scent of strong spices. The restaurant offers a satisfying meal, whether the patron desires a falafel plate or a hearty serving of kallaya, a stew of beef, chicken, or lamb sautéed with tomato, garlic, onion, and green pepper and served over a bed of basmati rice. The founder of Aladdin Pita, Naseeb Mohammed, immigrated to the United States from Palestine in 1967 after the Israeli invasion. Beginning as a busboy, he eventually opened a string of conventional diners and built a home for his family in Munster. His ultimate dream came to fruition when he opened Aladdin Pita and, in fulfillment of his highest professional ambition, introduced Middle Eastern cuisine to Northwest Indiana. Mohammed's trajectory from impoverished immigrant with English language difficulties and without marketable credentials to successful entrepreneur and father of five typifies the inspirational essence of what previous generations summarized with the phrase "American dream."

Mohammed's family wished they were dreaming on September 9, 2006. They entered Aladdin Pita to find their father murdered. He was shot dead—a mysterious as well as mournful development given that he had no enemies, and the killer, or killers, neglected to remove the cash from on his desk or steal the portable safe within clear view of the corpse. A small amount of money was missing from the register. The night before the murder a mosque in Merrillville hosted a memorial for the five-year anniversary of the 9/11 terrorist attacks. Local members of law enforcement, including Indiana FBI field agents, attended the ceremony. A sizable minority of Lake County residents expressed outrage. Without the ability to make intelligent distinctions, they viewed not Islamic terrorism, or even extremism, as the problem, but Islam itself. Any practicing Muslim, according to the familiar refrain on Fox News and right-wing radio, was a potential terrorist. At a minimum, he was a supporter of violent plots against the United States and its allies.

The police have not solved Mohammed's murder. They've entertained theories that it was a robbery gone wrong and have also investigated the more probable explanation of a hate crime. Regardless of their motive, the murderers remain at large. One of Mohammed's sons recalls two white men in a van outside the restaurant while police processed the crime scene. They were videotaping the events and laughing.[24]

Hate crimes have steadily increased throughout the United States since 2015. One study showed that whenever Donald Trump held a rally, hate crimes immediately multiplied in the hosting county.[25] As anti-Semitism rises so do assaults against Jews. Blacks and Latinos remain favorite targets of fascist fanatics, and in a period of escalating homophobia, gay and transgender Americans are facing greater dangers. During the worst months of the COVID-19 pandemic, streetside attacks on Asians became alarmingly common.

Northwest Indiana and the Chicago suburbs are not immune to the worsening trend of violence and terror. In recent years, hate crimes have increased with incidents ranging from the shouting of racial epithets at children to gang assaults. Indiana is one of four states that have failed to pass a comprehensive hate crime law. In 2019, the state government made modest progress by adopting policy that "allows" judges to consider sentences of greater severity for crimes with a "bias motive." The Anti-Defamation League, the Brennan Center for Justice, and the Movement Advancement Project, a think tank focusing on efforts aimed at equality at the local and state levels, have independently concluded that the sentencing provision falls far short of the criterion necessary for it to qualify as a hate crime law.

While Indiana is in slim and shameful company, its refusal to adopt sufficient hate crime legislation as law is not contradictory of a persistent American attitude. Christian Picciolini, the former neo-Nazi leader turned anti-racist advocate and extremist disengagement specialist, has repeatedly discussed that when he lectures to police departments, the officers often appear bored, preferring to talk about Muslims, Black Lives Matter, and Antifa instead of white racists. In 2009, Daryl Johnson, an intelligence analyst with the Department of Homeland Security, warned that white supremacists and right-wing radicals constituted the greatest national security threat. He also implored the Department of Defense to pay closer attention to the extremists within the ranks of the military who, like Timothy McVeigh, could use their expert training to declare war on the American people. For his trouble, the Obama administration suppressed and denounced his report. The American Legion led a hysterical campaign, amplified by the right-wing media, to act as if Johnson had smeared every military enlistee and officer as a Klansmen. The first Black president, fearful of attracting the enmity of white voters early in his presidency, retreated from a fight he knew was important, and which would become more important during the term of his successor when hate crimes continued to rise.

Ten years after Johnson's termination, he lamented that the crisis was getting worse, the hate movement was "mushrooming," and the political response wasn't even approaching adequate. Mass shooters who kill according to a reactionary ideology of hate are rarely called "terrorists," and reports indicate that the FBI and local law enforcement agencies refuse to invest sufficient resources into combatting right-wing extremism. Meanwhile, the Republican Party has all but celebrated militias, armed organizations, and even hate groups, like the Proud Boys. No New York or California liberal should feel smug when considering Indiana's inability to progress alongside modern society. While it is a crime to give "material aid" to a foreign terrorist organization, there is no comparable law targeting supporters of domestic terrorism. Committing a violent crime in the name of ISIS receives greater punishment than violent acts in accordance with white supremacy. The absence of a domestic terrorism law, and the resources it could marshal, is one reason why the Ku Klux Klan enjoyed a free reign of terror from the era of Reconstruction to the height of the civil rights movement. Leaders of the Oath Keepers, Three Percenters, and Proud Boys colluded in acts of sedition, violence, and insurrection on January 6, but even after their convictions, the FBI and police departments lack the legal means to treat their members as suspects providing "material aid" to terrorism.

Javed Ali, the national security expert mentioned earlier, believes it is unlikely that the United States will suffer through another attack on the scale of the January 6 insurrection in the near future. He still cautions that smaller acts of terror—like the one the FBI disrupted when Governor Whitmer was the target, mass shootings against political targets, and hate crimes—will happen with greater frequency and severity before the movements that encourage them begin to suffocate under their own weight.

As suburbia gains greater racial, cultural, and ideological diversity, the beleaguered and estranged reactionaries who once viewed it as a refuge will retreat further into the exurbs, exercising politics that enhance radical and dangerous partisanship and rancor. The suburbs of Atlanta, Las Vegas, and Phoenix helped deliver the 2020 election to Democrats. Demographic data indicate the pattern will only progress in future political cycles, especially given that the predominantly white suburbs of Philadelphia, Milwaukee, and other cities in swing states are growing grayer. As younger professionals and college graduates make homes in suburban counties, they will import liberalism into their districts. Meanwhile, the reactionary and authoritarian right will continue its metamorphosis into an insurgency. In exurban and rural districts, the insurgency will elect representatives and senators like those who attempted to serve the interests of the insurrection by preventing the inauguration of President Joe Biden—insurgents who reject the premise of constitutional democracy and despise the secular and multicultural electorate that it represents.

The insurgency has an entire institutional apparatus, propaganda system, and communication network to strengthen and solidify its presence and influence. While it will continue to lose at the polls and further alienate itself from younger, more secular, more educated, and more multiracial voters, its desperation could spell even greater societal trouble. Liberals, moderates, and even apolitical Americans might come to view certain towns or even counties as off-limits for political activity or even seemingly mundane events, like Juneteenth celebrations or "drag queen story hour" at the local library, as too risky to attend. The more violent that the minority insurgency becomes, enlarging its already established tendency to commit mass shootings, hate crimes, and brandish weapons at protest rallies and inside capitol buildings, the less safe the country will feel. A much deeper and more malevolent "cancel culture" will continue to threaten free speech as many would-be demonstrators will succumb to intimidation, electing to stay home from the march. When the Proud Boys announced plans to protest a drag queen story hour at a library in Columbus, Ohio, a coalition of LGBTQ organizations cosigned a statement urging gay and transgender Ohioans and their allies to refrain from counterprotest. "The situation is potentially dangerous and volatile," the statement warned.[26]

In Crown Point, Indiana, and many other small towns across the United States, marauders with assault rifles, shotguns, and handguns formed perimeters around Black Lives Matter protest march routes in 2020. Like Kyle Rittenhouse, they claimed that they were there to protect private and public property. The gun laws of the United States, particularly in lenient states like Indiana, and the paranoid conspiracy mentality of the far right have transformed nearly every event of political participation into a tinderbox.

At a Turning Point USA gathering in Idaho, an audience member asked Charlie Kirk, "When can we use the guns? How many elections are they going to steal before we kill these people?" Kirk advised the lunatic, who could likely win a congressional seat on a Republican ticket, that violence is "wrong." Revealingly enough, Kirk didn't cite moral reasons to support his condemnation of assassinating political opponents. Instead, he cautioned that it would "play into all their plans."[27] What happens if leaders like Kirk change their minds? What happens if couch commando fascists like the audience member no longer seek guidance but begin to act on their own accord? Perhaps Donald Trump gave an answer during the 2016 campaign when he offered speculation about Hillary Clinton's presidency: "If she gets to pick her judges, nothing you can do, folks. Although the Second Amendment people, maybe there is."

The most terrifying but urgent question is one that undoubtedly stayed on the minds of the Black Lives Matter protesters in Crown Point. Other than the obvious human suffering, no one is quite sure of the answer as it pertains to the future of American politics and culture. What happens if they start to shoot?

NOWHERE, USA

One of the most fascinating and exciting intersections in Chicago is the meeting ground of Lawrence and Broadway. At the heart of the Uptown neighborhood, not far from the former home of the late Studs Terkel, is a stoplight surrounded by streetlamps illuminating an Ethiopian restaurant, a taco stand, a French-themed night club, and one of the oldest jazz clubs in the country, the elegant and noirish Green Mill. Visible from the same intersection is the legendary Riviera Theatre, where bands like Gov't Mule and Snarky Puppy conquer the stage. When music fans empty out of the 2,500-seat theater, they can enjoy libations at the adjacent Uptown Lounge, open until four o'clock in the morning. Lawrence and Broadway dazzles locals and tourists with a moving, singing, and transacting tribute to music, the entrepreneurial spirit, and, most of all, social liberalism. Ethiopian immigrants, Mexican Americans, late-night drinkers of all colors and preferences, and jazz afficionados dine, imbibe, dance, and conduct business without descending into any petty wars of tribalism, religion, or ethnic bias. For all of the stories of crime, poverty, and racism that often dominate headlines, and weigh heavily on the minds of voters, in big cities, there is still the borderline miraculous achievement of what Adam Gopnik calls "the liberal idea of community."[1] The liberal community rests not on the conservative foundation of "blood ties and traditional authority" but on the execution and aspiration of "shared choices" informed by a "sense of sympathy."

During a break in a Saturday night performance by Sabretooth, a magnificent Chicago jazz band, I stepped outside the Green Mill into the wee small hours of the morning. A gay Black man smoking a cigarette pontificated at length on the skill and soul of Pat Mallinger, Sabretooth's saxophone player, and a blonde woman and Indian man flirted against the wall the way young lovers do. It was two in the morning, and even the nearby diner had closed. Luckily, a man with a heavy accent and cowboy hat pushed a cart full of tamales next to us. I selected pork and chicken before heading back inside for the final set. That scene under the sparkling emerald sign advertising the Green Mill might not seem profound, but it is pedestrian only because the steady victories of liberalism have made it possible and endlessly replicable.

The suburbs formed for reasons laudable, detestable, mundane, and scandalous. Families wanted more room, elderly people hoped to find life at a quieter and slower pace, and some people merely prefer sleepier surroundings. Political scandal and historic trauma are the dark side of suburban development; a set of policies enforcing the desire to maintain authority and establish borders of exclusion. The leaders who enacted those policies, and the home buyers who affirmed them, were rejecting and leaving the liberal community. It is exactly an intersection like Lawrence and Broadway that they hoped to avoid. While it is difficult to find a spot as eclectic in suburbia, the victories of liberalism made its march impossible to deter. There is no panacea to various forms of hatred, but the revolutionary triumphs of the civil rights movement enabled Black, Latino, and Asian people to find greater opportunities for freedom, prosperity, and communal participation in cities and small towns alike. Feminist reformation of legal, economic, and educational institutions, and the cultural changes that occurred as by-product, forever altered the idea and interests of "suburban women" and "soccer moms," and the gay rights movement conquered territory for residency and liberty outside of major metro areas and into the suburbs that surround them. When Highland, Indiana, has an LGBTQ Pride festival, various suburbs throughout the Chicagoland area celebrate Juneteenth, and coffeehouses like Sip are more vibrant than the average church, it becomes clear that "liberal community" is ascendant. Escape might seem impossible, but the vast scale of the United States always keeps the option open, and the conservatives and reactionaries with the greatest desire to flee have enough money to buy a ticket.

According to *The Wall Street Journal*, the median household income in the US exurbs in 2019 was $74,573—10 percent higher than the median household income for the entire country. The yawn is expected to widen, due to what the real estate industry calls "the great reshuffling." In 2020, white-collar professionals began to leave cities and suburbs in large numbers and relocate in the exurbs. The great reshuffling is the exodus of middle-class and upper-class wealth from the metros into more detached and distant communities.[2] Some experts are predicting that exurbia will experience a "boom" similar to what transpired in 1950s suburbia. Like the suburbs in the middle of the twentieth century, exurbia will become richer and denser. The great reshuffling will not only apply to real estate trends and taxable wealth but also politics. Exurbia will soon become a battleground between the young professionals who have flocked there for newer houses and the old guard that elected the authoritarian cultists of Republican Congress. If escape is no longer possible, the political and cultural fight will only intensify. Maniacs screaming "unmask our children" while threatening school board members at the height of a deadly pandemic and religious bigots insisting on the removal of novels with gay protagonists from library shelves act as a preview of the collision between liberal community and fight-or-flight politics of authority. The means already in place to preserve the isolation of exurbia also demonstrate the sociopolitical priorities of its inhabitants.

Driving from Chicago, through the immediate suburbs, and into the exurbs, a commuter will notice that traffic becomes much lighter. The roadway sparsity is for reasons obvious and more subtle. Fewer people and less activity produces lighter traffic, but anyone making the trek through Northwest Indiana will observe that the farther south and/or west they drive, the fewer buses they will see. Typically, the only bus in sight is yellow and full of children. Drivers in a hurry will also feel free from the anxiety of getting caught by a train. The Metra line transports workers and visitors from Chicago into the Illinois south suburbs, and the South Shore crosses the border into Indiana, but the furthest south that it goes is East Chicago, Indiana—a mere twenty-three miles from the Loop, and only ten miles from South Side neighborhoods. The city of Gary operates its own public transit bus service, with routes making stops at schools, hospitals, VA clinics, government buildings, and popular recreation venues. No bus ventures into exurbia. The routes into wealthier suburbs are less frequent than those running through Gary proper and its immediate surroundings.

The university where I teach—Indiana University Northwest—is located in Gary, and I regularly have students miss class, or have to rearrange their entire semester schedule, after coursework has already begun because their automobiles need costly repairs. Without a reliable public transportation system, they operate in isolation without communal assistance. The hardship grows more onerous, and the damages enlarge from the personal to the familial and, finally, to the social, when workers lose employment, parents lose access to day care, and students cannot complete their academic programs.

My students do not struggle alone. One Region, a nonprofit organization dedicated to "increasing household income" in Northwest Indiana, reports that the ragtag jumble of public transit in the area is "fragmented, underfunded, and underutilized."[3] Disabled rights advocate Raymond Fletcher, a former Hoosier who moved to Las Vegas, was more blunt and colorful at a 2018 town hall meeting devoted to discussion of public transportation. After explaining that it is easy for him to find bus routes to take him anywhere he desires to go in Vegas, he said, "When I come home to Northwest Indiana, it's like I'm back in the 1800s."[4] The ostensible purpose of the meeting was to give Democratic officials ammunition to advocate for increased funding for public transit from a Republican state government that exercises a religious devotion to the reduction of social services. Democratic mayors, Democrats on city councils, organizations committed to helping the poor, and the chancellors of local universities regularly argue for the establishment of one comprehensive regional bus network. Neglect of public transit amounts to a socioeconomic assault that will only worsen as residents, taxable wealth, and commercial opportunity move into exurbia. For the poor, the last bus route or train stop will act as an iron wall, prohibiting not only the movement but also the pursuit of employment for anyone without a private vehicle.

Among progressive intellectuals and activists, there is often justifiable condemnation of food deserts—areas without a grocery store selling nutritional food within a ten-mile radius—and bank deserts—a neighborhood lacking a bank within ten miles. There is far less conversation about what sociologists refer to as "transportation apartheid." The severe stratification of transportational resources according to class and race restricts the freedom and capital of mobility to those who can afford their own private means of travel. As the sociologists who coauthored *Sprawl City* contend, the struggle for universal public transit access is inseparable from the mission to establish and preserve "civil rights and human rights" in accordance with the charter of participatory democracy.[5]

"America has become a suburban nation," the authors explain. "As jobs and opportunity migrate to the distant suburbs, where public transit is inadequate or nonexistent, persons without cars are literally left by the side of the road." The beleaguered job seekers thumbing for rides stand alongside other citizens who suffer civic and economic exclusion either because they lack an automobile or lack the ability to operate a motor vehicle. Adults with physical and/or developmental disabilities that prevent them from driving rely on the favors of family or public transportation to get anywhere—work, school, day programs, the movies, parties. If a region is a public transit desert, like the exurbs of Northwest Indiana, it imprisons its disabled residents within its confines and effectively bars the disabled who live elsewhere.

As a state senator, Frank Mrvan, a Democratic businessman who was later elected to Congress, championed the creation of a "dial-a-ride" program for the poor, infirm, and disabled. The service allows residents in need to call a toll-free number to request a bus ride. While Mrvan's creation is admirable and laudable, the dial-a-ride program has its own disability—severely insufficient funding, which leads to a shortage of vehicles and drivers. Adults with disabilities routinely report waiting thirty minutes to even hours past the requested pickup time for a ride. Excessive tardiness is not only inconvenient, but intolerable if one is trying to get to work or class. Many of the adults with physical or developmental disabilities were born with their debilitating conditions; others develop chronic illnesses or disabilities as they age. In exurbia and within suburban sprawl, if a senior loses her ability to drive, she typically loses her independence. Now reliant on relatives or friends to take her to the grocery store, church, or the beauty salon, she no longer enjoys unrestricted or improvisational freedom of movement.

Public transit deserts inflict the psychic damage of attaching identity to a driver's license. Northwest Indiana is far from alone in creating the sociology of public transportation apartheid. The three authors of *Sprawl City* made the suburbs and exurbs surrounding Atlanta, Georgia, their case study. Scholars and activists at the Urban Information Lab at the University of Texas at Austin have found that the worst transit deserts, where up to one out of every eight residents lives in an area without an alternative to driving, are cities as far apart as Orlando, Florida; Colorado Springs, Colorado; and St. Louis, Missouri. The Urban Information Lab has also found that even in cities like San Francisco, where the municipal government robustly funds public transit, there is the equivalent of a transit desert, because the system cannot meet the rapidly growing needs of the people.[6] As the cost of housing becomes prohibitive in San Francisco, Portland, and similar cities, an increasing number of poor and blue-collar workers are commuting into the city from more affordable suburbs. The buses and trains that are available cannot keep up with increasing demand. While inadequate options for public transportation in major cities is an economic, social, and civic problem, the transportation apartheid in exurbia takes on an entirely different characteristic. It generates a dead zone.

The geography and culture of exurbia coalesce to conceive an everywhere and anywhere aesthetic, commerce, and politics. The typical exurb is often "Nowhere, USA." Transportation apartheid keeps exurbia physically remote and also minimizes sight of or interaction with those most in need of the minority rights, representation, and services that democracy is supposed to provide—the poor, the disabled, and the infirm. The culture and commerce that dominates exurbia maintains a "nowhere" quality by emptying out anything that generates a unique identity. Big-box retailers dominate the topography and economy of exurbia largely out of necessity. As their nickname would suggest, Walmart and Costco, are too architecturally large to open in crowded city neighborhoods with only small storefronts available to lease. Mayors, city councilmen and women, and, most significantly, residents of New York's Brooklyn or Chicago's Lincoln Park would grow apoplectic if they learned that the Walton family planned to take a wrecking ball to an entire city block and erect a big-box edifice in its place.

The small shops of the "mom-and-pop" variety, whether they are selling clothes or kitchen supplies, struggle to compete against a corporate giant committed to slashing prices in order to expand its costumer base. As many reports show, exurban wealth is on the rise, but in surrounding rural areas, and small towns dealing with privation since the 2008 Great Recession, another retailer has emerged as ubiquitous: dollar stores. Under the monikers of Dollar Tree, Dollar General, and Family Dollar, there are over thirty-seven thousand dollar stores throughout the United States, many of them located in what one geographer calls the "dollar store belt"—"running from Ohio and Indiana in the north, via Kentucky and Tennessee, to the Gulf Coast."[7] TODT, an artist collective in Cincinnati, Ohio, found creative inspiration in the dollar store belt. Their 2011 exhibit, *Exurbia*, used "dollar store waste" as part of its installations. As real as the waste in TODT's artistry is the economic refuse in small communities. In Haven, Kansas—an exurb between Wichita and Hutchinson—an independent grocer lamented that his business survived only "three years and three days" after a dollar store opened in a neighboring town. "Sales dropped and just kept dropping," he explained.[8]

The same reverberation of destruction—although not as extreme—happens with restaurants in distant suburban and exurban towns. The charming neighborhood diner or bar has to fight for every consumer dollar against corporate chains like Applebee's and Chili's that can afford to seduce families with "buy one, get one free" and "half off burger" specials. Recent numbers outline a grim story for aspiring restaurateurs: From 2010 to 2013, 7,158 independent restaurants closed in the United States. During the same period, chain restaurants opened 4,511 more franchises.[9] The COVID pandemic only worsened the disparity, and there are now over three hundred thousand chain restaurant locations in the country. An observant patron of these chains, especially TGI Fridays, Applebee's, and Chili's, will recognize a familiar aesthetic.

Corporate restaurants rely on recreating a flat, uniform version of neighborhood warmth. Adding insult to injury, the full name of the most ubiquitous chain in the Midwest is "Applebee's Neighborhood Grill and Bar." Applebee's is as much of a neighborhood hangout as the casino is a part of the local economy. Most of the profits go to corporate headquarters, and unlike the neighborhood bar with an owner who lives on your block and attends your high school reunion, Applebee's operates under the authority of characters as loathsome as former executive director of operations Wayne Pankratz, who celebrated high gas prices and inflation in 2022, because according to his sinister logic, the rising cost of living would "force workers to accept jobs with low pay."[10]

In 1984, singer/songwriter Don Henley released a jazzy synth-pop song, "Sunset Grill." On his second solo album, the lead singer of the Eagles drew on the inspiration of his favorite burger joint in Los Angeles. Joe Froelich opened the tiny outdoor eatery and beer stand after immigrating to California from Vienna. The burgers were dripping with Velveeta cheese and, according to Henley, the best in the city. The song's urban bop feels like it is facing a corporate invasion as the synthesizer grows louder and more ominous. Henley's blues-inflected vocal eventually paints a dark comparison with the Sunset Grill's competition: "These days the man makes you something / And you never see his face." At a 2004 concert, during his spoken introduction to "Sunset Grill," Henley warned fans against dining at the current California edifice that bears its name. Because of its corporate ownership, Henley explained that it's "not the same Joe, not the same burger, not the same beer, and definitely not the same place."

The farther one drives out past the suburbs, a more dramatic cultural and commercial transformation takes place. Joe Froelich and Don Henley's "Sunset Grill" vanishes, and in its place is Son Volt's "Exurbia." In 2018, Jay Farrar, songwriter and lead singer for the alt-country band, wrote about the surroundings outside his hometown of Belleville,

Illinois—a small town not far from his current place of residence, St. Louis. Farrar sings plaintively of exurbia as a"nightmare dream." As tearful guitar notes ring like a bell, he describes the exurban pattern of life as "Just work, car, interstate and house." One of the most striking lines of "Sunset Grill" is when Henley sings, with raspy delivery, "There is no hiding place / Down at the Sunset Grill." Farrar's "Exurbia" is nothing but a hiding place. The two songs, even with their musical arrangements—the jazz and pop bombast of "Sunset Grill," the sparse Americana of "Exurbia"—act as an inadvertent conversation between two opposed aesthetics, communal projects and attendant sets of politics.

Without walkable downtowns, large public parks, small businesses, and hospitable neighborhoods, exurban towns become epicenters of individualism, typifying the isolation that Robert Putnam described in *Bowling Alone* as "divorced from community, occupation, and association." Lonely individuals who, as Farrar would suggest, move alone from the car to the office to the house will have few opportunities to contemplate and experience what literary scholar Ed Folsom, in his interpretation of Walt Whitman's poetry calls, "urban affection." "Whitman feels the power of the city of strangers," Folsom explains. "He's looking at a city of strangers and how something we might now call 'urban affection' begins to develop. How do you come to care for people that you have never seen before and that you may never see again?"[11]

Urban affection can electrify the sociology of not only Whitman's Brooklyn but Mellencamp's Seymour or my Highland. It is present anywhere that people leave their homes and assemble, interact, and even argue. People starved of urban affection are, Putnam warns, "first and foremost among the supporters of extremism." He also cautions that "social dislocation breeds reactionary nostalgia." Nowhere, USA, has and forever will become the breeding ground for constituents who vote, donate, march, and threaten to create Never, USA—an imaginative construct of an America that never truly existed.

*

POLITICAL RESEARCHERS MADE AN ODD DISCOVERY
during Donald Trump's term in office. "The foodscape is political,"
Xiaofan Liang, a PhD candidate at Georgia Tech's School of City and
Regional Planning, offered as a summary of her recent scholarship with
Georgia Tech professor Clio Andris. "Places with a high percentage of
Trump voters have a higher percentage of chain [restaurants]." In so-
called "Trump country"—the fifth of the United States where the former president and his neofascist brethren won at least 63 percent of the
vote in 2020, 37 percent of all restaurants were corporate franchises. In
the fifth of the country where Trump was least popular, earning below
32 percent of the vote, only 23 percent of restaurants were chains. *The
Washington Post* inspected the data in an attempt to extrapolate a clean
conclusion. After controlling for region—rural versus urban, suburban
versus exurban—they found that the pattern did not break. Suburbs
with a larger number of chain restaurants voted for Trump at greater
rates, and even rural precincts with fewer franchises voted for Biden in
higher percentages. The variables of population density and education
also failed to settle the question over why counties with the most chain
restaurants also support Trump with the most enthusiasm. Liang and
Andris confessed that they "did not expect" to find the correlation, and
refused to speculate. Their interlocutor, in his story for the *Post*, called
it a "compelling mystery."[12]

With acknowledgment that I have not closely studied the data,
and I am not an academic specialist, only a writer who has lived in
suburbia my entire life, and spent a good amount of time in the exurbs,
I offer a theory.

There are corporate chains that offer enjoyable dining experiences
and those that are best avoided, but what they all share is a customer
service approach of familiarity, stability to the extent of calcification,

and an antiseptic aesthetic. Applebee's, Chili's, and TGI Fridays attempt to replicate the neighborhood bar, but with such commitment to uniformity, routine, and bland delivery that the design team and executives have missed the ingredients most crucial to the charm, fun, and communal affection of the local watering hole—an organic personality, slightly unpredictable evening, and eccentric cast of characters. The corporate chain offers little variety, adopts a menu that will please the broadest range of customers, and provides the cold comfort of conformity—an Applebee's in Munster, Indiana, is exactly the same as an Applebee's in the border town of Weslaco, Texas. I've had many pleasurable meals at corporate franchises, and I don't look down on them with any snobbery. They certainly serve their purpose, and it is often a good one. It is still impossible to deny that they appeal to an unadventurous palette and conservative social comportment.

One of my and my wife, Sarah's, favorite restaurants is the Schererville Lounge. An actual neighborhood bar and grill under local ownership, for decades the Schererville Lounge has served delectable steaks, fish, barbecue ribs, and burgers and a wide variety of specials alongside a long list of liquors to patrons ranging from blue-collar workers nursing beers after a hard shift to professional couples celebrating their anniversary. When Sarah and I first visited the regional treasure, we quickly fell into a conversation with our waiter, who now greets us by name, and the bartender—a pretty and casually dressed young woman who is the picture of Midwestern affability. On some nights the lounge plays country music, other nights rock and roll, and occasionally no music at all. The conversation, company, and service are not always entirely the same, and because the Schererville Lounge is not a national brand, we aren't exactly sure what we are getting when we order a new item on the menu. In stark contrast, the corporate chain, whether outstanding or awful, will feature no surprises, while most of the food, even for newcomers, will have predictable flavor. I'm sure there are exceptions, but never in all my years of dining have I heard, seen, or personally experienced camaraderie with a corporate chain employee. A report about the nationally popular chain Texas Roadhouse found that servers, under threat of termination, had to adhere to a strict set of rules, including how to greet customers, what dishes to recommend, and even when to dance to the country music blaring on the internal speaker system.[13] The scripted protocol not only takes what might appear like a spontaneous moment of joy—dancing—and transforms it into a dull workplace requirement but negates any hope for authentic communication. How can two people connect when one is reciting canned corporate lines?

Disconnection, like the standardization of the menu and decor, is precisely what the corporate chain most effectively sells. Donald Trump, like the larger right-wing movement he represents, treats diversity as a threat, preaches paranoia as a religious edict, and, from rejection of masks at the height of a pandemic to celebration of murderous gun culture, advances an individualistic mindset that ignores, neglects, or outright damages public safety, any coherent notions of community, and the welfare of other human beings. Major corporations are opening more franchises in counties with large potential consumer bases. They leave very little to chance, especially when they heavily fund market research firms to determine where their success is likeliest to multiply. The suburbs and exurbs where chains proliferate are those with voters and consumers whose antisocial tendencies overlap in political choice and restaurant preference. The corporate chain attracts customers of all kinds, but those who seek their services out with enthusiasm most likely enjoy a highly sanitized environment, predictable interactions, and stock flavors. The loyal right-wing voter desires a stagnant America in which politics and pop culture remain fixed so as not to disturb a familiar hierarchy or disrupt comfortable standards of expression. Applebee's is the neighborhood bar for Nowhere, USA. Texas Roadhouse isn't Texan as much as it is Nowherean.

*

A QUIET AND YET INTOXICATING REVOLUTION HAS occurred in the past few decades of American life. In the 1970s, beer drinkers had little choice when perusing the selection at a local tavern. Rather than thinking according to flavor, they separated their preferences into two broad categories—domestic and import. Among the former were only a handful of similar lagers and ales with names instantly recognizable to anyone who has watched a football game: Budweiser, Miller, and Old Style. An absence of competition ensured that few beer brands could go national, and most regions had only a small number of competing breweries. Colorado had Coors, Michigan had Stroh's, and Texas had Shiner, but large swaths of US territory offered little beyond the big three national brews to, using an appellation of a ZZ Top song, "beer drinkers and hell-raisers." There was hardly a shortage of customers, and given the long list of defunct beers from the 1960s and '70s, undoubtedly a steady supply of ambitious entrepreneurs ready to push their hoppy product on the market. The impenetrable obstacle for most would-be brewers was excessive and prohibitive federal regulation. Home brewing was illegal, and the cost of compliance with governmental standards, levying exorbitant fees for equipment and inspection, rendered the entire industry inaccessible for the average businessperson. President Jimmy Carter considered the corporate, and, as a consequence, stagnant and exclusive, status of the beer industry outrageous, and in 1978 signed a bill legalizing home brewing. He also recommended that states revoke their laws forbidding "brewpubs," meaning a restaurant or bar with an alcoholic inventory of its own beverage products.

Beginning in 1982, states began acting on Carter's advice. The former president's deregulatory policy was significant, because 90 percent of craft brewers begin as home brewers. The stunning cultural and commercial transformation of domestic beer provides all the necessary vindication of Carter's 1979 decision. At the time of his signing the bill, there were ninety breweries in the United States. In 2022, there were 9,552 According to one study of the craft beer boom, craft breweries contribute upwards of $76.3 billion to the US economy on an annual basis and employ nearly half a million people.[14] Carter receives barely any acclamation for his innovative and liberatory policy. Republicans are loathe to treat any Democrat as if he is not a spawn of Satan, and because the GOP acts as if the word "regulation" is a witches' spell, liberals are reticent to champion a sterling example of deregulation. The least an enterprising brewer could do is pay homage to the Nobel Prize winner with a beer named "The Carter." It should have a cartoon depiction of the smiling president on the label. The closest I have seen to a beverage tribute is a framed photograph of Jimmy Carter behind the bar at Beer Geeks, a hole in the wall in Highland that exclusively serves regional craft beer.

As one could gather from the craft brewery statistics, Beer Geeks has a large variety of options when determining their bottled and draft lists. In Lake County, Indiana, alone, there are twelve craft breweries. When adding the breweries in neighboring Porter County and the nearby Chicago suburbs of Illinois, the number more than doubles. The craft brewery revolution has not only provided livelihoods for thousands of people. It has preserved and enhanced the vitality of local, artisan, and independent culture during a suburban and exurban epoch of corporate-sponsored homogeneity. As chain franchises populate, and often pollute, the commercial and cultural environment, the craft brew revolution has demonstrated that there is an unsatisfiable thirst (forgive the pun) for the small-scale, creative spirit that once generated unique identities for countless small towns. At Fuzzyline Brewing in Highland, patrons can enjoy a robust selection of fruit-infused beers while eating gourmet hot dogs. Byway Brewing in Hammond has a food menu with items named after literary icons, most delightfully the extra-spicy beef sandwich, Executioner's Song. It also has the best pale ale for hundreds of miles. In Munster, 3 Floyds hosts an annual festival to celebrate its annual release of Dark Lord—a beer so heavy that it makes Newcastle Brown look and taste like lemonade. Heavy metal bands, of course, perform ballistic hymns to praise the Dark Lord throughout the afternoon and evening.

Craft beer culture counters the conservatism that critics have long associated with suburbia, and that those exercising the politics of escape would prefer forever dictate life in the exurbs. David Faris, a political scientist at Chicago's Roosevelt University, notes that the politics of craft beer culture are "generally left leaning."[15] While there are certainly reactionaries in the craft beer sphere, the research Faris has conducted for his podcast, *Electing to Drink*, indicates that a sizable majority of microbrewers are progressive, many of them expressing their ideology through their craft. A significant number of breweries designed beers to protest the gruesome presidency of Donald Trump, while many others donate proceeds of certain beer sales to Planned Parenthood and organizations that advocate for the rights and inclusion of LGBTQ Americans. Hundreds of brewers have also articulated support for strengthening the Clean Water Act. In the early stages of the COVID-19 pandemic, several of the Northwest Indiana brewers used their equipment to produce bottles of hand sanitizer that they donated to local hospitals, schools, libraries, community centers, and religious institutions.

While political activism always carries a risk for business, consumer surveys show a strong correlation between liberal politics and preference for craft beer. The majority of Republican beer drinkers opt for familiar national brews. A frosty mug of beer cannot expiate the existence of public transportation deserts, nor can it soften the effects of right-wing policies that undermine small business, paralyze the poor, and assault the aspirations of workers. It can make a meal taste better, add to a night's pleasure, and give golden representation to the restless spirit of those yearning to breathe free. It can represent the boundless potential to transform Nowhere, USA, into the liberal community.

Samuel Adams, an American revolutionary and beer entrepreneur, said that the central question of the anti-colonial revolution was whether "there shall be left to mankind an asylum . . . for civil and religious liberty." And so it remains.

IGNORANCE IS HELL

My first writing job was for the *Herald-News* in Joliet, Illinois. One month after my graduation from the University of St. Francis, I walked into the newspaper offices with a folder full of clipped columns I wrote for the USF student paper, the *Encounter*. I had no appointment or history with the *Herald*, only the knowledge of the editor in chief's name. When I approached the receptionist, I did my best to disguise myself as a confident professional and requested to see Dave Monaghan. After waiting approximately twenty minutes, a figure out of central casting emerged: hair over his ears, slightly paunchy, a pack of Marlboro Lights in the chest pocket of his dress shirt alongside a pen, sleeves rolled up to his elbows. He sat down and asked what I needed. Before I could begin my rehearsed sales pitch, he recognized my name and told me that he enjoyed my political columns for the *Encounter*. Barely able to utter an expression of gratitude before he continued, he asked if I would like to write a weekly column to run every Thursday. The only caveat was that no matter my topic, I had to find a way to connect it to the town of Joliet. I shook his hand and returned to my car a newspaper columnist.

The compensation was a controversial $20 per week. The miserly sum courted controversy, because every other local columnist earned only $10 as weekly payment. When I let my rate slip to a fellow *Herald* writer, he insisted that he would "let the other guys know," and together they would cosign a complaint to Monaghan. My editor, Roy Bernard, was from Indianapolis, wore a Mike Ditka–style mustache, never ventured anywhere without a mug of coffee, and matter-of-factly gave minor editorial notes on each column. The only interference he ran with my choice of topics or delivery was to suggest "taking a break" from Jerry Weller, a corrupt, sleazy, and reactionary Republican congressman who I attempted to transform into my personal punching bag. After the publication of my series of columns on Weller, the *Chicago Reader* reported on several financial improprieties involving the congressman and his father-in-law, former Guatemalan dictator José Efraín Ríos Montt. He did not seek reelection.

Bernard allowed me to break the Joliet rule when I wrote a tribute to George Carlin after the comedian's death, but otherwise it was easy to make local associations with most issues of national consequence. Joliet is the third-largest city in Illinois with a population of just over 150,000 people. Most famous for its historic prison and as the setting of the original *Blues Brothers* film, it has an increasingly diverse and steadily blue-collar profile. Sections of its east side have more signs in Spanish than English, thanks to the entrepreneurial and creative spirit of a large influx of Mexican immigrants. The downtown surrounding the courthouse hasn't significantly changed, other than the construction and opening of a casino, since it inspired the opening scene of one of America's greatest films, *The Sting*.

Meanwhile, the far west side typifies modern suburbia stretching into exurbia: strip malls, townhome complexes, heavy traffic, and chain stores. Like many Rust Belt cities of its size, it never fully recovered from the slow erosion of its manufacturing base, even though it offers a few attractions to visitors and families in search of a home: the country's oldest community college, a Catholic university, a downtown concert theater that hosts performers like Jerry Seinfeld and Lyle Lovett, a minor league baseball team, and a NASCAR race track. While much of Joliet retains a 1970s aesthetic, its politics have undergone an evolution that captures much of the suburban story in the United States. In 2000 and 2004, George W. Bush won a majority of Joliet votes in the respective presidential elections of those years, and the congressional district in which it sits at the center decisively reelected its Republican representative. Beginning in 2008, Joliet's younger and growing Latino and Black populations began electing Democratic congressional representatives and giving the town's presidential advantage to Barack Obama, Hillary Clinton, and Joe Biden. The exurban towns neighboring Joliet, farther from Chicago, remain Republican strongholds.

My favorite part of Joliet is the Chicago St. Pub, a downtown Joliet business, social institution, and communal artery that injects life into an otherwise staid scene. The owners, Mike and Kathy Trizna, dedicate themselves to making their neighborhood Irish bar a "Third Place" home for the rowdy, rebellious, and warmhearted. They host talented regional musicians, including local favorites John Condron and Brent James, and emphasize the arts whenever possible. The friendships that form inside the walls of the Chicago St. Pub feel as inalterable as genetics. When Dean, an elderly bartender with a quick wit, died one Wednesday morning, I drove to Chicago St. Pub to raise a toast to a barroom ambassador whose presence, humor, and storytelling were always as fun as they were comforting. Expecting not to find many fellow day drinkers on a Wednesday afternoon, I reacted with shock and tears when I entered the doors to find that the bar was packed wall-to-wall with patrons. Everyone told their most cherished Dean story, while the jukebox kept screaming his favorite songs. John Condron, taking in the scene of mourning and solidarity, gave me a hug and said, "Isn't it amazing that everyone knew to come here?"

Political scientist Robert Putnam defined "social capital" as "connections among individuals—networks and the norms of reciprocity and trustworthiness that arise from them." In his modern classic, *Bowling Alone*, he explained exactly how important social capital is to the establishment and maintenance of democracy. The Chicago St. Pub is a bank vault of social capital. People of various ethnic backgrounds, religious beliefs, income strata, and political opinions enjoy fellowship at the pub. When one of them dies, they grieve together. When one of them falls ill, they offer support. When one of them has good news, they celebrate. Because it was so important to our romance, my wife and I had our wedding reception at the pub. A Third Place, as everyone from de Tocqueville, who wrote of the need for "voluntary associations," to Putnam would understand is an essential element of social cohesion, communal vitality, and political efficacy. Suburbs and small cities, like Joliet, often have a Third Place where like-minded, and even un-like-minded, residents can assemble for the shared purpose of pleasure and conversation. Chain restaurants, and changing social habits of Americans, place them in jeopardy. Even in large cities, such as Chicago and Philadelphia, reports indicate that the "corner bar" is quickly becoming a relic of nostalgia—more visible in Edward Hopper paintings and old television shows than on the city block. In exurbia, the Third Place barely exists. Its danger and decline places democracy in peril, especially when coupled with the disappearance of another critical source of democratic energy: the local newspaper.

One late evening, or perhaps by then it was early morning, I stood outside the Chicago St. Pub, having a conversation with friends, when a middle-aged woman with curly gray hair, librarian spectacles, and a rollicking volume of energy introduced herself. She recognized my headshot from the newspaper and told me how much she enjoyed reading commentary from the left in an otherwise "conservative" newspaper. Her name was Jodi, and we remain friends to this day. I had similar exchanges with an Arab American who managed a Joliet convenience store, a server in Al's Steak House (a fine Joliet establishment), and a passerby outside a coffeeshop. I also received a steady stream of hate mail—the most memorable of which was from a gentleman with the signature "Not a Good Fan of Yours." He informed me that I knew nothing about politics. In fact, I "don't even know why I am alive." He advised me to quit writing for the newspaper and, instead, sell candy on the streets.

The *Herald-News* had a purpose and presence in Joliet. "Not a Good Fan" thought my contribution damaged its legacy, while Jodi believed I enhanced it. The newspaper began informing residents of important developments in 1877, issuing reports on everything from the next mayoral race to high school sports. Former reporter Ted Slowik wrote a series of articles exposing a previous bishop of the Joliet diocese as culpable and complacent in the face of widespread and credible pedophilia accusations against several diocesan priests. The investigate journalism provoked an intellectual and spiritual earthquake in the predominantly Catholic town. I was proud to send a weekly missive, via the *Herald*, to Joliet's townspeople, and I found joy and gratification in meeting the challenge of attracting the attention of not only leftists, like Jodi, but also right-wingers like "Not a Good Fan," and everyone in between who, no matter their ideological divergence, shared the same community.

I did not resign from my columnist post to pursue a lucrative career as a candy salesman, but instead I received an apologetic and sympathetic phone call from Roy Bernard a little over a year into my stint. He explained that due to budgetary constraints, the *Herald* staff made the "difficult decision" to eliminate local columnists and reduce its opinion section to a single page of syndicated writers. The $10 writers and I were the first brick to slip in a wall that was already crumbling down. Since my departure in 2009, the paper has diminished to the size of a hospital brochure. Containing more advertisements than articles, it has continually reduced its politics, business, and sports sections. My friend, Brent, refers to it as the "Hardly News." The *Hardly News* has fared better than most of its peers by its mere survival.

From 2004 to 2018, 1,800 newspapers, representing, at the time, a fifth of all American papers, ceased printing.[1] In the three years that followed, 360 newspapers closed their offices and ended production.[2] Many of the papers that remain, especially in midsize cities and small towns, resemble the *Herald*—barely enough reportage to qualify for the term of its medium, and under the ownership of a large, faceless corporate entity that exercises its authority without much concern for the local population. Shaw Media can currently count the *Herald* among its holdings of eighty newspapers and websites. The same company owns eight Illinois radio stations. Similar to the corporate raiding strategy in manufacturing, what former steel worker and labor organizer Terry Steagall called "strip-mining of companies," the media conglomerates that purchase newspapers maximize short-term profit by cutting staff and expenses while increasing prices for advertisers and subscribers. Fully expecting the paper to close within years, they adopt a "short-term gain, long-term death" business model, giving yet another real-life illustration of *Wall Street* villain Gordon Gekko's flippant answer to why he decided to wreck a small airline: "Because it's wreckable."

Not even a storied newspaper of a major city is safe from demolition. When Alden Global Capital acquired Tribune Publishing, the umbrella company for the *Chicago Tribune*, the *New York Daily News*, the *Orlando Sentinel*, and other publications, the injection of poison into the newsroom was swift and severe. In Chicago, several veteran journalists and opinion columnists accepted buyouts. Younger writers did not fare as well. They were either laid off or forced into accepting roles of greater work for inferior compensation. The *Chicago Tribune* never achieved national influence alongside *The New York Times* or *Washington Post*, but it did compete at that level, providing the important service of a Midwestern, "Third City" perspective on national developments and debates. Coverage of the federal government in the *Chicago Tribune* now derives from the wire services. Brian Hieggelke, a mainstay of Chicago journalism who currently edits the digital version of an alternative monthly, *Newcity*, wrote that the destruction of the *Chicago Tribune* offers a particularly grim sketch of how "all media are alternative." Plaintively, he adds, "But there's nothing left to be alternative to. The center is gone."[3]

When the center was under occupation from a handful of daily newspapers, three or four large-circulation magazines, and a few television networks, there were certainly problems. One does not need the expertise of Noam Chomsky and Edward S. Herman, coauthors of *Manufacturing Consent: The Political Economy of the Mass Media*, to understand that the mainstream press often excluded anti-war and anti-corporate stories from its pages, reduced the range of acceptable political opinion to a narrow center-right versus center-left spectrum, and, in previous decades, mirrored the racism, sexism, and homophobia of the broader culture. It isn't exactly ancient history when most media outlets reacted to the HIV/AIDS epidemic with indifference or hysterical ridicule of gay men. It is even more recent that the editors of *The New York Times* and *Washington Post* publicly apologized for not adopting a more skeptical approach toward covering the Bush administration's justifications for preemptive war in Iraq. The center was in desperate need of improvement and enlargement, but not vanquishment.

A journalistic ecology without a strong nucleus creates the fragmentation that has already proven so devastating to knowledge and consensus during the crises of the COVID-19 pandemic and Donald Trump's attempt to subvert the democratic system with bogus allegations of voter fraud. It also struggles to prevent toxic substances and bacteria from infecting public consciousness. While the new media system has allowed insightful analysts to amass large public followings, like historian Heather Cox Richardson, who gained notoriety on Facebook, and

Rachel Bitecofer, a political scientist who attracted a sizable audience on Twitter, it also enables deranged conspiracy theorists, white suprema- cists, and brazen misogynists to acquire followers on the scale of major publications that, for all their flaws, at least attempt to adhere to basic journalistic standards of honesty and decency.

Americans no longer share a culture, a prevailing sense of truth, his- tory, and identity, or a political framework for reacting to critical events. The compromise, mutual respect, and trust necessary to maintain life in a free society have suffered steady erosion. As Hieggelke concludes, "The weaker our journalistic institutions become, and the greater the diversity of news providers, the more likely we'll find that we have nothing in common anymore. And that is dangerous for democracy."

The absence of a local newspaper, along with other institutions of journalism, allows local and regional power brokers to get away with murder, perhaps even literally, and removes a crucial instrument of citizenry control on elected leadership and boardroom executives. Without a small-town paper, residents are unlikely to learn the truth of nearby political maneuvering, and unless they routinely attend town council meetings or mayoral sessions, they will not understand the stakes of seemingly mundane governmental procedure. It is impossible to imagine, barring some catastrophic incident, *The New York Times* or *The Wall Street Journal* sending a reporter to Highland, Indiana, or Lansing, Illinois, to report on change in public policy. Beyond the check and balance of otherwise unaccountable operators of political or economic power, the local newspaper can function as a surveyor of common ground. In the words of the authors of a Medill School of Journalism study on the importance of local newspapers, the publica- tions can contribute to the establishment and maintenance of a "shared agenda."[4] The announcements of local births and deaths, the report on the high school football game, and the profiles of neighbors involved in interesting or charitable enterprises spotlight the community and, in so doing, inculcate a sense of community. Allowing a culture to descend into perpetual anonymity where neighbors are strangers, and the activities of one's hometown are unknown or mysterious, enables stereotyping, heightened partisan hostility, and personal isolation.

Where local newspapers are not actively dying, they are often losing their readership. According to one survey, only 23 percent of Americans read a daily newspaper (print or online), and nearly 60 percent do not read beyond the headlines.[5] A disproportionate amount of readers are elderly. Gore Vidal once quipped, "Fifty percent of people won't vote, and fifty percent don't read newspapers. I hope it's the same fifty percent . . ." His sardonic wish resounded long after its utterance in the midterm elections of 2022. George Santos, a Republican elected to Congress to represent a traditionally Democratic district in Queens/Long Island, is a character out of a film that Christopher Guest and Oliver Stone might collaborate to create. He lied about nearly everything on the campaign trail—his employment history, his academic record, his ethnicity, his sexuality, and even the death of his mother, falsely claiming that she was a victim of the 9/11 attack. When national media outlets began to expose his series of fabrications and falsehoods, it was too late. He had already won the election. Observers wondered with alarm, "How could this happen?"

The publisher and staff of the Long Island newspaper *The North Shore Leader* had no reason for surprise, but plenty of justification for anger. The paper reported on the various lies, half-truths, and financial improprieties of Santos long before anyone cast a vote in his favor. No one in the Democratic Party or the national press paid any attention, and, evidently, too few voters read the unflattering stories to make a difference. The publisher of the newspaper speculated that Santos made a bet that "no one would check" the veracity of his outlandish claims.[6] He initially won the bet, and prepared to collect winnings in the amount of $348,000 taxpayer dollars (the annual salary for a congressional representative is $174,000, and he was elected to a two-year term).

The region of Northwest Indiana features three newspapers—the *Northwest Indiana Times*, the *Post-Tribune*, formerly the *Gary Post-Tribune* until its namesake office closed in 2009, and the *Chesterton Tribune*. The *Northwest Indiana Times* is the most traditional and robust paper of the three. Its reporters are often insightful, and its pages cover stories ranging from local environmental issues to business developments. The *Gary Post-Tribune* was once a fine paper, but since its renaming in 2009, has continually made cuts similar to the Joliet *Herald-News*. The *Chesterton Tribune*, covering the small town of Chesterton and the surrounding exurbs, typically runs no more than fifteen pages, half of which are advertisements and classifieds. A local "news" website, *Valpo.Life*, is a reliable source to learn about activities and personalities local to Valparaiso, but there is relatively no hard news or journalism. State after state—from Massachusetts to Minnesota—has announced in recent years the death and/or decline of suburban newspaper companies. The endangerment of local news creates "news deserts," where no journalism exists. Seventy million Americans live in a news desert, or in areas that are on the verge of becoming barren. Given that an average of two newspapers shut down on a weekly basis, it is only a matter of time until almost one-third of Americans have no source of local news.

Exurbia, a region founded upon the desire for isolation, is especially unobserved. It seems appropriate that Nowhere, USA, will receive attendant journalistic treatment. Its residents, hoping to detach themselves from the nucleus of American culture, will live on a map of invisibility. Few Americans will understand what transpires in the remote exurbs, including their own inhabitants. They will live in a perpetual fog, brushing at the thick air like a dazed Edgar Allan Poe wandering the streets of Baltimore in his mysterious final hours. They will find answers where they look for them and where algorithms, acting as a flashlight in an alley, direct them.

In the strange and ephemeral universe of the exurban news vacuum, Tucker Carlson becomes the local reporter. The vision that he imagines and outlines is imposable upon a provincial domain devoid of communal identity. The paranoid style of politics, particularly without a local perspective, invades consciousness. In Christian eschatology, the devil is omnipresent—a superpower more palpable and believable, according to devotees, because we cannot see him. The exurban reactionary only sees his enemy on television, distorted through a propagandistic lens. The enemy, as Richard Hofstadter explained, "is a perfect model of malice, a kind of amoral superman: sinister, ubiquitous, powerful, cruel, sensual, luxury-loving." The same qualities are attributable to Lucifer, and like the source of all evil, "the enemy is not caught in the toils of the vast mechanism of history . . . he controls the press, directs the public mind, has unlimited funds, has a special technique for seduction, and is gaining a stranglehold on the educational system."

It is a challenge to believe the paranoid story living in Chicago, where the so-called enemy is walking and living among you. In exurbia, the enemy is absent but still malevolent and, somehow, more powerful—threatening to undermine "traditional values" with school curricula, expansion of the franchise, and television entertainment with Black and gay characters. Given that far-right ideology is at a low point of popularity in American culture, and that at the national level the Republican Party is suffering significant decline among those under the age of fifty, aggrieved, white Christian voters, often living in self-imposed isolation, have turned hostile to the traditions, norms, and procedures that give representation and power to "enemy" groups or constituencies allied with the enemy.

Right-wing propaganda can only succeed on a large scale if there are sufficient numbers of Americans living in an intellectual and communal void. The design of exurbia not only creates but celebrates the void—no walkable downtown, no sidewalks in housing subdivisions, little cultural activity, and no newspaper coverage of local events. The communal void complements intellectual vacuity. When I asked Mike Lofgren why a significant minority of Americans have adopted the antidemocratic politics of insurgency, he replied, "It's not as if, in their spare time, they are reading Madison and Montesquieu." Lofgren's assumption might provoke grim laughter, but national surveys routinely indicate widespread historical and civic ignorance among the general population. An amusing irony is that recently nationalized immigrants score better on civics exams than the "Real Americans" of white, provincial territory. Despite all of the discussion of Fox News, fewer than 2 percent of the public regularly tunes into even the most popular cable news programs. Even still, Fox and its cyber cousins have managed to indoctrinate and radicalize a previously apolitical constituency. "Right-wing media has taken heretofore apolitical people, who were mainly interested in their jobs, families, sports, and what sitcoms were on TV, and politicized and mobilized them," Lofgren said, describing a particular breed of American male who has replaced fervor for the NFL with fanaticism for MAGA. It is not happenstance.

Fred Boenig, a radio talk show host and DJ in Emmaus, Pennsylvania, has remarked that a lifetime of working in mass media prepared him to understand the appeal of Fox News on the average white American man over the age of forty. "They [Fox] have good-looking women in short dresses, there are quick-moving flashy graphics, and everything happens with a loud, aggressive delivery," Boenig told me before concluding, "It's ESPN!" Jen Senko, in 2015, made a documentary, *The Brainwashing of My Dad*, telling the story of how her father transformed from a moderate, largely disinterested Republican whose passions were his children and professional baseball into a fascist maniac. She describes him kicking her out of his vehicle while yelling, "Feminazi!" the late Rush Limbaugh's preferred derogation of liberal women. When Senko's father quit Fox News and Limbaugh's daily radio broadcast cold turkey, after a family intervention, he slowly and steadily returned to his previously affable personality. Millions of other Americans remain inebriated.

There are many reasons why polls continue to indicate historically low levels of trust in the mainstream media. Leading newspapers and television stories wrongly reported on critical events, with their pundits making shallow, and ultimately incorrect, predictions—Iraq had weapons of mass destruction and the war would end quickly, the 2008 financial collapse was unlikely to cause long-term economic damage, Donald Trump had no chance to win the 2016 presidential election. Another reason, rarely discussed, is the decline of local media. When Americans use the phrase "the media," typically as a pejorative, they refer to the national press that they believe operates according to a loathsome ideological agenda. The allegation ranges from inarguably true, such as is the case with Fox News or any of the publications in the Murdoch empire, to paranoid. Contrary to popular opinion, *The New York Times* and CNN, with the exception of social issues, do not display a left-wing "bias" in their journalism or even commentary (even on social issues, is support for LGBTQ rights "left-wing" or mere decency?).

If a robust local media does not maintain presence in the lives of suburbanites, exurbanites, and small-town inhabitants everywhere, then the media transforms into a large, mysterious, and faceless machine, acting in concert with a spooky plan on the part of the well-connected. According to the typical cynic, journalists do not make mistakes. They lie in service of the "elite." Networks and newspapers don't focus on certain stories to increase readership and viewership and thereby maximize profits; they collaborate to move the country closer to a communist or capitalist, depending on the critic's perspective, dictatorship. Localities, particularly in the exurbs, no longer exist. The village has metamorphosized into the nation. National issues are now local issues. Local issues are insignificant and meaningless.

The nationalization of provincial life became increasingly evident and insidious during the COVID-19 pandemic. A sizable minority of Americans did not first think of their neighbors when learning of mask requirements in public places but instead took a crowbar, broke open the public health case, and jammed inside a narrow right-wing conception of "freedom." The school board meeting also became a staging ground for reactionary protest against perceived grievances regarding an international scheme to assault personal liberty. Gatherings across the country became shouting matches, often culminating in threats against school board members, teachers, and administrators. The enraged parents mouthed complaints regarding curricula and public health policies that had little or no connection to local decisions or regulations, but instead derived from far-right media appealing to a national audience. The national obliteration of local issues and culture has also inflicted severe damage on the political process, leaving facilities that acted as bipartisan meeting places dilapidated and empty. President John F. Kennedy secured sufficient votes to pass an educational aid program through Congress by persuading Southern Democrats and Northeastern Republicans to form a supportive coalition based upon their local and regional interests in the program. To imagine such a unified effort in contemporary Congress is nearly impossible. Most legislation passes along partisan lines with, perhaps, a few defectors from the opposing party. Meanwhile, congressional campaigns are increasingly focused on abstract and controversial national debates, more and more divorced from local realities. It is now common on the Hill for a newly elected congressional representative to have a large communication staff, working overtime to earn social media followers and cable news airtime, but only one or two staffers dedicated to policy. In a political culture where national issues almost always overshadow local concerns, Instagram is more important than institutions; Twitter triumphs over township.

NO ESCAPE

Joliet is running out of water. The sentence seems like the opening line in a dystopian novel, but it captures a cruel reality of modern life. Industry, climate change, ecological destruction, and exploitation of land and water have left millions of people in small towns and large cities around the world struggling to find a source of clean, safe, drinkable water. Children who spent their formative years in Flint, Michigan, undergo testing for brain damage due to drinking and bathing in water with high quantities of lead. The residents of Benton Harbor, Michigan, often rely on the largesse of the state government or private charity to bring them bottles of water when their taps spray out only sludge, and now those who live in Joliet must make a tough decision as to how they will proceed into a grim future where something as essential and elemental as water might elude them.

The story hasn't received much coverage in the Joliet *Herald-News*—an absence that gives sad demonstration to how the local media well is running dry. A few national and regional publications with an environmental focus have reported on the literal drought, as well as, *The Blazer*, a student newspaper for Joliet Junior College.[1] One of the community college's professors, Maria Anna Rafac, is a member of the water conservation subcommittee for Joliet. For several decades, she explains, the midsize city has relied upon an underground aquifer for its water supply. The first signs of trouble with the aquifer appeared in 1980, but in typical American fashion, leaders and the majority of voters ignored the problem until it screamed in their collective face. Joliet is now collapsing into a crisis.

"The aquifer will be unable to supply Joliet at peak demand," Rafac warned, before explaining that during sweltering days in the summer months, many homeowners, renters, and business owners might find their faucets empty. The proposed solution is to construct a water pipeline that will connect the city to Lake Michigan. Residents will have to meet the financial burden of the pipeline, even if they did nothing to create the situation it is intended to solve, with higher taxes and increased water fees. The Joliet City Council has also recommended that residents "take shorter showers."

It is unclear what advice, if any, Joliet city managers are giving to Amazon, Walmart, Dollar Tree, and Home Depot—all multinational corporations with a presence in Joliet's massive warehouse and logistics industry. Few shoppers realize when they make a purchase online that Joliet houses the country's largest inland port, moving $735 billion worth of product through its town on an annual basis. Twenty-nine percent of water usage in Joliet is due to warehouse activity, rendering the "short shower" solution rather dubious. Like the products that leave the warehouses of Joliet, the corporate drain of the American water supply will likely go national.

According to the Department of Energy, warehouses are the most common building in the country, second only to private residencies. The Joliet water department reports that Amazon alone uses one hundred times the amount of water of the average Joliet household. Devin Cooley, a Joliet resident and former Joliet Junior College employee, offered a succinct summary of the issue, telling the campus newspaper, "All I'm hearing from city council is use less water, even if we were all to do that, it wouldn't solve the issue. It's systemic. Corporations come in, use our water, exploit our labor, dirty up our air... When is it going to stop? Our wages aren't going up, only our cost of living."

Joliet is emblematic of the entire United States. To spur development, create a middle-class community, and ensure its economic prosperity, it invests, and continually doubles down, on the most pollutant industries in the world—oil refineries, chemical plants, distribution centers—and high levels of automobile traffic. In an exact execution of the "short-term gain, long-term mess" ideology of quarterly fixation, Joliet enhances fossil fuel extraction, even as it strangles the planet. It is not as if the poisonous effects are merely the subject of national debate, far out projection, and abstraction. Signs and symptoms of painful death are easy to identify. *Grist*, an environmental news and commentary publication, reports that diesel air pollution in Joliet is worse than in 90 percent of the country. Exxon's Joliet facility is currently under federal decree to reduce its sulfur dioxide emissions, and Ozinga, a concrete mixing company, is facing similar federal penalties for its excessive dust and particle pollution.[2]

Meanwhile, Midwest Generation, a coal-fired power plant, dumped toxic coal ash near Joliet for over forty years. It isn't rare to see a black film of dust coloring vehicles, buildings, and sidewalks as if a god has taken a giant pencil and shaded parts of the town. Many residents have told *Grist* that they routinely struggle with nosebleeds, blisters, migraine headaches, mercury poisoning, and many other ill health effects. The Sierra Club lists Joliet as one of the most contaminated cities in the country.

While it is true that Joliet's environment includes a shocking and egregious level of toxicity, it is far from alone in its inability to give residents, despite repeated protests, clean air and ample water. Suburbia and later, after diversification and the triumph of liberalism, exurbia became epicenters of escape—sanctuaries where Americans, predominantly white, could flee the consequences of creating an unequal society where poverty and racism transform phrases like "land of opportunity" and "American dream" into taunts of ridicule. Suburban and exurban towns also promised escape from smog, collapsing infrastructure, and other environmental troubles so often associated with urban streets.

As the local debate surrounding the Joliet pipeline project gathers steam, few of its proponents acknowledge that Lake Michigan is not an eternal reservoir. Climate change has made volatility the most dominant characteristic of the Great Lakes. A consortium of Canadian scientists studied Lakes Michigan and Huron, and predict that water levels will fall by 3.5 feet before 2030, only to rise again by 2040. An American scientist told National Public Radio, "What we are seeing with climate change now in the Great Lakes region is more rocking and rolling in water levels—higher highs and lower lows and a much more rapid transition between the highs and lows."[3]

The heavy rains followed by droughts create a situation of extreme oscillation, and the rapid swings in climate have already led to erosion. Coastal properties, often valued in the millions, are facing unprecedented damage, threatening the stability of lakeside towns. Despite the volatility of water levels, few experts expect the lake to fall below normal range, meaning that the Midwest might become a domestic climate migration center, attracting residents from other regions in search of fresh water. Several towns in Michigan itself are already losing groundwater, making issues affecting the nearby lake ever more urgent. The threat of overuse and excessive draining will not only alter the lake itself but radically re-form the communities that surround it.

A top tourist attraction in the region is Indiana Dunes National Park—a beautiful beach full of luxurious sand dunes located in the distant suburbs and exurbs of Northern Indiana. It is a popular destination for families, young singles, and students off for the summer. It is also the fourth most biodiverse national park in the United States, home to hundreds of species of birds, nearly fifty mammals, sixty butterflies, and dozens of reptiles, fish, and dragonflies. The intensity of storms from climate change, attendant erosion, private development, and large-scale sand mining endanger the national treasure and local recreational destination. Carl Sandburg likened the dunes to the "Grand Canyon of the Midwest," bearing a "signature of time and eternity." He also cautioned that their loss would prove "irrevocable."[4]

Sandburg would have cause for concern if he suddenly rose from the dead. Many of the species of the dunes are already endangered due to the reduced breeding cycle resulting from climate change (warmer winters, shorter springs, sweltering summers). "Ice cover that was fortifying the beach during the winter is not there as long," a climate scientist from Chicago's Field Museum explained when summarizing yet another threat facing the dunes.[5] There is no escape from Earth, and no matter how far exurbanites attempt to drive out of the city, and away from the suburbs, they will, eventually, have to reckon with ecological destruction. Not even Fox News can convince a viewer that beach territory exists where it does not, that a species is proliferating when it is dying, and that flooding is not a concern when their house is underwater.

A flood might have brought comfort to the residents of East Chicago, Indiana—a small, predominantly Latino suburb situated along Lake Michigan, immediately west of Gary. Like its neighbor, it suffered years of decline after the downfall of steel and manufacturing employment. In 2017, a community organization found that the drinking water in East Chicago contained high levels of lead contamination, similar to the crisis residents of Flint suffered a few years earlier. East Chicago contains a heavily contaminated Superfund site. Arsenic and lead poison the water supply primarily for residents of a public housing complex in East Chicago, but also homeowners, many of whom don't have the funds to move, given that their property value has plummeted due to the contamination.[6] The Biden administration has vowed to rectify the situation, already allotting $1 billion for Great Lakes restoration, which includes East Chicago, and an additional $200,000 for a pollution-monitoring project in East Chicago. Efforts to remove the lead have begun, but there is no potential reversal of the medical damage East Chicagoans have already incurred.

In nearby Highland and Griffith, city governments are determining how to afford federally mandated improvements to their sewer systems. After the EPA found that the two towns were directing excessive amounts of wastewater to neighboring Hammond, another predominantly Latino town, polluting the Little Calumet River, they issued a decree forcing infrastructural development. They also slapped Highland with a civil penalty of $175,000, and Griffith with $33,000. Highland and Griffith will share the combined costs for the project, predicted to total over $100 million.[7] For a long time, it was foolish but fashionable to fabricate a binary choice between environmentalism and sound economics. In middle-class suburbia, and later exurbia, the dichotomy was easy to accept as long as the symptoms of ecological disease were subtle and barely visible. Thanks to the wrath of Mother Nature it has become obvious that the hippies and tree huggers were right all along. Neil Young sang about human beings putting "Mother Nature on the run" in the 1970s. In the 2020s, the Pope warns that Mother Nature strikes back, calling extreme weather a "chorus of anguish." For the first time in a long time, the cries are audible in suburbia and exurbia. Now Mother Nature has everyone on the run. The only problem is that there is nowhere to go.

SINCERE FASCIST AND OTHERWISE FRAUD STEVE BAN-non issued a call on his podcast for fellow reactionaries to "flood" local election offices, and other municipal positions. Meanwhile, well-funded organizations, like Moms for Liberty, adopt the name and pose of grassroots popular appeal, but actually draw crucial monetary support from national networks with ties to the Republican Party and rely on right-wing media, namely Fox News and podcast hosts, like Bannon, to spread their message. In the case of Moms for Liberty, the organization dedicates itself to banning books about Black history and LGBTQ rights from school curricula and libraries. During the worst months of the COVID-19 pandemic, Moms for Liberty also led the effort to "unmask our kids," as their signs proclaim, and reopen school buildings. It is often true, especially outside large cities, that the political right is much more active at the local level than liberals and leftists. The dangerous pattern dates back to the late 1960s when Richard Viguerie, a far-right organizer most famous for pioneering direct mail campaigns, took a look at the national map and noticed that the right wing was in shambles. Republicans winning elections were moderates or, like Richard Nixon, making concessions to moderates in order to appeal to the national mood. To engineer a far-right revival after the success of the Kennedy administration, and following the disgrace of Nixon, Viguerie recommended the establishment of local power structures. If far-right Republicans could overtake school boards, suburban mayorships and town council positions, and typically neglected offices, like sheriff, they could work in concert to fortify a political infrastructure, pooling each others' resources, influence, and power to assist hard-line Republicans running for the House of Representatives, the Senate, and gubernatorial mansions. Viguerie's strategical tactic was not the only reason that the far right steadily regained power throughout the 1970s, culminating with the presidential election of Ronald Reagan, but it did play a sizable part.[8]

Having neglected local, and in some cases even state, offices for too long, the liberal majority often finds itself at the mercy of the governing minority. Highland, Indiana, is no exception. Even though the majority of its residents have voted for the Democratic presidential nominee in the previous four elections, its town council, by four to two, is under Republican control. The disparity between national interest and local institutions is especially destructive to the natural environment. It is often town councils and city governments that approve of development projects, issue construction permits, and, within federal constraints, control natural resources within their jurisdictions. National elections and debates are critical to the survival of democracy and the advancement of human rights, but local battles also have high stakes.

Thomas Linzey, the cofounder of the Community Environment Legal Defense Fund, has dedicated himself to the adoption of ecological sustainability as a guiding public policy principle, town by town, county by county. His organization's manifesto advocates for activists to enshrine sustainability into local law, allowing village, municipal, and county governance to "provide a template for new state and federal constitutional structures."

"Much like using single matches to illuminate a painting in a dark room," Linzey writes, "enough matches need to be struck simultaneously (and burn long enough) so that the painting can be viewed in its entirety. Each municipality is a match."[9]

According to one national survey, nearly a third of local governments have adopted sustainability standards as part of their governing protocol. While the efficacy of these measures varies, the Sierra Club can still reasonably assert that "a green new deal is already underway in states and cities." In the same report, the Sierra Club spotlights environmental reforms in New York, Los Angeles, Pittsburgh, Portland, and other major cities, but they are far from alone. Kaid Benfield, a former director of sustainable communities with the Natural Resources Defense Council, writes that many small towns—suburban and exurban—are making strides to ensure that future generations will enjoy their natural resources and beauty. After a tornado destroyed much of Greensburg,

Kansas, town leaders decided to allocate federal and state funds to not only rebuild but make "green infrastructure" the top priority. It now has the most LEED-certified buildings (efficient, cost-effective, environmentally friendly) per capita in the country. The small town of Columbus, Wisconsin, made wise use of grant funds to install and create "high-efficiency LED street lighting, hybrid electric municipal vehicles, plug-in stations at municipal parking lots, energy-efficiency audits and upgrades of municipal offices and services, and small subsidies for energy and water efficiency efforts and for tree planting by homeowners." Other small cities, like Corning, New York, have heavily invested in "bringing back Main Street," recognizing that a walkable downtown creates communal belonging and possesses charm that will attract visitors. It is also much healthier for the environment than sprawl, strip malls, and city planning that promotes more automobile traffic and development.[10]

Highland might now join their laudable company. A small but influential group of Highland residents, ranging from retirees to high school students, forms the Highland Neighbors for Sustainability, a local assembly of citizens who commit to conservation projects and advocate for policies at the local level that enshrine environmentally sustainable standards in development, use of resources, city planning projects, and town ordinances. Highland Neighbors for Sustainability stands in stark contrast to Moms for Liberty, an organization that maintains a "grassroots" appearance but receives heavy funding from Republican billionaires and also benefits from promotion on Fox News. Bottom up in its origin and operational methods, Highland Neighbors for Sustainability receives no outside funding and, unlike many reactionary organizations that operate in suburbs and exurbs, does not rely upon national strategists for political direction or rhetorical tactics.

The local environmental group has created rain gardens in public spaces, distributed native plant seeds at town gatherings, connected with the public high school's green student club, and organized park and bike trail cleanup events. My wife and I volunteer for Highland Neighbors, and when we first attended meetings, we were pleased to learn that the organization also had a commitment to interaction, and even agitation, with the Highland town council. More than a conservation club, the Highland Neighbors for Sustainability expressed the ambition to bring pressure to bear on public policy.

Connie Wachala, a retired educator and newspaper reporter, founded the Highland Neighbors for Sustainability, along with her husband, John, due to worry, fear, and anger over climate change and ecological destruction. The details underscore the importance of local involvement, gathering face-to-face in a shared room, and, as clichéd as it might seem, without any pun intended, meeting your neighbors. When I spoke to Connie, she recalled attending two environmental conferences in Indianapolis, and at each conference learned about how various Indiana towns were reacting to escalating flood damage from extreme weather events.

"I remember one community had to close their hospital for nine months, due to water flowing into downtown, and damage to the facility," Connie said. "Flooding was becoming a real concern for mayors and town councils," she added, before explaining that, despite having major floods in Northwest Indiana, "no one was talking about it here."

The practical and unavoidable interest in mitigating flood damage could serve, according to Connie, as an entryway into further governmental discussion on the crises of climate change, conservation, and pollution. "So, John and I organized a mini-conference called the Climate Blitz with the goal of getting people in the same towns talking to each other. We sat everyone by their zip codes, and we had twelve people at the Highland table." They developed the goal of "doing something environmentally, but we didn't know quite what to do."

An attendee of the conference, whom Connie met that evening, was Alexandro Bazán. More than a mere interested party, Bazán had worked on sustainability projects in South Bend, Indiana—a midsize city in the northern part of the state most famous for its university, Notre Dame, and former mayor, Pete Buttigieg. Bazán informed the budding activists that Indiana University has a program, the Resilience Cohort, that, at no cost, will take an inventory of greenhouse gas emissions within a town to help residents and leadership adopt more climate-friendly policies.

The twelve members of the Highland table decided to meet on their own. They adopted the name Highland Neighbors for Sustainability, and dedicated themselves to convincing the Highland Town Council to participate in the Climate Cohort. Without much resistance, the city government agreed—demonstrating how many activists can learn from the Bible verse that proclaims, "You have not, because you ask not." Certainly not always, and perhaps not even in the majority of cases, but with surprising frequency, local power is amenable to good ideas if only those ideas are placed in front of them. "So many people have goodwill," Connie said while reflecting on her experience since creating the local advocacy organization in 2020. "They want to do something positive, but they often don't know how, and they feel isolated."

When I asked Connie why she felt it was essential to locally organize, especially when the troubles facing the planet are not only national but global, she said, "What really drove it home for me was Trump's presidency. Once Trump became president, we realized that we aren't going to do very much, at least for the next four years, at the national level. It isn't going to happen. So, let's see what we can accomplish at the local level."

It has become typical to read demoralizing studies about significant numbers of young people, along with some of their parents and even grandparents, learning the grim projections of the planet's future while observing the devastating effects of extreme weather and natural disaster and feeling an overwhelming sense of despair. Convincing local government to implement more effective and thorough conservation policies will not alone solve the ecological crisis; it will contribute to the solution, and, in the words of Connie, "help with climate doom." "We not only organize and work toward our goals, but we have fun," she added.

My wife, Sarah, and I attended the Highland Neighbors for Sustainability Christmas party at the home of Connie and her husband, John. They served vegan and non-vegan pizza, had plenty of beer and wine available, and Terry Steagall, the retired steelworker, encouraged everyone to imbibe with his hearty laugh and shouts of joy at the mere entrance of another member. After his prodding succeeded, John, a musician who plays flute in a local orchestra and teaches children how to play a variety of instruments, picked up his guitar. He sang Christmas classics, James Taylor songs by request, and a few of the protest anthems by underrated master of the form Phil Ochs.

The broader mainstream of American culture has imposed an impression upon millions of minds that activism is a dull and tedious chore, and that when activists assemble, they will inevitably scold each other about use of pronouns, dietary preferences, and adherence to an ideological maxim of personal purity. Most grassroots, citizen-led organizations defy the stereotype. The Highland Neighbors for Sustainability includes a retired preschool teacher, an administrator at Indiana University Northwest, two high school seniors, the owner of a landscaping business, and a former fire chief—all intelligent and committed people, passionate about the environment, but without any formal position or training in public policy or political organizing. They've overcome their lack of professional experience to not only form friendships, and combat the growing loneliness of American society, but also make a sizable dent in the armor of Highland's Republican-led governing body.

The group succeeded in organizing and enacting several small projects involving rain gardens and native plants while also hosting a climate change protest event on Earth Day in cooperation with another environmental group in neighboring Hammond. Membership agreed that they needed to formulate a larger focus that would enable them to work toward a more significant political objective. Bazán, the same professional who advised the group at its impetus, explained that many town councils throughout the United States, including in South Bend, Indiana, and Flossmoor, Illinois, have adopted "sustainability commissions" that provide counsel, recommendations, and expert opinion to municipal leadership on any and all issues involving the environment. A sustainability commission enshrines the voice of ecological concern into governing institutions, giving priority to conservation just as school boards, police unions, and library trustees amplify the needs and protests of their constituents.

In 2022 the Highland Neighbors for Sustainability, with only fifteen to twenty members, began petitioning the Highland town council to create a sustainability commission.

They had monthly meetings at the aptly named Green Witch Café. Liz, the Green Witch's owner, became a member of the group herself. Most of Green Witch's menu is vegan, and the café is full of locally sourced honey, hemp, and cannabidiol products. Wearing her trademark purple bandana, which is an accessory to her colorful variety of tattoos, Liz is happy to walk customers through the benefits of turmeric tea or collect donations for the Northwest Indiana Food Bank while the grunge rock stylings of Soundgarden or Nirvana fill the room from an overhead speaker. It isn't as if The Green Witch is a political advocacy operation; rather Liz's support for environmentalism, social liberalism, and farm-to-fork initiatives complements the services of her enterprise. It is the kind of business that, when I was in high school, would have been impossible to imagine existing with a solid customer base in the south suburbs of Chicago. Anyone looking for a Green Witch–like experience would have had no choice but to jump on the highway, fight traffic, and search for parking in a North Side neighborhood. Now it is the Third Place for the Highland Neighbors for Sustainability, representing the transformation of the suburbs from denizens of white, conservative homogeneity into havens for modern, progressive values.

Local government in Democratic-leaning suburbs often resembles the tyranny-of-the-minority US Senate, where despite representing forty million more Americans, Democrats struggle for senatorial control, and often lose it to a Republican Party that benefits from a system that gives greater weight to land than voters. The majority of townspeople are left of center, to varying degrees, but through their lack of engagement and participation allow Republican council members to dictate local policy, regulation, and ordinance.

The Highland Neighbors for Sustainability, with an environmental focus, has attempted to alter the askew arrangement of power in their town. At the end of 2022, they won a big victory. After months of attending town council meetings, collecting petition signatures, and giving presentations to skeptical town council members, they secured favorable votes for the sustainability commission from not only one but two of the Republican members of the council. Along with the two supportive Democrats, the tally was sufficient to create the commission and fold it into local government. The only caveat was that in order to guarantee its passage the Highland Neighbors for Sustainability agreed to the stipulation of one Republican councilman that it would exist on a trial basis for a one-year period—upon expiration the council would review the work of the commission to determine whether or not it can continue. The threat of disbandment that hangs overhead the commission spotlights the need for involvement in not only local issues but electoral politics.

As Alexandro Bazán told the Neighbors when he proposed the sustainability commission as a political goal, "Local government decisions are often made through a very top-down approach. A commission could decentralize power and change the dynamic of top-down decision-making. By elevating sustainability issues you can strengthen and grow grassroots groups that can accelerate change. A commission can help inspire and mobilize more members of the public to join a sustainability commission, join a sustainability related group, start a sustainability group, run for an elected position with a sustainability agenda, and incorporate sustainability in their everyday decisions."

The plan is already bearing fruit. Three members of the Highland Neighbors for Sustainability, including the owner of Fuzzyline, a local craft brewery, are running for the town council. Should they win, they would not only make the commission permanent but aggressively and officially advocate for a "green" emphasis in local development, use of taxpayer funds, and communal activity. Given that they are environmentalists who subscribe to a set of liberal ideas, they are also unlikely, should these battles eventually land in Highland, to ban books about Black history or novels featuring transgender protagonists from libraries and schools.

It might not have the excitement, and score the ratings, of the culture wars, but genuine politics and the survival of American democracy depends upon the quality of work that groups like the Highland Neighbors for Sustainability project and promote. For the United States to continue its advancement into "the liberal community," exercising the mechanism of constitutional democracy to enlarge the conception of freedom for everyone, expand opportunity for prosperity, and bring into existence a working model of justice, the progressive promise must operate not only in Chicago but Highland; not only in the hustle and bustle of metropolitan streets but on the quiet back-roads of the suburbs and exurbs.

When Steve Bannon called for a fascist infusion of activists at the local level, he implored his radio audience, "It's going to be a fight, but this is a fight that must be won. We don't have an option. We're going to take this back village by village, precinct by precinct." Bannon hoped for the demolition of voting rights and the upheaval of the American electoral system. His words, even still, apply equally to the fight in favor of democracy, the fight in favor of a clean environment, and the fight in favor of a multiracial, multigendered coalition committed to peace and hospitality.

To quote a better messenger, Rachel Carson, the author of *Silent Spring*, wrote, "The more clearly we can focus our attention on the wonders and realities of the universe about us, the less taste we shall have for destruction." Where better to focus than in one's backyard?

THE BOHEMIAN SUBURB
VERSUS EXURBISTAN

A common cliché in political discourse is the phrase "all politics is local." Though he did not coin the expression, former Speaker of the House Tip O'Neill is its most famous messenger. In 1982, the larger-than-life Irish American politician successfully steered the Democrats to national midterm victory by speaking in Republican House leader Robert H. Michel's home district within Peoria, Illinois, about how many jobs Republican opposition to O'Neill's infrastructure bill cost the city. He also made heavy weather out of the crumbling roads and bridges that, due to right-wing ideological obstinance, would continue to suffer from disrepair and neglect. Chris Matthews, former chief of staff to O'Neill who would later host a nightly television program on cable news, explained that the savvy maneuver "translated a wholesale debate about national economic policy to the local, retail level."[1]

There is an ongoing argument over the origin of a similar admonition, "think globally, act locally." Environmentalist activists, futurist theoreticians, a theologian, and a Scottish town planner all uttered the phrase and would later claim invention. The authorial disputes might no longer have much meaning to the various parties. Like "all politics is local," "think globally, act locally" is quickly becoming a philosophical relic. Much to the detriment of political culture and legislative procedure, millions of Americans no longer think or act locally. Due to the dominance of national media, the demise of local media, and the poisonous influence of social media, "all politics is local" has transformed into "no politics is local." All politics is now national. A University of Chicago study found that from 1998 to 2023, the percentage of Americans who believe that "community involvement" is important crashed from 47 to 27 percent.[2] Even when many Americans begin to participate at the local level, their motivational impetus operates out of New York or Washington, DC. The zealots who storm school board meetings, demanding book bans and censorship of teachers—similar to the fascists who threatened the lives of election workers in 2020 and 2021—are not responsive to any local scandal or development but are accepting marching orders from national media personalities and political agitators who have never even visited their hometown.

Contrary to Tip O'Neill's 1982 triumph, the massive infrastructure expenditure that President Biden signed into law in 2021 had no effect on his approval rating or support for Democratic officials in Congress. At $1 trillion, Biden's Building a Better America is the largest infrastructure program in the country's history. It is funding the repair of roads, bridges, harbors, school buildings, and public hospitals while also allowing mayors and town councils to invest in new bus stations, train depots, and environmentally friendly renovations of existing buildings, power grids, and water supply systems. As much as it is improving the lives of people and the communities where they live, in political terms, it might as well not even exist.

In the early 1960s, after reading the poverty journalism of Pulitzer Prize winner Homer Bigart, and political scientist Michael Harrington's enduring treatise on deprivation in the world's wealthiest nation, *The*

Other America, President John F. Kennedy articulated and enacted an agenda to resuscitate beleaguered sections of Appalachia, the Heartland, and other declining regions that were losing any trace of connection to American productivity and prosperity. A critical plank in the platform was 1961's Area Redevelopment Act (ARA). When Kennedy signed the ARA into law, the federal government earmarked $400 million—quite substantial for the time—to identify regions ranging from bankrupt farmland to Native American reservations in desperate need of economic vitality and communal improvement. Private companies, agreeing to operate in financially troubled territory and train and hire local workers, could qualify for generous, low-interest loans to open new plants, warehouses, or office parks. Meanwhile, city and state governments could also apply for loans or, if they were so depressed that they could not reasonably foresee repaying the loans, collect grants to invest in community infrastructure. The public-private alliance created hundreds of thousands of jobs in four years, providing sufficient incentive for large companies to conduct business in small towns like Metropolis, Illinois; Price, Utah; and many others.

During the same duration, the infrastructural arm of the ARA created over thirty thousand jobs repairing water and sewage systems, constructing airports, and allowing for the renovation of public clinics. To enhance the popular program, the Kennedy administration also authorized the funding of ambitious research projects, including a marine center in Yaquina Bay, Oregon, to help the town's then-struggling fishing industry; the establishment of a graduate training laboratory in Wilkes-Barre, Pennsylvania, to attract engineers to work for tech firms in the downtrodden mid-sized city; and a large grant to the University of Kentucky for the creation of a timber conservation center.

One of the program's administrators said that, among the public and their local representatives, it was so successful and popular that it "went like a house afire." For four years it generated momentous energy, partially due to a bipartisan coalition of support. Southern Democrats, New England Republicans, and Midwestern officials of both parties applauded the Kennedy effort, because the triumphs were visible in their districts, and they were able to boast to voters, correctly or incorrectly, that their leadership was responsible. The Area Redevelopment Act was one of the most effective and massive governmental programs of poverty relief in the nation's history. The past tense provokes an unavoidable inquiry: What happened?

Influential Republican leaders turned on the program when they accurately ascertained that the political benefits were accruing at the White House doorstep rather than their own offices. Kennedy lost support within his own party at the same time, because many ARA programs relied upon nonunion workers. The main culprit in the death of area redevelopment, far beyond self-centered partisanship and the narrow interests of organized labor, was much more dangerous and sinister.[3]

In the first two years of his presidency, Kennedy made major contributions to the struggle for civil rights. He made possible a civil rights division in the Department of Justice by recruiting hundreds of lawyers to look specifically at issues of racial discrimination and voting suppression. He summoned the National Guard on two occasions—once in Mississippi and once, more famously, in Alabama—to intervene on behalf of students and civil rights protesters, and quietly attempted to steer civil rights legislation through Congress—an effort that failed. Despite these acts of policy, Kennedy did not make an overt, public statement to address the ongoing catastrophe of Jim Crow until June 11, 1963. On that summer evening, Kennedy gave a televised address from the Oval Office. He spoke eloquently and forcefully about the "crisis" of racist law, ordinance, and custom, calling on the nation—at the local, state, and federal levels—to demolish the Jim Crow regime and adopt new laws that would make the promises of the Bill of Rights applicable to all citizens. He highlighted the hypocrisy of a country that "preaches freedom" in juxtaposition to the Soviet Union, but does not grant it to anyone with dark skin within its own borders. He identified the economic and political damage that racism was inflicting on the entire country—not only the South—but focused, primarily, on the moral disaster of apartheid. Challenging white Americans to show empathy, he presented the following inquiry:

> The heart of the question is whether all Americans are to be afforded equal rights and equal opportunities, whether we are going to treat our fellow Americans as we want to be treated. If an American, because his skin is dark, cannot eat lunch in a restaurant open to the public, if he cannot send his children to the best public school available, if he cannot vote for the public officials who will represent him, if, in short, he cannot enjoy the full and free life which all of us want, then who among us would be content to have the color of his skin changed and stand in his place? Who among us would then be content with the counsels of patience and delay?

Many white Americans accepted the president's imperative and became allies in the civil rights movement. With only a few exceptions, Southern Democrats in the House and Senate were not among this number. The very next day, members of Kennedy's own party who had previously supported the Area Redevelopment Act voted as a bloc to eliminate funding for the program. The betrayal of their president and, more important, their constituents was a racist revolt to punish Kennedy for his support of racial equality. Arthur Schlesinger, historian and friend of the Kennedy family, recalls praising Kennedy for his moving speech on civil rights. The president replied, "Yes, and look at what happened to area development the very next day in the House. But, of course, I had to give that speech, and I'm glad that I did."

One of the most consistent follies of some white leftists, particularly podcast ramblers and internet scribblers of Marxist stripes, is the article-of-faith assumption that if only progressive organizers and officials would emphasize class, and speak little of race and gender, a socialist revolution would break out among the reactionary rank and file. The suffocation of the Area Redevelopment Act, the exodus of Democrats to the Republican Party after the passage of the Civil Rights Act, and the religious right's lowly origin of bigotry demonstrates that the fabulists who envision a raceless and sexless transformation of society have their sequence in exactly the opposite order. Even hostility toward the Affordable Care Act is inseparable from racism. Not only do many elected officials oppose the program because it is central to the legacy of the country's first Black president but average right-wing voters, even the uninsured who would most benefit from its largesse, look at it with hatred.

Jonathan Metzl, a psychiatrist and sociologist, toured the South and Midwest to write his study *Dying of Whiteness: How the Politics of Racial Resentment is Killing America's Heartland*. He met many men like Trevor, a white Tennessean who drove a cab until abdominal pain from hepatitis C rendered him unable to complete even the most elementary of tasks. Even while preparing to expire, with jaundiced eyes and gray skin, he told Metzl that he would "rather die than sign up for Obamacare." "We don't need government in our lives," he said, "And no way I want my tax dollars paying for Mexicans and welfare queens." Metzl, transitioning from journalist to medical professional in the next paragraph, wrote that while the hepatitis virus is what physically killed Trevor, another cause of death was "toxic dogma."[4]

Toxic dogma is also causing entire counties to take sick leave of the twenty-first century. One of the statistics to draw the most attention following Donald Trump's election in 2016 was that the counties that Hillary Clinton won were responsible for two-thirds of US economic activity. In 2020, the divide grew wider, with Biden's counties representing 71 percent. Perhaps even more significant than dollars and cents is cultural sense. Educated Americans, especially those under the age of forty, look at the exurban epicenter of reactionary politics as an alien planet. Having taken racial diversity for granted while coming of age with admiration for Black athletes and gay and transgender pop stars, and recalling that the country enjoyed far better leadership under a biracial man with an Arabic name than when it suffered under the likes of Donald Trump, most city dwellers and large-metro suburbanites want nothing to do with right-wing culture or the America that it mythologizes.

Due to the outsize influence of right-wing media, and the institutional encroachment of Republican power and influence in the Supreme Court, Congress, and the Electoral College, the United States cannot progress according to the trajectory that the majority of its voters support. Instead, the entire political culture is in a freeze-out. The arguments that attract the most attention, and amplify the most deafening shrieks, have little to do with the welfare of the average person. Meanwhile, many quality-of-life issues that affect the day-to-day existence of millions are on mute. If the most agitated Americans cannot even settle on the survival of liberal democracy, any attempt to provoke conversations regarding the sustainability and happiness of small communities will fail to find a voice over the culture war cacophony.

*

I WORK FOR THE LARGEST EMPLOYER IN THE STATE of Indiana—Indiana University. It has multiple campuses spread throughout the state, along with ancillary offices and online services. Another top-ten employer is IU's fiercest rival, Purdue University. Even if Indiana is small, it is not unique. The largest employer in the state of Michigan is the University of Michigan, the largest in Iowa is the

University of Iowa, and the largest in Wisconsin is the University of Wisconsin. Outside of the Midwest, public university systems are also the largest employers in Colorado, Nebraska, New Mexico, and Vermont.[5] To state institutions of higher education, one could add public schools, police and fire departments, the postal service, public and VA hospitals, public works departments, public libraries, and public transportation services to employers that provide stable jobs with generous benefits at a living wage. Every four years, various candidates vying for the presidency expound on the need for "economic stimulation," "job growth," and giving incentives to "job creators," and yet it is rare to hear policy proposals involving public universities or governmental expansion in the form of public services as part of an economic agenda. Even if one wouldn't know it from listening to political debate, "big government," it turns out, is a big employer. The efficacy of government is almost always kept secret.

If people started telling secrets and could overcome their stultifying pathologies of hatred, a real recovery program for the troubled sections of the Heartland could emerge. It would demand robust investment in public goods—not only because they create jobs and stimulate private business—but also because they act as fertilizer for communities with desirable standards of living that translate into a pleasurable lifestyle. Even in times of extreme political division, people share certain interests and sources of recreation. Live music does not adhere to any ideological border, and as ticket prices for national and international acts continue to rise to unaffordable levels, local music becomes more attractive to fans of all genres, particularly young listeners. Public libraries in Madison, Pittsburgh, Nashville, Austin, Fort Worth, and Davenport have exercised creativity under the economic weight of monopoly by partnering with the private company Rabble to form local music streaming services for library members. Each qualifying artist enters into a licensing agreement with the library, receives higher payment than anything Spotify or Amazon offers, and can take full advantage of prominence on a locally centered, communal streaming service to book shows, sell records, and build a regional audience. The public library system in Edmonton, Canada, enhanced the project by collaborating with nearby businesses to sponsor vinyl pressings and sales and host music events throughout the city.

One could imagine how a thriving music scene—not to mention with the addition of visual arts, theater, and poetry—could revive small metro areas and their surrounding suburbs. An artistic renaissance could even reach exurbia, inspiring its adolescents and challenging the parochial prejudices of its home and business owners. Patti Smith suggested as much when she told interlocuter Jonathan Lethem during a public conversation in New York that one of the most enlivening aspects of the city she made her home as an aspiring artist was that it was cheap for the youthful and downtrodden. "You could get an apartment and build a whole community of transvestites, artists, or writers," she said, before making a juxtaposition and recommendation: "Now, New York has closed itself off to the young and struggling. But there's always other cities. I don't know—Detroit, Poughkeepsie, Newark. You have to find the new place, because New York has been taken away from you. It's still a great city, but it has closed itself off from the poor and creative burgeoning society. So, my advice is find a new city."[6]

Smith's advice, for its poetic beauty, falls into the common category of "easier said than done," but it is not an unreasonable fantasy. Even in Joliet, when the owners of the Chicago St. Pub turned it into the staging ground for the local music scene, the consequence was cultural growth and transformation. In only a few years, two microbreweries opened in Joliet, also regularly featuring local musicians, a local music and craft beer festival took place at the nearby minor league baseball stadium, and a group of artists received permission from the city government to commandeer a shuttered historical prison for the purpose of art fairs and music performances.

The only thriving neighborhood of Gary, Indiana, is Miller Beach, which not only benefits from its shoreline location but also a unique regional focus on the arts. One of the highlights of Miller Beach is the world's only Nelson Algren museum, named after the legendary writer who had a home in the neighborhood. One can further activate the political imagination by envisioning what regeneration might transpire if municipal and state governments actually operated with the goal of stimulating the arts, rather than merely granting permits as a passive observer or harming grassroots stimuli by concentrating on casino construction or corporate capture of local markets.

A group of civil engineers, journalists, city planners, and environmentalists have formed a national organization, Strong Towns. Together, they advocate for livable city planning that is better for ecology and city inhabitants. They propose incremental housing projects that address local needs while guarding against sprawl, shaping downtown priorities around pedestrians rather than the automobile, and an end to highway expansion. The Strong Towns agenda coalesces with the average experience of vacationers, television producers, and successful real estate agents. Everyone seems to know that a charming, walkable downtown in a tightly knit community with a thriving arts scene is the most appealing small town commercial and environmental landscape, and yet few plan for it, let alone adopt zoning laws and business and housing incentives that make it a reality.

One of the most powerful reasons that quality of life issues cannot enter the political discussion is that the politics of exurban escape are dominant among the Republican Party and, as a consequence, influential on all discourse, from presidential campaign rhetoric all the way down to the village council meeting. My hometown of Highland tried to adopt the Patti Smith–Strong Town approach, but continually collided with the brick wall of right-wing obstinance.

A few of my fondest memories from high school involve dates or outings with friends at the Town Theatre in downtown Highland. The multiplex monstrosity had already conquered Northwest Indiana suburban territory, rendering the Town, a one-screen theater with an old-fashioned marquee hovering over the sidewalk and ticket window, the lone source of independent, art, and foreign films. To make the experience even more idyllic, the Town had an intermission for every evening showing during which the staff would provide, free of charge, cakes, brownies, and coffee from the local bakery. Due to years of neglect from ownership, the Town was in desperate need of repairs and renovation. The last movie that I saw at the theater was riddled with technical problems—scratchy sound, odd shadows obstructing the images in the frame, and collapsing chairs in the auditorium.

Around 2013, Highland residents began to propose that the town council purchase the theater, pay for renovations, and use the newly upgraded and furnished movie palace to create an arts district. A popular record store with a large consumer base of vinyl obsessives was on the same block. There were proposals for the Town to double as a small concert and live theater venue. In 2016, when a majority of Highland residents voted for Hillary Clinton and the Democratic candidate for Congress, Republicans still managed to overtake the town council. Citing concerns about property taxes, they aborted all the plans surrounding the Town. It is now on schedule for demolition, and a condominium will replace it, bringing no vitality or stimulation to the community.

After the September 11 terrorist attacks, reactionaries who sought to fuel hostility toward Muslims warned of major cities in the United States and Europe falling under the control of Islamic fanatics, none more so than "Londonistan." Like most right-wing moral panics of racial and religious animus, the fears were without justification, but the language is interesting. It suggests that, hypothetically, if enough people of shared values impose their ideas on a town, they will transform the very nature of the community. In suburbs that are rapidly diversifying with young residents longing for a more progressive, Patti Smith–Strong Towns agenda, there is the presence of "Exurbistan."

A leader of Exurbistan in Highland is a man who obsessively monitors and attempts to interfere in town council procedure. He uses his considerable wealth to fund the campaigns of far-right proxies—two of whom sit on the governing body. Even with his allies on the council, he remains a fixture at town meetings, perhaps to watch his minions do his bidding. His commentary is extreme and indicative of the antisocial tendencies that now pass for "politics" on the American right. He almost derailed one meeting by protesting that he cannot carry his gun inside the chambers. "Do my constitutional rights not apply to this room?" he asked with indignation. When the Highland Neighbors for Sustainability proposed the sustainability commission, he would often object, insisting that "no one is going to tell me that I can't eat meat in my own house and no one is going to come to my driveway to check how many miles I put on my car that week." His paranoid ravings would shock even Richard Hofstadter and possibly arouse the ghost of Rush Limbaugh, as they have become an enemy of sanity in local governance.

The good news is that his ideology is losing ground with the American public. Given its access to massive amounts of political lobbying money, and its navigation of a political system that serves its interests, Exurbistan will not surrender without a fight. The Exurbistan ideology of escape, individualism, and repression recently won a battle in Highland. A referendum appeared on the local ballot seeking an infinitesimal increase in property taxes, which are already quite low, to create a teacher recruitment and retainment fund. As the family and child populations of Highland grow, the schools face an urgent need for additional staff. Despite the rather elementary economics and communal concerns of the referendum, it failed. The voter turnout for the election was 14 percent. Based upon my observations at the ballot box and my subsequent conversations with locals, the 14 percent included a disproportionate number of elderly Republicans. Until young (and youngish) Americans who represent the diverse American polity, and adhere to beliefs that are generally liberal and secular, begin voting in equal and greater numbers than reactionaries—at the local, state, and federal levels—Exurbistan will remain on the march.

One of the most foolish clichés inhibiting American politics originated with the late right-wing provocateur and muckracker Andrew Breitbart. When starting his website, which has since turned into a cesspool of white nationalism and misogyny, he said, "Politics is downstream of culture." Elements of the left have embraced this mindset with equal force as the right. Those who believe it demonstrate how little they know about politics or culture. The reality is that politics and culture are two streams running parallel into the ocean of history. It is ironic that for all of the right-wing punditry's bellowing about culture, they do seem to understand the fundamental importance of voting and institutions. Even if they comprise a minority of Americans, they enter the political arena with various advantages. First, the US Senate empowers Exurbistan. Nearly forty million people live in California. Approximately 1.6 million people live in North and South Dakota combined, and yet the Dakotas have more representation in the Senate than Californians. The House is more democratic, but gerrymandering creates and emboldens political exurbia, enabling the election of far-right insurgents and diluting the power of progressives, especially Blacks, Latinos, and Native Americans. Finally, the Electoral College is exurbia's greatest friend, giving Exurbistan partisans in swing states like Pennsylvania, Georgia, and Arizona massive influence over the selection of the president. Due to the results of recent presidential elections, Exurbistan now controls the Supreme Court of the United States.

The ossified institutions of American democracy create an ongoing fiasco where the majority rightfully feels under siege from an extreme minority. Institutional ossification allows for the political calcification of oligarchic economics and evangelical social policy. Under such an asymmetrical arrangement of power, liberals and leftists cannot afford to stay on the bench during any electoral competitions, and they cannot have any illusions about the extreme menace of contemporary Republican politics. "Voting is a militant apparatus," Jesse Jackson often says. If it wasn't, the right-wing would not expend ample dollars and energy in making it more difficult for people of color and college students. Voting is not the only political tool—far from it—but as the histories of civil rights, women's rights, Latino rights, and LGBTQ rights demonstrate, it is essential to the formation of multicultural coalitions that make peace, justice, and improving standards of living possible. The recent catastrophes of President Bush's invasion and occupation of Iraq, Donald Trump's lethal mismanagement of the COVID-19 pandemic, and the insurrection of January 6 prove that rapper and business mogul Sean Combs, otherwise known as Diddy, was not hysterical when he encouraged voter registration with the slogan "Vote or Die."

Many people, especially Black, Latino, Asian, Jewish, and LGBTQ Americans, will become victims of attack and exploitation, but the war launching out of Exurbistan is not against any particular group of people as much as it is against the future. In an odd postmodern twist, the ideological inhabitants of Exurbistan also seek to destroy any sense of history that could create a future of equality, justice, and pervasive happiness. The struggle for American democracy and prosperity calls to mind a lyric of one of the world's greatest musicians, Warren Haynes, "You can't get to the future . . . / Without going through the past, my friend."

WHEN THE WALLS COME
CRUMBLING DOWN

The small, exurban town of Chesterton, Indiana, would make an ideal setting for a Hallmark television movie. At the center of its bucolic surroundings is a downtown commercial district attracting visitors with restaurants inside converted Victorian mansions, elegant wine shops, an antiquarian bookstore, and barrooms with neon lights in the windows, oak finishing, and rock and roll on jukeboxes. At its edge is Indiana Dunes State Park—over two thousand acres of dunes and forestry at the coastline of Lake Michigan. It is also one of many battlegrounds for reactionary forces staging an assault against the dignity of democracy and the people it is designed to represent.

In 2021, the Duneland School Corporation, in its authority of the Chesterton public school system, voted to forbid teachers at Chesterton Middle School from displaying anything related to Black Lives Matter or LGBTQ pride in the classroom. Even the innocuous rainbow flag was found impermissible. Hundreds of students, parents, teachers, and Chesterton residents protested the ordinance. Elsa Estridge, at the time an eighth grader, said that the act of censorship felt like a "personal attack." One parent held a sign with headshot photos of Walt Whitman,

James Baldwin, Lorraine Hansberry, and other LGBTQ literary icons underneath the words, "Unfortunately, history has set the record a little too straight." The rally ended without incident, but prohibition remains part of Chesterton school policy.[1]

Three years earlier, another student-led protest activity was not nearly as tranquil. More than two hundred Chesterton High School students walked out of their classes to hold a rally on school grounds to demand more swift and aggressive action on gun control from local, state, and national leadership. The hour-long event included seventeen minutes of silence; at each minute mark, a student recited the name of a victim of the Parkland school shooting. The teenagers demanded more restrictions on firearm ownership and transactions, and also admonished Indiana officials for accepting donations from the National Rifle Association.[2] Local members of the organization did not take kindly to the students' peaceful protest rally. They surrounded the students, hurled insults, and even issued threats. According to one former student of Chesterton High School who participated in the protest and gave me her firsthand account, one man's mania swept him into such a frenzy that he began charging at the students. When police told him to cease and desist, he refused. He was handcuffed and escorted away from the premises in a squad car.

The Chesterton native who now studies at Indiana University Northwest explained that the entire crowd of counterprotesters was crude and hostile, but the man who police arrested is a known irritant in Chesterton. His idea of recreation includes attempting to pay local businesses with "Trump money"—fake dollar bills with Trump's loathsome mug at the center. He also demands that fast food and retail employees accept his brochures promoting a reactionary form of Christianity. If they refuse, he insists on receiving a full refund for his purchase. "There are two Chestertons," the IUN student told me. "There is the Chesterton of the downtown and the protests, and people trying to make it more progressive, and then there is the Chesterton that is MAGA crazy." *The New York Times* detailed election map shows that, in 2020, the downtown area of Chesterton leaned Democratic, but the surrounding hinterlands were solidly in the "MAGA crazy" camp.

The two protest stories give revealing complement to each other. When the fascistic right can exercise the civil process of political procedure, debate, and peaceful adoption of legislation in its favor, it will use democracy as a cudgel against its enemies. The Duneland School Corporation disapproves of Black Lives Matter and relegates gay and transgender students to roles of silent inferiority. The policy forbidding and punishing teachers who would display a BLM logo or equal sign sticker meant to represent the Human Rights Campaign, an LGBTQ advocacy organization, informs Black students and staff, and their LGBTQ coworkers and classmates, that they are, to use the words of one student at the protest, "unsafe and unwelcome."

If law fails, as it has consistently, to kill the momentum of the civil rights, feminist, and LGBTQ rights movements to enlarge the promise of freedom and expand the measure of democracy, the parties of reactionary backlash can resort to using actual weapons. As Republican politicians and pundits, as well as the executive board of the NRA, will explain, the reckless laissez-faire accessibility of firearms is not about home defense in case of burglary, and it is especially not about hunting and the outdoorsman lifestyle. It is a political intimidation tool for a minority guarding against delusions of "tyranny" that is intent on imposing tyrannical ambitions on the majority. Chesterton is an exurb with a significant percentage of its population preparing to enter into a future of cosmopolitan equality, but it also has a contingent, with representation on the school board, seeking to undermine the future by erasing all memory of the past. The history that they are attempting to expunge is right next door.

*

BARBARA COTTON WAS RAISING HER CHILDREN IN
the Cabrini-Green public apartment complex in Chicago during the
turbulence and terror of the 1960s. Her minister introduced her to
members of a Lutheran organization, Prince of Peace, which was modeled after President Kennedy's Peace Corps program within the federal
government. Prince of Peace operated with the support of Valparaiso
University in Valparaiso, Indiana. As part of the program, Barbara
Cotton would take her children to Valparaiso for recreational and educational activities, and the Prince of Peace volunteers and staff would
visit Cabrini-Green to learn directly about racism and poverty from
inner-city Black families. In 1968, a tragic crime occurred that Barbara
Cotton's son, Robert, describes as a "dream dasher"—the assassination
of Martin Luther King Jr. For the Cottons, even under the weight of
national catastrophe and personal despair, there was cause for hope. "As
we left school on the day that King was killed, people were turning over
anything white, and harassing light-skinned kids—a lot of them were
Hispanic, but it didn't matter in that stage of rage and ignorance. But I
remember, and I'll always be thankful for what my mom exhibited. She
alone challenged that crowd. She said, 'Get away from those kids,' and
walked them over to North Avenue [where riots were not taking place]."

Another brilliant flash of solidarity shot color through the darkness when Walt and Lois Reiner, the Chicago administrators of the
Prince of Peace program, announced that they were moving back to
Valparaiso. Barbara Cotton asked if she and her children could also
move to Valparaiso. The only problem was one with the same source of
violence and hatred that troubled America's fragile democracy, and had
caused the dream-dashing disasters of the decade. Valparaiso did not
have a single Black resident, and it did not want one. It was a "sundown
town," meaning that local leadership, the police, and the majority of
townspeople made it clear through threat of pain that any Black person
caught within its borders after the sun set was unwelcome.

Throughout the United States, Blacks who found themselves in sundown towns after nightfall would spend the night in jail with trumped-up charges or suffer an extralegal fate far worse. Barbara Cotton had the defiance and courage to resist the onslaught of exclusionary law and violence, and she possessed a mother's fierce power of love. The Reiners had the compassion, as well as their own supply of bravery, to assist in the Cotton journey of integration. "We were looking for the promise of America through the promise of Valparaiso," Robert Cotton told me when I asked him to reflect back on his childhood. "We were given additional support that was not forthcoming in Chicago, and we had a Candyland for kids all around us—green spaces, parks, better schools, organized Little League baseball. In Chicago, we were playing 'strike 'em out' baseball, which was one kid up against a wall in a parking lot, and a pitcher would try to strike him out. In Valparaiso, it was like *The Sandlot*. We had uniforms and ballparks. We were fortunate enough to be nestled in the bosom in a neighborhood of young kids, and we lived in the university area, where we were befriended by many kids. I don't think that helped my mom, though, who was still pretty isolated."

Cotton's fond memories do not encapsulate the entire story of the first family to integrate Valparaiso. Lois Reiner recalls Barbara Cotton saying, "You can go home to your safe schools and good community. Why can't my kids have the same thing?" In 1969 the Cotton family moved to the "reputable sundown town," to use Robert Cotton's words. He added: "We trusted Walt Reiner with our lives." No local realtors would sell a house to a Black person, and no landlord would agree to rent a unit to the Cotton family. Undeterred, the Cottons and Reiners purchased a lot of land, and enough locals volunteered their time and services to "rig up a house," as Cotton describes it. Of his earliest allies, he said, "they were marvelous people who broke the mold." Despite the alliances the Cottons were forging, the mold was still out of favor with democracy, equality, and justice.

"It was a Candyland for kids during the day, but the night was pretty threatening," Cotton recalled. "One night I heard a scream, and I ran toward the back door, where I saw my mother buckle in fear. She said that there was someone staring at her through the window." As a young boy, Cotton grabbed a "meat cleaver," believing he could guard his family. The severity and frequency of the threats and harassment went far beyond the protective capacity of a child. Prince of Peace, with some irony given its name, assigned its volunteers to act as armed guards outside the Cotton home. The Reiners also received threats. Their daughter remembers receiving multiple calls a week from enraged maniacs promising to shoot them.

"Barbara Cotton is a remarkable woman," a former Prince of Peace volunteer said, "somebody who wanted a better life for her kids and herself. She came to a place that was largely unknown. It had its challenges, but she did it for the benefit of her family." She would eventually graduate college and, as Robert Cotton explains, "inspire a whole new set of ambitions. It was an emboldening transformation that, by proxy, was an extension of the dream that Martin Luther King set us on. It was also something that helped change the consciousness of the city. We've become a more functional, well-rounded community rather than an all-white city. Children of different races can grow up together, and children who are Black are not cursed or damned by the perpetuating nature of what segregation has meant to this country."

As much as Barbara Cotton was the groundbreaking force for inclusion and integration in Valparaiso, Robert Cotton is a critical agent of acceleration in Valparaiso's movement toward freedom, peace, and democratic fruition. In 2009, he was elected to the Valparaiso City Council, where he currently sits as the first and only Black city councilman in the history of the community. During his swearing-in ceremony, his mother stood at his side, failing to hold back tears. As she cried, Robert held his head high and took the oath of office.

Cotton told me that he employs his presence and assertive personality in service of making Valparaiso more diverse, equal, and just. He dedicates himself to increasing local services, making public education the top priority in the town budget, and using every opportunity to highlight multicultural hospitality as part of Valparaiso's recreational and political comportment. The stunning trajectory of his life, growing from a boy trying to protect his mother against terrorists with a meat cleaver into the town's first Black city councilman, representing women like his mother with public rhetoric and legislative vote, is one of many examples illustrating America's soft revolution. In fifty years, the United States has radically changed for Blacks, Latinos, Asians, women, the disabled, and LGBTQ citizens, mainly due to social movements, voter participation, and nonviolent agitation of otherwise obstinate power. The essential and ultimate question is whether the soft revolution will continue to advance into American households, schools, companies, and governmental chambers or if the paranoid and prejudicial forces of backlash will prevail. Those forces cry out from the corners of towns similar to Robert Cotton's home.

"There is a core of resistance against what we've achieved, because of protecting privilege, and also protecting against fear of what our bodies know that our minds do not consciously know," Cotton said when I asked why an American backlash remains influential and destructive, and why it so often happens at the behest of voters who live in small towns and exurbs. "It has to do with old trauma that is now defused," he elaborated. "It transferred itself from Europe into the time when immigrants were able to escape into the Americas. The first 'white flight' happened from Europe to the United States. They were escaping class trauma, governmental persecution trauma, religious trauma, and they never resolved it. They came here, and were able to flush their ethnic and class differences, and were absorbed into something called 'white.' So, instead of healing their trauma, they subjugated Blacks and others.

There is trauma on the Black side, and that trauma survives to accommodate harsh treatment. There is an instinctive tendency of Black mothers to protect their sons and raise their daughters. But the one thing that is unique to whites is a fight-or-flight fear response to Blacks."

The flight instinct has taken reactionaries out into the exurbs—an American journey that began with movement from cities to suburbs and now lands in the isolated precincts of exurbia. As Cotton's life and achievements demonstrate, the struggle will continue to traverse all geographical boundaries. The civil rights leader Jesse Jackson has said, "When the walls go up, it creates a shadow effect. In the darkness, what lives is fear, resentment, ignorance, hatred. When walls come down, the sunlight gets in, and justice, equality, and solidarity can grow."

Cotton has witnessed and participated in the demolition of walls, and he is now enrolled in the effort to prevent the construction of new ones. Those chanting, "Build the wall!" are demanding far more than an oppressive and exclusionary physical edifice at the American border. They are longing for a reversal of time and the subversion of what Cotton called, with hope, "the promise of America." Cotton argues that the "narrow construct of race inhibits us all and makes us complicit in the perpetuation of an identity crisis." "How do you move out of the paradigm" of the identity crisis, Cotton asks before giving a simple first step: "You start treating your neighbors of a different color as real neighbors."

Exurbia operates as a shadowland, preferring to live behind the walls of fear and resentment. Not all of its voters, but many, work to extend the shadows far beyond their surroundings. The story of the Cotton family and Valparaiso might act as an allegory of defiant joy and faith in better possibilities. As Robert Cotton put it, "It's been a slow process, but it is a process that has happened in one of the most stringent, segregationist cities in the country. From the deepest depths of what was construed as a sundown town, you can have the sunrise."[3]

CRY FOR HOPE

Jerry Garcia attributed the Grateful Dead's surprising stadium success in the 1980s and '90s to widespread resistance to the "passionless America" that had taken shape during the Reagan revolution of mass commercial culture, suburban political dominance, and the resurgence of the religious right. People seeking an alternative of passion, authenticity, community, and improvisation could find it in the parking lot of the Grateful Dead's nearest concert and in the seating pavilions themselves. The American spirit of defiant creativity that had birthed jazz, beat poetry, and rock and roll was on life support in the broader society, but at a Grateful Dead show it was exploding with vitality.

Many Grateful Dead fans had assembled at Central Park in Griffith, Indiana—a small town between Gary and Highland (not quite far enough from Chicago for exurban classification, but too far for suburbia). Central Park is nestled within a residential area and frequently the site of farmers markets, art fairs, and live music performances in the summer. In July 2022, Central Park was the location for Rockopelli Music Festival—an annual gathering, mostly of local musicians, to benefit the PelliPlay foundation, which funds music lessons for low-income children and supports arts programs for children in schools and other community networks. That year featured the exhilarating surprise of a headline performer: George Porter Jr. Backed by his band, the Runnin' Pardners, and in collaboration with funk and jazz guitarist Joe Marcinek, who hails from Crown Point, Indiana, the legendary bassist and vocalist who electrified audiences with the Meters, and inspired several Grateful Dead covers, put on a lively, imaginative, and ferocious set of music. Playing in the open space between order and ad-lib, Porter's raspy howl echoed throughout the park. He and his musical company injected the drama and joy of the blues into the audience through renditions of his own material—songs like "Crying for Hope" and "Hey Pocky A-Way"—and energetic, ribald covers of Bill Withers and Billy Preston. As the night became darker, the audience grew larger, its members ranging from twentysomething couples in tie-dye to the more predictable "touch of gray" ponytails. Latino teenagers and white elders danced, pairs of women and men stood in line for beer, and cheers of excitement and awe erupted when Porter and Marcinek traded licks and phrases during extended jams. The music was good, and it promised the power of transcendence—no matter how corrupt, unjust, or plain stupid politics and religion render the urban, suburban, exurban—American—headlines, a great band can exercise veracity that is more eternal. It unites multiple generations and races of people and gives a glimpse into the possibilities of communal solidarity and democracy. By the time Porter closed with "Fire on the Bayou," the few hundred assembled were in a frenzy—dancing, waving their hands in the air, and responding with high volume to Porter's request for them to sing along with the chorus.

It was hard to reconcile George Porter Jr., a legend of the funk and jam scene, performing in Griffith—an event that would have seemed like the property of fantasy twenty years earlier. But flying from a post above the stage was an American flag. The Stars and Stripes offered a reminder that the patriotic spirit and symbol belongs not only to the passionless, hateful, and warlike but also to George Porter Jr. and Joe Marcinek, the Grateful Dead, and Carlos Santana, whose "Soul Sacrifice" the band teased for a few joyous bars. It belongs to the gay, Latino, Black, Asian, and raucous teenagers dancing on the grass in front of the stage, and the parents, teachers, and neighbors who love and nurture them. It belongs not only to the "founding fathers," but to Martin Luther King, Jesse Jackson, and Ella Baker. It belongs to Puerto Rican resistance leaders, like Antonia Pantoja and Frank Espada, as well as his son, the poet Martín Espada. It belongs to Harvey Milk, Marsha P. Johnson, and Channyn Lynne Parker, the CEO of Chicago's Brave Space Alliance, an LGBTQ center in the South Side of Chicago. With work, discipline, and commitment, their heirs and executors will transform cities, suburbs, and exurbs, and in so doing, they will continue to transform the United States.

During a brief pause between songs, George Porter Jr. praised the enthusiasm of the crowd in Griffith, looked around at the houses that surrounded the park, and said, "This reminds me of home. We have all kinds of cool parks like this where cool things happen right in the middle of neighborhoods." Home for George Porter Jr. is New Orleans.

Could Northern Indiana become New Orleans? It might seem unlikely, but so did the civil rights movement, the LGBTQ rights movement, the Chicano movement, the disability rights movement, and the feminist movement. As Porter once told an interviewer, "There is truth in rhythm."

ACKNOWLEDGMENTS

Thank you to my agent, Mark Falkin, for his intelligence, dedication, and ferocious energy. He makes a great advocate, intellectual sparring partner, and confidant. Thank you to Carl Bromley, at Melville House, for his early belief in this book, and his consistent support, which makes its existence possible. Thank you to all of my generous and insightful interview sources, especially Mike Lofgren, Sidney Blumenthal, Robert Cotton, Javed Ali, Anthony DiMaggio, Bruce Bartlett, Christian Picciolini, Christy Allen, and Connie Wachala. Thank you to Fr. Edward R. Ward for many years of friendship and insight. Thank you to Rev. Jesse Jackson for the friendship, inspiration, and, most of all, for keeping hope alive for all of us. Thank you to Alanna Ford for her faith and friendship, and all the laughs. Thank you to all of my family and friends whose support is the most precious and vital resource, especially my mother and father (Pearl and Lou). Finally, thank you to my wife, Sarah, who gives me strength, joy, and a world of dreams.

ENDNOTES

WELCOME TO THE EXIT: A SUBURBAN-EXURBAN TOUR

1   Devon Marisa Zuegel provides a primer on government subsidy and suburbia for Strong Towns: Devon Marisa Zuegel, "Financing Suburbia: How Government Mortgage Policy Determined Where You Live," Strong Towns, August 16, 2017.

2   For more detail go directly to Sheryll Cashin's excellent book *White Space, Black Hood: Opportunity Hoarding and Segregation in the Age of Inequality* (Boston: Beacon Press, 2021).

3   See the seminal *The Color of Law: A Forgotten History of How Our Government Segregated America* (New York: Norton, 2017) by Richard Rothstein

4   For the full story of blockbusting, read W. Orser's *Blockbusting in Baltimore: The Edmondson Village Story* (Lexington: University Press of Kentucky, 1997).

5   Although difficult to track online, the most comprehensive and informative story about white flight from the Chicago suburbs in the 1990s is Danielle Gordon's "White Flight Taking Off in Chicago Suburbs," for *The Chicago Reporter*, December 1997.

6   See "As Majority Black Population Increases in Affluent Flossmoor, Whites Are Moving Out," from *The Crusader*, October 7, 2021, by Erick Johnson.

7   Read the late Mike Davis's masterpiece, *City of Quartz: Excavating the Future in Los Angeles* (New York: Verso, 1990).

8   Binyamin Appelbaum, "Long Island, We Need to Talk About Housing," *The New York Times*, February 4, 2022.

9   Andres Duany, Elizabeth Plater-Zyberk, and Jeff Speck, *Suburban Nation: The Rise of Sprawl and the Decline of the American Dream* (New York: North Point Press, 2010).

10   Pew Research Center: / https://www.pewresearch.org/social-trends/2020/07/29/prior-to-covid-19-urban-core-counties-in-the-u-s-were-gaining-vitality-on-key-measures/

11   The Cleveland Clinic explains the psychology of "fight or flight" in the article "What Happens to Your Body During the Fight-or-Flight Response?," *Health Essentials*, December 9, 2019.

12   Find Robert Pape's work at the University of Chicago's Chicago Project on Security and Threats, specifically the study *American Face of Insurrection: Analysis of Individuals Charged for Storming the US Capitol on January 6, 2021* (Chicago: Chicago Project on Security and Threats, January 5, 2022).

13   Jacob Whiton, "Where Trumpism Lives," *Boston Review*, January 19, 2021.

14   Carol Anderson, *White Rage: The Unspoken Truth of Our Racial Divide* (New York: Bloomsbury, 2016).

15   Voting data is easily accessible at the Lake County website. An essential resource for learning voting patterns in the 2016 and 2020 elections, which I cite throughout this book, is *The New York Times* election result map, available at "An Extremely Detailed Map of the 2020 Election," *The New York Times*, March 30, 2021, https://www.nytimes.com/interactive/2021/upshot/2020-election-map.html.

16   Will Weissert, "GOP Eyes Indiana Upset amid Push to Diversify Party," AP News, October 26, 2022.

17   *BuzzFeed News* reported on the Crown Point fiasco with the story "Armed White Men Showed Up to a Black Lives Matter Protest in Indiana," June 4, 2020, as did *Politico*, "White Bystanders Armed with Rifles Watch Floyd Protesters March in Indiana," June 6, 2020.

THE CONFEDERACY STRONGHOLD OF NORTHERN ILLINOIS

1   Read Tejeda's recollection of his high school years at TFS at his own blog: Gregory Tejeda, "I Was Once a Rebel, Chicago-Style," *Chicago Argus* (blog), January 22, 2008, http://chicagoargus.blogspot.com/2008/01/i-was-once-rebel-chicago-style_22.html.

2   The Village of Lansing provides crime statistics from 1996 to the present: "Yearly Analysis of Crime," Village of Lansing, accessed August 7, 2023, https://www.villageoflansing.org/village_departments/yearly_analysis_of_crime/index.php.

3   For additional details consult Lindsay Haines's study: "The Effects of White Flight and Urban Decay in Suburban Cook County," *Park Place Economist* 18, no. 1 (2010): 18–27.

4   All data derive from US Census reports.

5   See Lawrence Rosenthal's book on the subject, *Empire of Resentment: Populism's Toxic Embrace of Nationalism* (New York: The New Press, 2020).

6   See Alexander Laban Hinton's book on the subject, *It Can Happen Here: White Power and the Rising Threat of Genocide in the US* (New York: NYU Press, 2021).

7   David Foster Wallace made his prescient remarks in the 2004 interview "To the Best of Our Knowledge: Interview with David Foster Wallace," which is available in the interview collection Stephen J. Burn, ed., *Conversations with David Foster Wallace* (Jackson: University Press of Mississippi, 2012).

8   For more information on Christian Picciolini, read his riveting memoir, *White American Youth: My Descent into America's Most Violent Hate Movement—and How I Got Out* (New York: Hachette Books, 2017).

9   Samuel Kye's study "The Persistence of White Flight in Middle-Class Suburbia," was published in *Social Science Research* 72 in May 2018.

10   Anastasia Loukaitou-Sideris is quoted by Eleanor Cummins in "The Surprising Politics of Sidewalks," published by *Popular Science* on April 10, 2018.

11   The Maxmin-Maher exchange took place on *Real Time with Bill Maher*, season 20, episode 14.

12   Historian Rick Perlstein writes about the infamous Atwater assertion at *The Nation*, "Exclusive: Lee Atwater's Infamous 1981 Interview on the Southern Strategy."

13   Mark Muro, Eli Bryerly-Duke, Yang You, and Robert Maxim of the Brookings Institute reported on Biden's victory and commercial activity with "Biden-Voting Counties Equal 70% of America's Economy. What Does This Mean for the Nation's Political-Economic Divide?," on November 10, 2020.

14   Carisa Crawford Chappell writes about Lansing for *Chicago* in "Where to Buy Now: Suburbs," published on June 1, 2022.

GODZILLA JESUS

1   Matthew 6:6.

2   See Randall Balmer's outstanding book *Bad Faith: Race and the Rise of the Religious Right* (Grand Rapids, MI: Eerdmans, 2021).

3   David Foster Wallace's amusing and deeply moving essay on his experience during the September 11 attack, "The View from Mrs. Thompson's," is included in the essay collection *Consider the Lobster and Other Essays* (New York: Little, Brown and Company, 2005).

4   Pew Research Center reported on rates of religiosity and the decline of Christianity in the October 17, 2019, report *In U.S., Decline of Christianity Continues Apace*.

5   For Kristin Kobes Du Mez's complete thoughts on the subject, see her salient book *Jesus and John Wayne: How White Evangelicals Corrupted a Faith and Fractured a Nation* (New York: Liveright, 2020).

6   See the October 14, 2021, article by Yonat Shimron on *Religion News Service*: "Study: Attendance Hemorrhaging at Small and Midsize US Congregations."

7   Charity R. Carney's essay about exurban churches was reproduced in the *Utne Reader* on August 10, 2015. Her essay is called "Megachurches, Suburbia and the Prosperity Gospel."

8   Jonathan Mahler's story is "The Soul of the Exurb," published by *The New York Times* on March 27, 2005.

9   Tim Alberta wrote about FloodGate for *The Atlantic* in his May 10, 2022 story, "How Politics Poisoned the Evangelical Church."

10 Mulder is quoted in *The Atlantic*'s July 26, 2021, story "The Fastest-Growing Group of American Evangelicals," written by Meaghan Winter

11 The Associated Press reported on Litton and the SBC. See the story "Southern Baptists Elect a New President, Ed Litton, Who Is Seen As a Bridge Builder," NPR, June 15, 2021.

12 See "Prosperity Gospel and Foreclosure" by Sarah Posner, published on February 27, 2013, by *Religion Dispatches*.

13 See "Prosperity Gospel's Steve Munsey's Great Yom Kippur Scam" by Bill Berkowtiz, published on September 25, 2015, on *The Smirking Chimp*.

14 See Marisa Kwik's story "Local Megachurch Navigates Precarious Path," *Northwest Indiana Times*, February 17, 2013.

15 Ibid.

16 See Sarah Reese's report, "Judge Dismisses Wrongful Death Lawsuit Against

Megachurch Pastors," *Northwest Indiana Times*, April 12, 2022. See also: Joseph Hartropp, "Family Sues Megachurch After Daughter Drowns in Pastor's Swimming Pool," *Christianity Today*, November 18, 2016.

17 See Mike Lofgren's essay "The Dangerous Rise of the Gullible American Cynic," *Common Dreams*, July 9, 2022.

18 John Harwood, "White Evangelicals' Dominance of the GOP Has Turned It into the Party of Resistance," CNN, February 28, 2021.

19 Wilson is quoted in Elle Hardy's story "The Rise of Christian Nationalism," *UnHerd*, June 21, 2022.

20 See Weinstein's interview with Paul Jay, "Jan 6th: The Real Threat Is Christian Nationalism in the Military—Mikey Weinstein," *theAnalysis.news*, January 11, 2022.

21 See Gorski's interview with Paul Jay, "Jan 6 Committee Ignores White Christian Nationalism," *theAnalysis.news*, July 26, 2022.

22 See Katherine Stewart's July 5, 2022, essay for *The New York Times*, "Christian Nationalists Are Excited About What Comes Next."

23 See Andrew L. Whitehead and Samuel L. Perry's book, *Taking America Back for God: Christian Nationalism in the United States* (New York: Oxford University Press, 2020).

24 Jason Luger summarizes his findings with "How the Radical Right Infiltrates Suburban Communities," *Rantt*, January 21, 2022.

25 Stephen Gossett writes about Kass's racism at the *Chicagoist*, "John Kass' Column About 'Feral Boys' Is a New Nadir . . . Even for Him," September 8, 2016.

26 Lara Krupicka of the *National Catholic Register* profiled the Shillings in the August 4, 2011 story "Following a Path of Faith to Shrine of Christ's Passion."

27 See James S. Bielo, *Materializing the Bible: Scripture, Sensations, Place* (New York: Bloomsbury, 2021).

28 Thomas Reese, "The Catholic Bishops Support Gun Control. Why Don't We Hear More About It?," *National Catholic Reporter*, June 14, 2022.

29 Richard Flory, "In the Age of Megachurches, Sometimes Less Is More" by Richard Flory, *Religious Dispatches*, March 7, 2016.

30 See Ray Oldenburg's book *The Great Good Place* (Cambridge, MA: Da Capo Press, 1989)

31 David Mamet writes about "the usual" in his essay collection *Make-Believe Town: Essays and Remembrances* (New York: Little, Brown and Company, 1996).

32 The story of the Voyles family is available in Northwest Indiana PFLAG brochures.

A POLITICAL TRAFFIC JAM

1   All quotes from Mike Lofgren, Sidney Blumenthal, and Bruce Bartlett derive from personal interviews. Aristotle, *Politics*.

2   Steve Benen, *The Impostors: How Republicans Quit Governing and Seized American Politics* (New York: Mariner Books, 2020).

3   Julie Carr Smyth, "Ohio Supreme Court Scraps 2nd GOP-Drawn Congressional Map," Associated Press, July 19, 2022.

4   Zack Beauchamp reports on North Carolina's gerrymandering for *Vox*: "North Carolina's Extreme New Gerrymander, Explained," November 9, 2021.

5   See the ACLU's online explanatory guide *Everything You Always Wanted to Know About Redistricting but Were Afraid to Ask* (Atlanta: American Civil Liberties Union Foundation Voting Rights Project, 2010).

6   See the summary of the study by Katheryn Royster at Vanderbilt University's website, titled "New Political Science Research Debunks Myths About White Working-Class Support for Trump," July 29, 2020.

7   Lisa McGirr, *Suburban Warriors: The Origins of the New American Right* (Princeton: Princeton University Press, 2015).

8   Kevin M. Kruse, *White Flight: Atlanta and the Making of Modern Conservatism* (Princeton: Princeton University Press, 2005).

9   "This Isn't Dennis Hastert's First Scandal" by Norm Ornstein for *The Atlantic*, June 3, 2015.

10 The Center for American Progress provides a thorough run through of the Clinton economic record with their report *Power of Progressive Economics: The Clinton Years* (Washington, DC: Center for American Progress, October 28, 2011).

11 The American Library Association press release on the report is available at the organization's website under "American Library Association Reports Record Number of Demands to Censor Library Books and Materials in 2022," March 22, 2023.

12 See Matthew Cantor's August 5, 2022, story at *The Guardian*, "US Library Defunded After Refusing to Censor LGBTQ Authors: 'We Will Not Ban the Books.'"

13 Gore issued the statement to Anderson Cooper during a CNN interview, available on YouTube: "Al Gore Predicts Impact of Democrats' Massive Climate Bill," CNN, August 14, 2022, https://www.youtube.com/watch?v=wQcx4dFyZwc.

14 See Richard Hofstadter's essential book, *The Paranoid Style in American Politics, and Other Essays* (New York: Knopf, 1965).

BUSTED ON A BAD BEAT

1 A good summary is available from *All That's Interesting*, written by Natasha Isak, "33 Haunting Photos of Gary, Indiana—'The Most Miserable City In America,'" updated December 18, 2019.

2 See Andy Cush's May 11, 2017, story for *Spin*: "Donald Trump Has a Shady Casino History in Gary, Indiana."

3 Umberto Eco's essay "Ur-Fascism" was originally published in *The New York Review of Books* on June 22, 1995, but is available for free at the online resource The Anarchist Library.

4 Chris Arnade writes about Gary for *The Guardian*: "White Flight Followed Factory Jobs Out of Gary, Indiana. Black People Didn't Have a Choice," March 28, 2017.

5 See Stepanie Mencimer's report for *Mother Jones*: "Trump's Casino Broke a Big Promise to Give Millions to Charity," July 8, 2016, and James Briggs's story for *The Indianapolis Star*: "In Gary, Memories of Donald Trump's Casino Promises," April 24, 2016.

6 Peter T. Kilborn, "An Illinois City, Once Down and Out, Finds Rebirth in Riverboat Gambling," *The New York Times*, March 9, 1996.

7 H. David Baer's essay "Was Dostoevsky a Simpleton?" was published by *The Cresset* in the Advent-Christmas issue of 2011.

8 See Chloe Taft's piece "Rust Belt Cities Gamble on Casino-Led Urban Development" at NextCity.org

9 The Chicago History Museum has an informative entry on the Thornton quarry in its encyclopedia of Chicago.

10 See citation 1.

11 Rachel B. Gross, "The Politics of Nostalgia," *Religion and Politics*, Feb. 2, 2021

12 Camus's insight is available in his classic book-length essay, *The Rebel*.

13 See Federica Cocco's story for the *Financial Times*, published on December 2, 2016, "Most US Manufacturing Jobs Lost to Technology, Not Trade."

14 The Carnegie Endowment for International Peace report was made available online on December 10, 2018, under the title *How Trade Did and Did Not Account for Manufacturing Job Losses*.

15 Dana Mattioli wrote about Kodak on January 6, 2012, for the *Wall Street Journal*: "As Kodak Fades, Workers Remember Their Moments."

16 Studs Terkel, *Working: People Talk About What They Do All Day and How They Feel About What They Do* (New York: Pantheon Books, 1974).

17 These insights derive from a conversation with labor historian and socialist journalist Paul Street.

18 See Zygmant Bauman's book on the subject, *Liquid Modernity* (Cambridge, UK: Polity, 2000).

MEN AT WAR

1   See Dan Kois's report at *Slate*, "Killer Truck, Dude," February 28, 2022, and also "The Hidden Danger of Big Trucks" by Keith Barry for *Consumer Reports*, June 8, 2021.

2   Brett Berk, "You Don't Need a Full-Size Pickup Truck, You Need a Cowboy Costume," *The Drive*, March 15, 2019.

3   Paul Waldman, "The Evolving Political Symbolism of the Pickup Truck," *The Washington Post*, November 1, 2022.

4   Dara Lind, "Who Owns Guns in America? White Men, Mostly," *Vox*, December 4, 2015.

5   Ibid.

6   See F. Carson Mencken and Paul Froese's study, "Gun Culture in Action," *Social Problems* 66, no. 1 (February 2019).

7   Allen's dissertation, "Living the Second Amendment," is unpublished. After I met her through a mutual friend, she allowed me to read and cite it.

8   See Ryan Busse's *Gunfight: My Battle Against the Industry that Radicalized America* (New York: PublicAffairs, 2021).

9   See my own article at *Salon*: "The Punisher Skull: Unofficial Logo of the White American Death Cult," April 28, 2019.

10 For background on the Three Percenters, read Alejandro Beutel and Daryl Johnson's March 2021 report, *The Three Percenters: A Look Inside an Anti-Government Militia*, available online from the Newlines Institute for Strategy and Policy.

11 See Cyril Mychalejko's story "Why Is Your Neighbor Flying That All-Black American Flag?" in *Philly Burbs*, October 27, 2021.

12 Carl Hoffman, *Liar's Circus: A Strange and Terrifying Journey Into the Upside-Down World of Trump's MAGA Rallies* (New York: Custom House, 2020)

13   See Kleinfeld's July 6, 2022 story, "The GOP's Militia Problem: Proud Boys, Oath Keepers and Lessons from Abroad," in *Just Security*, July 6, 2022.

14   Ibid.

15   See Ryan Busse's November 11, 2021, story for *The Bulwark*: "Prepare for the Shock Troops."

16   Whitmer made the accurate observation on the CNN program *Who's Talking to Chris Wallace?*

17   "Accused of Flirting, Juror Dismissed from Whitmer Plot Trial," Associated Press, October 15, 2022.

18   See Tresa Baldas's April 6, 2022 story, "Whitmer Kidnap Plot Trial: What We Know About Jurors Deciding Historic Verdict," for the *Detroit Free Press*

19   See the NBC News report from January 14, 2021 by Wilson Wong: "Kyle Rittenhouse, Out on Bail, Flashed White Power Signs at a Bar, Prosecutors Say."

20   See the Southern Poverty Law Center's 2022 report by Cassie Miller, "SPLC Poll Finds Substantial Support for 'Great Replacement' Theory and Other Hard-Right Ideas."

21   Steve Peoples, "Republican Senate candidates promote 'replacement' theory," Associated Press, May 17, 2022.

22   See Anthony DiMaggio's December 30, 2022, essay for *CounterPunch*: "White Supremacy and January 6: What's Missing from the Congressional Report." I've interviewed DiMaggio for the *Washington Monthly*.

23   Arie Perliger writes about his findings at *Medium* in the August 20, 2020, essay "Why Do Hate Crimes Proliferate in Progressive Blue States?"

24   Details are available in reporting from the *Northwest Indiana Times*.

25   See David Choi's March 23, 2019, story for *Business Insider*: "Hate Crimes Increased 226% in Places Trump Held a Campaign Rally in 2016, Study Claims."

26   The Associated Press reported on the story on December 3, 2022: "Ohio School Cancels Drag Story Time, Citing Security Dispute."

27   Media Matters reported on the frightening exchange on October 26, 2021: "Pushing Election Lies, TPUSA Audience Member Asks Charlie Kirk When They Can 'Use the Guns' and 'Kill These People.'"

NOWHERE, USA

1   See Adam Gopnik's book *A Thousand Small Sanities: The Moral Adventure of Liberalism* (New York: Basic Books, 2019).

2   See Laura Forman's June 25, 2021, story for *The Wall Street Journal*: "The 'Great Reshuffling' Is Shifting Wealth to the Exurbs."

3   One Region makes it data available on its own website: https://oneregionnwi.org/

4   See Tim Zorn's May 17, 2018, story in the *Chicago Tribune*: "Public Transportation Growth for Northwest Indiana Pushed at Summit."

5   Robert D. Bullard, Glenn S. Johnson, and Angel O. Torres wrote their report for the American Bar Association on July 1, 2007, available online, under the headline "Dismantling Transportation Apartheid in the United States Before and After Disasters Strike."

6   See Junfeng Jiao and Chris Bischak's March 13, 2018, report at *The Conversation*: "People Are Stranded in 'Transit Deserts' in Dozens of US Cities."

7   Tanvi Misra writes on the "dollar store belt" for *Bloomberg* on December 20, 2018: "The Dollar Store Backlash Has Begun."

8   Chris McGreal reporting for *The Guardian*, August 13, 2018: "Where Even Walmart Won't Go: How Dollar General Took Over Rural America."

9   See "The Pandemic Has Transformed America's Dining Landscape into an Oligopoly Dominated by Chains," by Adam Reiner for *The Counter*, May 12, 2022.

10 See Paul Blest for *Vice News*, March 4, 2022: "Applebee's Franchise Exec: High Gas Prices Are Great for Hiring."

11 Ed Folsom gives these thoughts in the PBS documentary *Walt Whitman: American Experience*.

12 Andrew Van Dam, "The most Common Restaurant Cuisine in Every State, and a Chain-Restaurant Mystery," *The Washington Post*, September 29, 2022.

13 See Meaghan Cameron and Steven John's July 9, 2022, report for *Eat This, Not That!*, "7 Strict Rules Texas Roadhouse Workers Have to Follow."

14 See the Brewer Association summary online: "The Craft Brewing Industry Contributed $76.3 Billion to the U.S. Economy in 2021, more than 490,000 Jobs."

15 See Bryan Roth's November 10, 2019, report for *Good Beer Hunting*: "A Show of Hands—Breweries Take Political and Business Risks Mixing Beer and Social Stances."

IGNORANCE IS HELL

1   See Liz Carey reporting in the *Daily Yonder* on October 22, 2018: "One-Fifth of U.S. Newspapers Close in Last 14 Years."

2   See the Pew Research Center report: "Over 360 Newspaper Closures Since Just Before the Pandemic."

3   See Brian Hieggelke's February 18, 2021, essay for *Newcity*: "The Tower Is Crumbling: What the Decline and Fall of the Chicago Tribune and the Shattering of Local Media Means."

4   See Medill's online summary, "Struggling Communities Hardest Hit by Decline in Local Journalism."

5   See Penny Abernathy of Northwestern University's June 29, 2022, report, *The State of Local News.*

6   See Richard Hall's January 23, 2023, story for *The Independent*: "'He Was Weird': Publisher of Long Island Newspaper That Exposed Santos Knew Something Was Up Years Before Election Win."

NO ESCAPE

1   Rodolfo Zagal's story for the *Joliet Junior College Blazer*, published on October 21, 2022, is "Joliet Running Dry; Residents Will Pay."

2   Adam Mahoney writing in *Grist* on February 24, 2022, "America's Largest Inland Port Is Running Out of Water."

3   See Monica Eng, "Climate Change Is Already Impacting Lake Michigan—Here's How," NPR, Septebmer 16, 2019.

4   "Indiana Dunes: Administrative History," *National Park Service.*

5   See Alex Ruppenthal's August 30, 2018, report for WTTW, "Climate Scientists Create Plan for Preserving Indiana Dunes."

6   Enrique Saenz wrote about East Chicago for the *Indiana Environmental Reporter* on March 31, 2021: "Decades of 'Missed Opportunities' Exposed Multiple Generations of East Chicago Residents to Lead Contamination, Federal Report Finds."

7   See the April 11, 2022, story at *WaterWorld*, "Two Indiana Towns Agree to Cut Untreated Sewage Discharges."

8   See the book *The Permanent Campaign: Inside the World of Elite Political Operatives* (Boston: Beacon Press, 1980) by Sidney Blumenthal.

9   See Thomas Linzey's pamphlet *On Community Civil Disobedience in the Name of Sustainability: The Community Rights Movement in the United States* (Binghamton, NY: PM Press, 2015).

10 See the Sierra Club's report, "A Green New Deal Is Already Underway in States and Cities."

THE BOHEMIAN SUBURB VERSUS EXURBISTAN

1   See Chris Matthews's book *Hardball: How Politics Is Played, Told by One Who Knows the Game* (New York: Simon and Schuster, 1999).

2   See Aaron Zitner's story in *The Wall Street Journal* from March 27, 2023, "America Pulls Back From Values That Once Defined It, WSJ-NORC Poll Finds."

3   See Irving Bernstein's excellent book *Promises Kept: John F. Kennedy's New Frontier* (New York: Oxford University Press, 1991).

4   Jonathan M. Metzl, *Dying of Whiteness: How the Politics of Racial Resentment Is Killing America's Heartland* (New York: Basic Books: 2019)

5   Melissa Turpin, "What Company Employs the Most People in Indiana?," WishTV, January 27, 2017.

6   Poet and social critic Jeremiah Moss wrote about Patti Smith's comments at his blog under the headline "Find a New City."

WHEN THE WALLS COME CRUMBLING DOWN

1   Liz Nagy covered the Chesterton development on April 13, 2021, for ABC Chicago: "LGBTQ Pride Flag, Black Lives Matter Poster Removed from Chesterton Middle School Causes Controversy Over Inclusion."

2   Meredith Colias-Pete and Carole Carlson wrote about the gun control rally on March 14, 2018, for the *Chicago Tribune*: "NW Indiana Students Face Detention, Praise During Walkout Advocating Gun Reform."

3   In addition to my own interview with Robert Cotton, the 2020 documentary *From Sundown to Sunrise*, directed by Pat Wisniewski, was an essential source.

INDEX